Q&A
English Legal
System

Routledge Questions & Answers Series

Each Routledge Q&A contains questions on topics commonly found on exam papers, with comprehensive suggested answers. The titles are written by lecturers who are also examiners, so the student gains an important insight into exactly what examiners are looking for in an answer. This makes them excellent revision and practice guides.

Titles in the series:

Q&A Company Law
Q&A Commercial Law
Q&A Contract Law
Q&A Criminal Law
Q&A Employment Law
Q&A English Legal System
Q&A Equity and Trusts
Q&A European Union Law
Q&A Evidence
Q&A Family Law
Q&A Intellectual Property Law
Q&A Jurisprudence
Q&A Land Law
Q&A Medical Law
Q&A Public Law
Q&A Torts

For a full listing, visit http://www.routledge.com/cw/revision

Q&A
English Legal System

Gary Slapper and David Kelly

Additional content supplied by Karen Davies

Routledge
Taylor & Francis Group

LONDON AND NEW YORK

Eleventh edition published 2015
by Routledge
2 Park Square, Milton Park, Abingdon, Oxon OX14 4RN

and by Routledge
711 Third Avenue, New York, NY 10017

Routledge is an imprint of the Taylor & Francis Group, an informa business

First edition published by Cavendish Publishing 1993
Tenth edition published by Routledge 2013

British Library Cataloguing in Publication Data
A catalogue record for this book is available from the British Library

Library of Congress Cataloging in Publication Data
Slapper, Gary, author.
Q&A English legal system / Gary Slapper and David Kelly. – Eleventh edition.
   pages cm. – (Routledge questions & answers series)
   Includes index.
   ISBN 978-1-138-77869-6 (pbk) – ISBN 978-1-315-77170-0 (ebk) 1. Law–England–Examinations, questions, etc.. I. Kelly, David, 1950– author. II. Title.
   KD663.S58 2015
   349.42–dc23   2014025514

ISBN: 978-1-138-77869-6 (pbk)
ISBN: 978-1-315-77170-0 (ebk)

Typeset in TheSans
by Wearset Ltd, Boldon, Tyne and Wear

Printed and bound in Great Britain by
TJ International Ltd, Padstow, Cornwall

Contents

Preface

This book has been written to assist students in their study of the English legal system. It has been composed for students of this subject, in general, and for undergraduates and those studying for professional examinations, in particular. The text is not a substitute for course books, law reports and legal journals, but aims to complement them by showing how typical examination and assignment questions can be answered.

The subject matter of the English legal system requires students to be familiar with our legal institutions and procedures, the criminal and civil processes, some substantive law, legal theories and debates in the realms of morals and politics. One thread running through all these topics is the requirement that students be evaluative and critical in their approach to the issues. It is also essential that answers take account of recent developments. Our answers in this book aim to show examples of such technique. This edition contains several new features including 'How the Read this Question' sections and 'Up for Debate' sections.

These answers will, perhaps, be most appreciated by students who have already acquired a good working knowledge of the relevant issues, principles and law and who desire clarification on the techniques that can be used to best present their knowledge in response to typical questions. The questions are modelled on those from a variety of English Legal System courses, including the University of London (External) LLB. We have chosen a mix of essay and 'problem' questions and concentrated on issues which have current significance.

There have been many changes made to the apparatus and processes of the English legal system since the seventh edition of this book was published in 2013. There have been changes to civil and criminal process, the court system, the funding of legal services, the jury, human rights law, and several important common law decisions in the Court of Appeal, the House of Lords, and the European Court of Human Rights. These have all been digested in this edition.

We have again greatly benefited from the encouragement and meticulous professionalism of Fiona Briden at Routledge. We are very grateful to the professionalism of Damian Mitchell, Emma Nugent, and Rebekah Jenkins at Routledge, and to Karen Davies for her expertise on the diagrams. The work of Kim Silver on the legal pedagogic aids and updates was superb. We are very grateful for the great work of Hayley Kennard, Deputy Production Editorial Manager at Routledge, and Allie Hargreaves, Senior Project Manager at Wearset and to Jackie Day for expertly managing the production at Routledge.

We are very grateful to our families for their forbearance in not asking too many questions while we were answering those in this book.

We have endeavoured to state the law as at August 2014.

Gary Slapper
David Kelly
August 2014

Table of Cases

Table of Legislation

■ Statutes

■ Secondary Legislation

■ International Instruments

Guide to the Companion Website

www.routledge.com/cw/revision

Visit the Law Revision website to discover a comprehensive range of resources designed to enhance your learning experience.

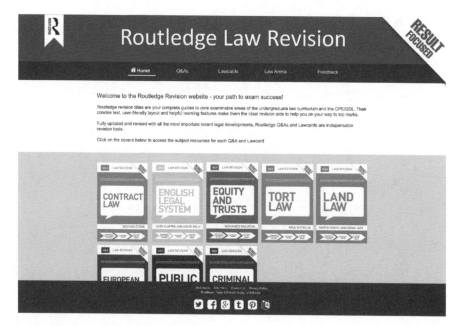

The Good, The Fair, & The Ugly

Good essays are the gateway to top marks. This interactive tutorial provides sample essays together with voice-over commentary and tips for successful exam essays, written by our Q&A authors themselves.

Multiple Choice Questions

Knowledge is the foundation of every good essay. Focusing on key examination themes, these MCQs have been written to test your knowledge and understanding of each subject in the book.

Bonus Q&As

Having studied our exam advice, put your revision into practice and test your essay writing skills with our additional online questions and answers.

Introduction

This book is intended to be of help to students studying the English legal system where they feel that they have acquired a reasonable body of knowledge and skills, but do not feel confident about using them effectively in exams. This book sets out to demonstrate how to apply the knowledge to the question and how to structure the answer. Students, especially first-year students, often find the technique of answering problem questions particularly hard to grasp, so this book contains a number of answers to such questions.

It is hoped that this book will be particularly useful at exam time, but it may also prove useful throughout the year. The book provides examples of the kind of questions that are usually asked in end-of-year examinations, along with suggested solutions. Each chapter deals with one of the main themes covered in legal system courses and contains typical questions on that area. The aim is not to include questions covering every aspect of a course, but to pick out the areas that tend to be examined because they are particularly contentious or topical. Many courses contain a certain amount of material that is not examined, although it is important for providing background knowledge.

PROBLEM AND ESSAY QUESTIONS

Some areas tend to be examined only by essays, some mainly – although not invariably – by problems, and some by either. The questions chosen reflect this mix, and the introductions at the beginning of each chapter cover the themes commonly examined. It is important not to choose a topic and then assume that it will appear on the exam paper in a particular form unless it is in an area where, for example, a problem question is never set. If it might appear as an essay or a problem, revision should be geared to either possibility; a very thorough knowledge of the area should be acquired, but also an awareness of critical opinion in relation to it.

LENGTH OF ANSWERS

The answers in this book are about the length of an essay that a good student would expect to write in an exam. Some are a little longer and that will be of assistance in explaining the topic during the course.

ADDITIONAL NOTES

Some essays are followed by additional notes exploring areas of the answer in more depth, which should be of value to the student who wants to do more than cover the main points.

EXPRESSING A POINT OF VIEW

Students sometimes ask, especially in an area such as the English legal system which can be quite topical and politically controversial, whether they should argue for any particular point of view in an essay. It will be noticed that some of the essays in this book do this. In general, the good student does argue for one side but he or she always uses sound arguments to support his or her view. Further, a good student does not ignore the opposing arguments; they are considered and their weaknesses are exposed. Of course, it would not be appropriate to do this in a problem question or in some essay questions but, where an invitation to do so is held out, it is a good idea to accept it rather than sit on the fence.

EXAMINATION PREPARATION

There are very few universally applicable tips for examination preparation and revision because people like to do these things in their own way.

If you are preparing for an examination you should however:

❖ Plan your revision programme so that you can tell, weeks from the examination, on what days you will be revising which subjects and topics. Allocating your time to revising different subjects on a random or intuitive basis is not good idea.

❖ Have a system for testing your powers of recall, e.g. see if you can recite the topic you have learnt to an imaginary audience and re-start this exercise if you falter on any point.

❖ Ensure with as many topics as you can that you know not only the law and its ambiguous points but also what critical commentary exists in the area.

In the examination:

❖ Stick rigidly to the time for each question, e.g. if you have to write four answers in three hours, do not exceed 45 minutes for any answer. It will be hard to pick up *extra* marks by slogging away at an answer to which you have already devoted 45 minutes; it will be significantly easier to gain *the first ten marks* awardable for the next answer.

❖ Focus on the precise question asked and frame your response to answer that question. Avoid simply reproducing in the script (however accurately) everything you have learnt about the relevant theme.

Common Pitfalls

The most common mistake made when using Questions & Answers books for revision is to memorise the model answers provided and try to reproduce them in exams. This approach is a sure-fire pitfall, likely to result in a poor overall mark because your answer will not be specific enough to the particular question on your exam paper, and there is also a danger that reproducing an answer in this way would be treated as plagiarism. You must instead be sure to read the question carefully, to identify the issues and problems it is asking you to address and to answer it directly in your exam. If you take our examiners' advice and use your Q&A to focus on your question-answering skills and understanding of the law applied, you will be ready for whatever your exam paper has to offer!

1 The Rule of Law and Human Rights

INTRODUCTION

The questions in this chapter may not appear in all English Legal System syllabuses. It is true that this chapter touches on material that will, traditionally, be considered more fully in other courses, such as public or constitutional and administrative law, civil liberties options or, indeed, some legal theory courses. The fact is, however, that the English legal system simply cannot be fully understood or placed in its contemporary context without a consideration of the points raised hereafter, and many syllabuses look to students to have at least a passing acquaintance with the matters that are considered in this chapter.

The English legal system cannot be treated as static; it is continuously responding to changes that take place in society as a whole. For example, to deny the relevance of European law in an English Legal System course would not only be restrictive, it would be wrong, to the extent that it ignores an increasingly important factor in the formation and determination of UK law. The same can be said of the change in the form and content of law that took place in the course of the twentieth century and which can be linked to the emergence of the interventionist state. The incorporation of the **European Convention on Human Rights (ECHR)** into UK law through the **Human Rights Act (HRA) 1998** has had profound implications for the operation of the English legal system and the relationship of the judiciary to the legislature and executive. Although how it finally works out remains to be seen, it can already be seen to have had a substantial effect since its implementation in October 2000.

Checklist
You should be familiar with the following areas:
■ What is actually meant by the term 'the rule of law'?
■ Does everyone agree as to the meaning?
■ To what extent has the meaning changed over time?
■ Is there an identifiable core meaning to 'the rule of law'?
■ Is law an end in itself, or simply a means to an end?
■ What does the HRA 1998 provide?
■ What are the implications of the HRA 1998?

QUESTION 1

Section 1 of the **Constitutional Reform Act 2005** specifically provides that it 'does not adversely affect the existing constitutional principle of the rule of law ...'.

▶ Explain what is meant by the 'rule of law' and its relevance in contemporary society.

How to Read this Question

The first thing to notice is that although this question refers to the **Constitutional Reform Act 2005**, it is not about that particular piece of legislation and can, and indeed should, be answered with no reference to it whatsoever.

It is commonplace for examiners to use quotations or other references to hang questions on and that is exactly what has been done here. The question is about the concept of the rule of law and that is what should be addressed in the answer.

How to Answer this Question

This question asks for a general consideration of the rule of law and, importantly, questions its relevance in contemporary times. Candidates must know what is understood by the concept and must offer an opinion as to its continued relevance; but they must be careful to substantiate any opinion and not resort to mere assertion and amorphous waffle. One way (and it is only one of many ways) to answer this question is as follows:

❖ offer a general definition of the rule of law, before going on to examine particular versions of the idea;
❖ explain AV Dicey's understanding of the concept;
❖ outline historical criticisms of Dicey;
❖ give an account of Friedrich von Hayek's view of the rule of law;
❖ describe Raz's critique of Hayek and his version of the rule of law;
❖ conclude by considering the possibility of there being some core meaning within the idea of the rule of law.

Answer Structure

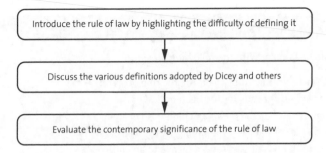

Introduce the rule of law by highlighting the difficulty of defining it

↓

Discuss the various definitions adopted by Dicey and others

↓

Evaluate the contemporary significance of the rule of law

ANSWER

In considering the meaning of the concept 'the rule of law', one is immediately drawn into a consideration of the work of the nineteenth-century writer on the English constitution, AV

Dicey, whose *Law of the Constitution* was first published in 1885. According to the chauvinistic Dicey, the rule of law was one of the key features that distinguished the English constitution from its continental counterparts. (The other essential element in the English constitution was the sovereignty of Parliament, an idea not completely compatible with the rule of law, for the idea that Parliament is sovereign and recognises no restraint is in conflict with a notion of the rule of law that sees it as primarily about controlling executive power.)

In setting out what was actually meant by the rule of law, Dicey considered three distinct elements. First, it involved an absence of arbitrary power on the part of the Government. Under the rule of law, the extent of the state's power and the manner in which it exercises such power is limited and controlled by law. This control is aimed at preventing the state from acquiring and using wide discretionary powers, because Dicey recognised that inherent in discretion is the possibility of its being used in an arbitrary manner.

The second of Dicey's elements related to equality before the law; the fact that no person is above the law, irrespective of rank or class, together with the related fact that functionaries of the state are subject to the same law and legal procedures as private citizens. Thus, the law, as represented in Dicey's version of the rule of law, ignores substantive differences and treats everyone as formally equal. In other words, the law is blind to real, concrete differences between people, in terms of wealth or power or connection, and treats them all the same as possessors of abstract rights and duties.

The third component of the rule of law, for Dicey, is related to the fact that the rules of the English constitution were the outcome of the ordinary law of the land and were based on the provision of remedies by the courts, rather than on the declaration of rights in the form of a written constitution.

It is essential to recognise that Dicey was writing not just at a particular historical period but, perhaps more importantly, he was writing from a particular political perspective. He was a committed believer in the free operation of the market and was opposed to any increase in state activity, particularly with regard to any attempt by the state to regulate the economy. It is at least arguable that at the time Dicey wrote his *Law of the Constitution*, he was misrepresenting changes that had already occurred in the UK polity, in a desire to curtail the burgeoning activity of the state and, at the same time, to justify that political stance on the basis of a spurious constitutional history.

Friedrich von Hayek's work became influential with the coming to power of the Thatcher Conservative Government in 1979, although it has to be said that in 1944, when his *The Road to Serfdom* was first published, he was almost a lone voice crying in the wilderness. As regards the rule of law, it is not surprising that Hayek followed Dicey in emphasising its essential component as the absence of arbitrary power in the hands of the state. According to Hayek:

> Stripped of all technicalities, the rule of law means that Government in all its actions is bound by rules fixed and announced beforehand.

Hayek, however, went further than Dicey in setting out the actual form and, at least in a negative way, the actual content of legal rules, in order for them to be considered as compatible with the rule of law. As Hayek expressed it in *The Road to Serfdom*:

> The Rule of Law implies limits on the scope of legislation, it restricts it to the kind of general rules known as formal law; and excludes legislation directly aimed at particular people.

Nor should law be aimed at particular goals. In other words, the Government has no place in usurping the authority of individuals by deciding their course of action for them. Within clearly defined and strictly controlled legal parameters, individuals should be left to act as they choose. The job of law is to set the boundaries of personal action, not to dictate the course of such action. Laws should not be particular in content or application, but should be general in nature, applying to all and benefiting no one in particular.

It is important to note that Hayek did not suggest that rules are not laws; they are legal, as long as they are enacted through the appropriate and proper mechanisms; they simply are not in accord with the rule of law. Other legal philosophers have recognised the need for, and have come to terms with, state intervention in the pursuit of substantive as well as merely formal justice and have provided new ways of understanding the rule of law as a means of controlling discretion, without attempting to eradicate it completely. Joseph Raz, for example, took Hayek to task for disguising a socio-economic argument as a legal one, in order to strike at policies of which he did not approve as being contrary to the rule of law, and he suggested that such reasoning was in danger of identifying the 'rule of law' with the rule of 'good law', that is, law/policy of which Hayek approved.

If both Dicey and Hayek laid great emphasis on government by law, rather than by men, Raz[1] recognises the need for the government of men as well as of laws and that the pursuit of social goals may require the enactment of both general *and particular* laws. Indeed, he suggests that it is actually inconceivable for law to consist solely of general rules. Raz claims that the basic requirement from which the wider idea of the rule of law emerges is the requirement that the law must be capable of guiding the individual's behaviour. On that basis, he lists some of the most important principles that may be derived from the general idea. These are as follows:

(a)   Laws should be prospective rather than retroactive, for the reason that people cannot be guided by and expected to obey laws that have not as yet been introduced. The laws should also be open and clear, in order to enable people to understand/guide their actions in line with them.

(b)   Laws should be relatively stable and should not be changed too frequently, as this might lead to confusion as to what actually is covered by the law.

(c)   There should be clear rules and procedures for making laws.

(d)   The independence of the judiciary has to be guaranteed, to ensure that it is free to decide cases in line with the law and not in response to any external pressure.

----

1   In addition to considering Dicey, Hayek and Raz, reference to the contemporary debate could be introduced by consideration of the views of Lord Bingham, which are discussed in Question 2.

(e) The principles of natural justice should be observed, requiring an open and fair hearing to be given to all parties to proceedings.

(f) The courts should have the power to review the way in which the other principles are implemented, to ensure that they are being operated as demanded by the rule of law.

(g) The courts should be easily accessible, as they remain at the heart of the idea of making discretion subject to legal control.

(h) The discretion of the crime prevention agencies should not be allowed to pervert the law.

Raz recognises the validity of, and the need to use, discretionary powers and particular goal-oriented legislation in contemporary society and, to that extent, he differs from both Dicey and Hayek. Yet, he also sees the rule of law as essentially a negative value, acting to minimise the danger that can be consequent upon the exercise, in an arbitrary manner, of such discretionary power. In seeking to control the exercise of discretion, he shares common ground with Dicey and Hayek.[2]

QUESTION 2

Assess Lord Bingham's contribution to the contemporary debate as to the meaning and content of the concept of 'the rule of law'.

How to Read this Question

In distinction from the previous one, this 'rule of law' question requires responses specifically to focus on the work of the late Lord Bingham, although it would be permissible to compare and contrast his ideas with others, perhaps most especially Dicey.

The point is that it is NOT a general question on the nature of the rule of law and should not be treated as such. In other words, if you do not know what Bigham had to say on the topic you would be ill advised to attempt it.

How to Answer this Question

This question clearly requires the respondent to have a detailed knowledge of Lord Bingham's *Sir David Williams Lecture* on the rule of law, but as this is likely to form a central component of any English Legal System module dealing with the rule of law, the specific nature of the question is not unexpected.

A structure for answering the question would be as follows:

❖ introduce the concept with a brief reference to the context in which the lecture was delivered;

❖ deal with each of Lord Bingham's sub-rules in some detail, but being careful to precis the content so as to keep the answer within the necessary limitations of length;

2 Don't underestimate the value of a conclusion which summarises your views and provides a brief answer to the specific question asked. (You may find it useful to re-read the question before beginning your conclusion.)

❖ provide a critical analysis/commentary on each of the points made in the lecture;

❖ finish with a general conclusion as to the relevance and success of the lecture.

Answer Structure

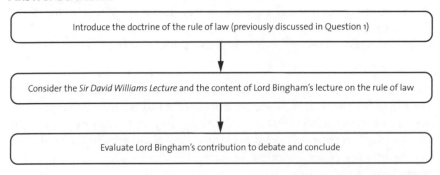

Introduce the doctrine of the rule of law (previously discussed in Question 1)

Consider the *Sir David Williams Lecture* and the content of Lord Bingham's lecture on the rule of law

Evaluate Lord Bingham's contribution to debate and conclude

ANSWER

While he recognised the difficulty in fixing a single meaning to the principle,[3] Lord Bingham nonetheless felt it appropriate to offer his own understanding of the rule of law. In his view, at the core of the concept of the rule of law is the idea that:

all persons and authorities within the state, whether public or private, should be bound by and entitled to the benefit of laws publicly and prospectively promulgated and publicly administered in the courts.

However, the vital element is the detail that Lord Bingham introduces through his consideration of the eight implications, or sub-rules, that he holds are particular aspects of the general principle of the rule of law. These sub-rules are:

❖ *The law must be accessible, and so far as possible, intelligible, clear and predictable*

The reasoning behind this requirement is that if everyone is bound by the law they must be able without undue difficulty to find out what it is, even if that means taking advice from their lawyers. Equally the law should be sufficiently clear that a course of action can be based on it.

❖ *Questions of legal right and liability should ordinarily be resolved by application of the law and not the exercise of discretion*

Lord Bingham does not share Dicey's complete antipathy to the exercise of discretion, and cites immigration law as an example where it has been advantageous. Nonetheless he does believe that the essential truth of Dicey's insight stands and that:

the broader and more loosely-textured a discretion is, *whether conferred on an official or a judge*, the greater the scope for subjectivity and hence for arbitrariness, which is the antithesis of the rule of law.

---

3   As previously highlighted in the answer to Question 1.

However, he is satisfied that the need for discretion to be narrowly defined, and its exercise to be capable of reasoned justification, are requirements that UK law almost always satisfies.

❖ *The laws of the land should apply equally to all, save to the extent that objective differences justify differentiation*

However, if the law is to apply to all, then governments should also accept the converse, that the rule of law does not allow for any distinction between British nationals and others. Unfortunately, the second part of the reciprocal link did not appear to have been considered when Parliament passed **Pt 4** of the **Anti-terrorism, Crime and Security Act 2001**, which was held to be incompatible with the **Human Rights Act 1998** in the *Belmarsh* case (*A v Secretary of State for the Home Department* (2004)).[4]

❖ *The law must afford adequate protection of fundamental human rights*[5]

This sub-rule goes beyond the formalistic approaches of Dicey to insist that the rule of law does in fact connote a substantive content, although Lord Bingham is less certain as to the particular detail of that content. However, he still maintains that:

> within a given state there will ordinarily be a measure of agreement on where the lines are to be drawn, and in the last resort (subject in this country to statute) the courts are there to draw them.

Consequently the rule of law must require the legal protection of such human rights as are recognised in that society.

❖ *Means must be provided for resolving, without prohibitive cost or inordinate delay, bona fide civil disputes which the parties themselves are unable to resolve*

As a corollary of the principle that everyone is bound by and entitled to the benefit of the law is the requirement that people should be able, in the last resort, to go to court to have their rights and liabilities determined. In stating this sub-rule Lord Bingham makes it clear that he is not seeking to undermine arbitration, which he sees as supremely important; rather he is looking to support the provisions of a properly funded legal aid scheme,[6] the demise of which he clearly regrets, as may be seen from what follows:

❖ *Ministers and public officers at all levels must exercise the powers conferred on them reasonably, in good faith, for the purpose for which the powers were conferred and without exceeding the limits of such powers*

....

4   This paragraph demonstrates the helpful use of specific legislation and case law in highlighting and/or strengthening argument.
5   As protection of human rights came to the fore following the end of the Second World War, it is a good example of the contemporary significance of the rule of law, as specifically highlighted in the question.
6   Further reference to the contemporary significance of the rule of law.

As Lord Bingham saw it:

> The historic role of the courts has of course been to check excesses of executive power, a role greatly expanded in recent years due to the increased complexity of government and the greater willingness of the public to challenge governmental (in the broadest sense) decisions. Even under our constitution the separation of powers is crucial in guaranteeing the integrity of the courts' performance of this role.

This judicial role has of course been met through judicial review.

❖ *Adjudicative procedures provided by the state should be fair*

In Lord Bingham's view decisions must be taken by adjudicators who are:

> independent and impartial ... free of any extraneous influence or pressure, and impartial in the sense that they are, so far as humanly possible, open-minded, unbiased by any personal interest or partisan allegiance of any kind.

However, a second element is involved, which relates to the presumption that any issue should not be finally decided against a person until they have had an adequate opportunity for their response to the allegation to be heard. In effect this means that:

> a person potentially subject to any liability or penalty should be adequately informed of what is said against him; that the accuser should make adequate disclosure of material helpful to the other party or damaging to itself; that where the interests of a party cannot be adequately protected without the benefit of professional help which the party cannot afford, public assistance should so far as practicable be afforded; that a party accused should have an adequate opportunity to prepare his answer to what is said against him; and that the innocence of a defendant charged with criminal conduct should be presumed until guilt is proved.

❖ *The existing principle of the rule of law requires compliance by the state with its obligations in international law*

This particular section of Lord Bingham's lecture is interesting for the indirect way in which he examined the involvement of the UK in the ongoing war in Iraq while, as he said,

> not for obvious reasons touch[ing] on the vexed question whether Britain's involvement in the 2003 war on Iraq was in breach of international law and thus, if this sub-rule is sound, of the rule of law.

The way he achieved this was through a comparison between the procedures followed in 2003 and those followed at the time of the Suez invasion of 1956. While he concluded that the comparison suggests that over the period the rule of law has gained ground in the UK it also allowed him to make some pointed comments in relation to the way the latter war was initiated.

In conclusion, Lord Bingham correlated the rule of law with a democratic society based on:[7]

> an unspoken but fundamental bargain between the individual and the state, the governed and the governor, by which both sacrifice a measure of the freedom and power which they would otherwise enjoy.

QUESTION 3

Explain the background and content of the **Human Rights Act (HRA) 1998**.

How to Read this Question

This is as straightforward a question as one could get on the Human Rights Act. The first part of the question requires some knowledge of the way the **European Convention on Human Rights (ECHR)** impacted on UK law and in particular the disadvantages of the convention not applying directly should be canvassed, although the greater part of the answer should focus on the actual provisions and operation of the **HRA 1998**.

How to Answer this Question

This question asks candidates to provide a brief consideration of the incorporation of the ECHR into UK law, through the mechanism of the **HRA 1998**. It requires a basic knowledge of the content and effect of the **HRA 1998**. The following points should be covered:

- ❖ explain what the **ECHR** is;
- ❖ explain the disadvantages of the UK's relationship to the **Convention** prior to the **HRA 1998**;
- ❖ list the various Articles that have been incorporated by the Act;
- ❖ consider the effect of the Act on public bodies;
- ❖ explain what is meant by a declaration of compatibility in relation to legislation;
- ❖ assess the role of the courts in relation to the Act;
- ❖ explain fast-track remedial action for legislation that is found to be incompatible.

Answer Structure

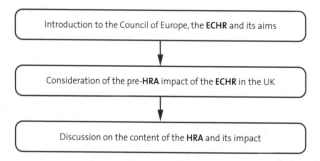

Introduction to the Council of Europe, the **ECHR** and its aims

↓

Consideration of the pre-**HRA** impact of the **ECHR** in the UK

↓

Discussion on the content of the **HRA** and its impact

7   Very relevant conclusion, which allows Lord Bingham himself to summarise the contemporary debate on the significance of the rule of law. (In an examination, you may find it difficult to provide a verbatim quotation: don't be afraid to paraphrase but ensure that you make it clear whether you are providing a quotation or paraphrasing.)

ANSWER

The UK was one of the initial signatories to the **European Convention on Human Rights (ECHR)** in 1950, which was created in post-war Europe as a means of establishing and enforcing essential human rights. In 1966, the UK recognised the power of the European Commission on Human Rights to hear complaints from individual UK citizens and, at the same time, recognised the authority of the **European Court of Human Rights (ECtHR)** to adjudicate in such matters. It did not, however, at that time, incorporate the **ECHR** into UK law. The **HRA 1998** corrected this anomalous situation by incorporating the rights enshrined in the **ECHR**, together with the protocols to it, into UK law. The rights incorporated are listed in **Sched 1** to the Act, and cover the following matters:[8]

- a general commitment to human rights (**Art 1**);
- right to life (**Art 2**);
- freedom from torture and inhuman or degrading treatment or punishment (**Art 3**);
- freedom from slavery and forced or compulsory labour (**Art 4**);
- right to liberty and security of person (subject to a derogation applicable to Northern Ireland) (**Art 5**);
- right to a fair and public trial within a reasonable time (**Art 6**);
- freedom from retrospective criminal law and no punishment without law (**Art 7**);
- right to respect for private and family life, home and correspondence (**Art 8**);
- freedom of thought, conscience and religion (**Art 9**);
- freedom of expression (**Art 10**);
- freedom of assembly and association (**Art 11**);
- right to marry and found a family (**Art 12**);
- prohibition of discrimination in the enjoyment of the Convention rights (**Art 14**);
- right to peaceful enjoyment of possessions and protection of property (**Art 1, Protocol 1**);
- right to education (subject to a UK reservation) (**Art 2, Protocol 1**);
- right to free elections (**Art 3, Protocol 1**);
- right not to be subjected to the death penalty (**Arts 1 and 2, Protocol 6**).

The above rights can be relied on by any person, non-governmental organisation or group of individuals. Importantly, it also applies where appropriate to companies which are incorporated entities and, hence, legal persons and other bodies. It cannot be relied on by governmental organisations, such as local authorities.

The general list of rights are not all seen in the same way. Some are absolute and inalienable and cannot be interfered with by the state, or, at least, only to a limited and tightly circumscribed degree. Others are merely contingent and are subject to derogation; that is, signatory states can opt out of them in particular circumstances. The absolute rights are those provided for in **Arts 2, 3, 4, 7** and **14**. All the others are subject to potential limitations; and, in particular, the rights provided for under **Arts 8, 9, 10** and **11** are subject to legal restrictions, such as are:

8   Don't panic if you can't remember all of the rights contained within the legislation. Examples of the most important would be acceptable.

necessary in a democratic society in the interests of national security or public safety, for the prevention of crime, for the protection of health or morals or the protection of the rights and freedoms of others [**Art 11(2)**].

In deciding the legality of any derogation, courts are required not just to be convinced that there is a need for the derogation, but they must also be sure that the state's action has been proportionate to that need. In other words, the state must not overreact to a perceived problem by removing more rights than is necessary to effect the solution. With further regard to the possibility of derogation, **s 19** of the Act requires a minister, responsible for the passage of any Bill through Parliament, either to make a written declaration that it is compatible with the Convention or, alternatively, to declare that although it may not be compatible, it is still the Government's wish to proceed with it.

The **HRA 1998** has profound implications for the operation of the English legal system.[9] **Section 2** of the Act requires future courts to take into account any previous decision of the **ECtHR**. It was at first thought that this provision would have a major impact on the operation of the doctrine of precedent within the English legal system, as it was thought effectively to sanction the overruling of any previous English authority that was in conflict with a decision of the **ECtHR**. However, in *Price v Leeds City* (2006) the House of Lords distinguished between decisions of the European Court of Justice and those of the European Court of Human Rights: the former are binding, while the latter are not.[10] As a consequence the House of Lords decided that the normal rules of precedent should apply, and lower courts should follow the House of Lords, even when their decisions have been overturned by the **ECtHR**. This does not apply, however, where the previous authority had been set without reference to the **Human Rights Act**.

Also, **s 3**, requiring all legislation to be read so far as possible to give effect to the rights provided under the Convention, has the potential to invalidate previously accepted interpretations of statutes which were made, by necessity, without recourse to the Convention. Thus in *Mendoza v Ghaidan* (2002), the Court of Appeal used **s 3** to extend the rights of same-sex partners to inherit a statutory tenancy under the **Rent Act 1977**. In *Fitzpatrick v Sterling Housing Association Ltd* (1999), the House of Lords had extended the rights of such individuals to inherit the lesser assured tenancy by including them within the deceased person's family. However, it declined to allow them to inherit statutory tenancies, on the grounds that they could not be considered to be the wife or husband of the deceased as the Act required. In *Mendoza*, the Court of Appeal held that the **Rent Act**, as it had been construed by the House of Lords in *Fitzpatrick*, was incompatible with **Art 14** of the **ECHR** on the grounds of its discriminatory treatment of surviving same-sex partners. The court, however, decided that the failing could be remedied by reading the words 'as

....

9 Although the question does not specifically ask for discussion of the impact of the **HRA**, it is implicit that consideration of its effect should be provided.

10 This distinction in very important. Students often confuse the **ECHR** with the law of the **EU** and, although the **EU** recognises and applies principles contained in the **Convention**, demonstrating that you understand the difference can only impress.

his or her wife or husband' in the Act as meaning 'as if they were his or her wife or husband'. The Court of Appeal's decision and reasoning was subsequently confirmed by the House of Lords in 2004.

Section 6 declares it unlawful for any public authority to act in a way which is incompatible with the Convention, and s7 allows the 'victim of the unlawful act' to bring proceedings against the public authority in breach. Section 8 empowers the court to grant such relief or remedy against the public authority in breach of the Act, as it considers just and appropriate. However, where a public authority is acting under the instructions of some primary legislation, which is itself incompatible with the Convention, the public authority will not be liable under s 6.

The Act expressly states that the courts cannot invalidate any primary legislation, essentially Acts of Parliament, which are found to be incompatible with the Convention. The courts can only make a declaration of such incompatibility and leave it to the legislature to remedy the situation through new legislation (s4). In this respect, the Act provides for the provision of remedial legislation through a fast-track procedure. This fast-track procedure gives a minister of the Crown the power to alter primary legislation by way of statutory instrument. This power is also available to implement judgments of the Strasbourg Court against the UK which are made after the coming into force of the HRA 1998. It is also available in urgent cases, where subordinate legislation has been quashed or declared invalid.

QUESTION 4

In relation to the European Convention of Human Rights and the European Court of Human Rights explain the following concepts:

(i)   derogation;
(ii)   margin of appreciation;
(iii) proportionality;
(iv)   the Convention as a living text.

How to Read this Question

This question requires candidates to be able to explain some procedural detail in relation to the ECHR. As it stands it requires quite a wide rather than a deep knowledge, but the question could be reformulated in any particular combination to assess greater depth of knowledge.

On reading this question you have to ask yourself whether you actually can answer all four parts. Three good answers out of four would be OK, but two out of four makes it a marginal question to tackle and certainly knowledge of only one part should make you look elsewhere if at all possible. That raises a point of general worth about doing exams. Marks are allocated according to the number of parts in the question, and remember, it is always easier to gain marks at the start of a question, So don't be tempted to spend most of your time on one part of a four-part question. You may be brilliant on derogation, but if you don't know the other three elements you still won't pass.

How to Answer this Question

Following on from the above it is essential to address each of the parts in the question. The first three parts of the question are of crucial importance and candidates should have some knowledge of them. Indeed they are of such importance that candidates might be tempted to spend too much time on any one aspect of the total question. Once again remember time management is important and you only have a limited period to provide a basic explanation of each of the terms.

Answer Structure

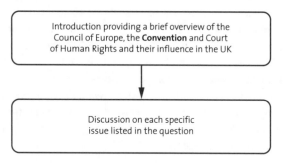

ANSWER

(i) Derogation

The rights listed in the **European Convention on Human Rights** are not all treated in the same way. Some rights are absolute and inalienable and cannot be interfered with by the signatory state to the **Convention**. Others rights, however, are merely contingent and are subject to derogation. This means that, in particular circumstances and to a limited and controlled degree, states can effectively opt out of those provisions they do not wish to comply with. For example and in particular, the UK **Humans Right Act**,[11] which implements the **ECHR**, provides that **Arts 8, 9, 10** and **11** are subject to legal restrictions such as are

> necessary in a democratic society in the interests of national security or public safety, for the prevention of crime, for the protection of health or morals or the protection of the rights and freedoms of others [**Art 11(2)**].

The UK entered such a derogation in relation to the extended detention of terrorist suspects without charge, under the **Prevention of Terrorism (Temporary Provisions) Act 1989**, subsequently replaced and extended by the **Terrorism Act 2000**. Those powers had been held to be contrary to **Art 5** of the **Convention** by the **ECtHR** in *Brogan v UK* (1989). In deciding the legality of any derogation, courts are required not just to be convinced that there is a need for the derogation, but they must also be sure that the state's action has been proportionate to that need. In other words, the state must not overreact to a perceived problem by removing more rights than is necessary to effect the solution.

11   Wherever possible, refer to legal authority in support of argument and to provide examples.

(ii) The Margin of Appreciation

This refers to the fact that the **ECtHR** recognises that there may well be a range of responses to particular crises or social situations within individual states, which might well involve some legitimate limitation on the rights established under the **ECHR**. The Court recognises that in such areas, the response should be decided at the local level, rather than being imposed centrally. The most obvious, but by no means the only, situations that involve the recognition of the margin of appreciation are the fields of morality and state security. For example, *Wingrove v UK* (1997)[12] concerned the refusal of the British Board of Film Classification to give a certificate of classification to the video film, *Visions of Ecstasy*, on the grounds that it was blasphemous, thus effectively banning it. The applicant, the director of the film, claimed that the refusal to grant a certificate of classification to the film amounted to a breach of his rights to free speech under **Art 10** of the **ECHR**. The Court rejected his claim, holding that the offence of blasphemy, by its very nature, did not lend itself to precise legal definition. Consequently, national authorities 'must be afforded a degree of flexibility in assessing whether the facts of a particular case fall within the accepted definition of the offence'. In reaching its decision, the Court clearly set out how the doctrine was to operate and its justifications. It also explained the different ranges of the margin of appreciation that will be allowed in different areas. Thus:

> Whereas there is little scope under **Article 10, para 2** of the **Convention (Art 10(2))** for restrictions on political speech or on debate of questions of public interest a wider margin of appreciation is generally available to the Contracting States when regulating freedom of expression in relation to matters liable to offend intimate personal convictions within the sphere of morals or, especially, religion. Moreover, as in the field of morals, and perhaps to an even greater degree, there is no uniform European conception of the requirements of 'the protection of the rights of others' in relation to attacks on their religious convictions. What is likely to cause substantial offence to persons of a particular religious persuasion will vary significantly from time to time and from place to place, especially in an era characterised by an ever growing array of faiths and denominations. By reason of their direct and continuous contact with the vital forces of their countries, State authorities are in principle in a better position than the international judge to give an opinion on the exact content of these requirements with regard to the rights of others as well as on the 'necessity' of a 'restriction' intended to protect from such material those whose deepest feelings and convictions would be seriously offended.

In *Civil Service Unions v UK* (1988), it was held that national security interests were of such paramount concern that they outweighed individual rights of freedom of association. Hence, the unions had no remedy under the **ECHR** for the removal of their members' rights to join and be in a trade union.

One point to note in relation to the operation of the margin of appreciation is that, by definition, it is a rule of international law, in that it recognises the different approaches of

---

12 Again the use of a relevant example can demonstrate understanding and aid explanation.

distinct states. Consequently, it is limited in operation to the supranational **ECtHR** and not to national courts. The latter may follow precedents based on the doctrine, but it is difficult to see how they could themselves apply it in a national context, although it would appear that the domestic courts' development of the doctrine of deference achieves similar ends to those allowed under the margin of appreciation.

(iii) Proportionality

Even where states avail themselves of the margin of appreciation, they are not at liberty to interfere with rights to any degree beyond what is required, as a minimum, to deal with the perceived problem within the context of a democratic society. In other words, there must be a relationship of necessity between the end desired and the means used to achieve it.

As the **ECtHR** stated in *Chorherr v Austria* (1994):

> The margin of appreciation extends in particular to the choice of the reasonable and appropriate means to be used by the authority to ensure that lawful manifestation can take place peacefully.

Proportionality is central to the jurisprudence of the **ECtHR** and as such is now central to the jurisprudence of the UK courts in relation to human rights issues. It is suggested that it will not be restricted to this limited sphere for long and that it will expand into judicial review and other areas as the **HRA** becomes increasingly understood and used.

(iv) The living instrument

It also has to be recognised that the **ECHR** as a legal document is not fixed text. As Luzius Wildhaber, the former president of the Court, stated:

On the question of evolutive interpretation, it is precisely the genius of the **Convention** that it is indeed a dynamic and a living instrument, which has shown its capacity to evolve in the light of social and technological developments that its drafters, however far sighted, could never have imagined. The **Convention** has shown that it is capable of growing with society; and in this respect its formulations have proved their worth over five decades. It has remained a live and modern instrument.

The 'living instrument' doctrine is one of the best-known principles of Strasbourg case law, the principle that the **Convention** is interpreted 'in the light of present day conditions', that it evolves, through the interpretation of the Court.

The recognition of this approach may be seen in the Court's legal recognition of transsexuals' new sexual identity in *Goodwin v UK* (2002). Until that decision, the Court had found that there was no positive obligation for the states to modify their civil status systems so as to have the register of births updated or annotated to record changed sexual identity. However, in *Goodwin*, the Court finally reached the conclusion that the fair balance now favoured the recognition of such rights, and ruled accordingly.

2 Sources of Law and Legal Reform

INTRODUCTION

There are different interpretations of the phrase 'source of law'. It can, in jurisprudence, refer to what it is in our nature or society that necessitates law. More generally, however, the expression refers to the procedural origin of the law which is applied in the courts. There are three main sources: parliamentary legislation, delegated legislation and the common law. Used in this sense, the latter phrase 'common law' connotes all judge-made law and therefore includes equity.

If you are covering this theme, you should be very familiar with the origins and modern role of both common law and equity. You should also understand the details of the process of enacting legislation from the stage before the publication of Green Papers to the final stage, the Royal Assent. However, the English legal system cannot be treated as static; it is continuously responding to changes that take place in society as a whole. To deny the relevance of European law in an English Legal System course would not only be restrictive, it would be wrong to the extent that it ignored an increasingly important factor in the formation and determination of UK law.

You should also have a good knowledge of the different bodies associated with reform: permanent institutions, that is, the Law Reform Committee, the Criminal Law Revision Committee and the Law Commission, and ad hoc bodies, such as Royal Commissions. You should also understand how the system resolves the interplay of several competing interest groups in order to produce legislation. This is a subject area where it is especially useful to have a sound knowledge of recent examples.

Checklist

You should be familiar with:

- the origin and modern operation of the common law;
- the origin and modern operation of equity;
- the stages of promulgation of legislation;
- parliamentary sovereignty and types of legislation;
- the types of delegated legislation and its advantages and disadvantages;
- the major institutions of the **European Union (EU)**, particularly the **European Court of Justice of the European Union (CJEU)**;
- the institutions of law reform, the **Law Commission**, ad hoc bodies, etc.

QUESTION 5

What are the main sources of law today?

How to Read this Question

This is a very general question and any answer has to cover a number of possible sources and allocate sufficient time to them to do them justice, while not concentrating too much on one particular source. The well-prepared candidate will have lots of detailed information on the various elements in this question but only a relatively superficial response can be given to each of those. It should also be noticed that the final word of the question is 'today'; the question might alternatively have asked about 'contemporary' sources. Those words indicate in particular that significant time should NOT be spend on the general development of the common law, which is all too often how students approach such a question.

How to Answer this Question

This is, apparently, a very straightforward question, but the temptation is to ignore the European Union (EU) as a source of law and to overemphasise custom as a source. The following structure does not make these mistakes:

Answer Structure

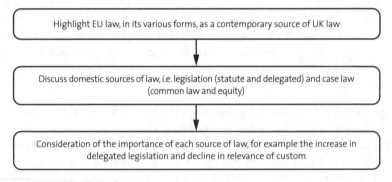

Highlight EU law, in its various forms, as a contemporary source of UK law

Discuss domestic sources of law, i.e. legislation (statute and delegated) and case law (common law and equity)

Consideration of the importance of each source of law, for example the increase in delegated legislation and decline in relevance of custom

ANSWER

European Law

Since the UK joined the **European Economic Community (EEC)** (now, following the Lisbon Treaty, the **European Union (EU)**), it has progressively but effectively passed the power to create laws which are operative in this country to the wider European institutions. The UK is now subject to Community law, not just as a direct consequence of the various treaties of accession passed by the UK Parliament, but increasingly it is subject to the secondary legislation generated by the various institutions of the EU.

European law takes three distinct forms: regulations, directives and decisions. Regulations are immediately effective without the need for the UK Parliament to produce its own legislation. Directives, on the other hand, require specific legislation to implement their proposals, but the UK Parliament is under an obligation to enact such legislation as will give effect to their implementation. Decisions of the **CJEU** are binding throughout the EU and take precedence over any domestic law.[1]

Parliamentary Legislation

Under UK constitutional law, it is recognised that Parliament has the power to enact, revoke or alter such and any law it sees fit to deal with and no one Parliament can bind its successors. The extent of this sovereignty may be brought into question with respect to the EU for such time as the UK remains a member, but within the UK, Parliament's power is absolute. This absolute power is a consequence of the historical struggle between Parliament and the Stuart monarchy in the seventeenth century. Parliament arrogated to itself absolute law-making power, a power not challenged by the courts, which were in turn granted an independent sphere of operation. It should be remembered, however, that the **Human Rights Act (HRA) 1998** has, for the first time, given the courts the power to question, although not strike down, primary legislation as being incompatible with the rights protected under the **European Convention on Human Rights (ECHR)**. It also allows the courts to declare secondary legislation to be invalid for the same reason.[2]

Parliament makes law in the form of legislation, that is, Acts of Parliament. There are various types of legislation. Whereas public Acts affect the public generally, private Acts only affect a limited sector of the populace, either particular people or people within a particular locality. Within the category of public Acts, a further distinction can be made between Government Bills and Private Member's Bills. The former are usually introduced by the Government, while the latter are the product of individual initiative on the part of particular MPs. Bills have to be considered by both Houses of Parliament and have to receive Royal Assent before they are enacted and become Acts of Parliament.

Delegated legislation has to be considered as a source of law, in addition, but subordinate, to general Acts of Parliament. Generally speaking, delegated legislation is law made by some person or body to whom Parliament has delegated its general law-making power. In statistical terms, it is arguable that at present, delegated legislation is actually more significant than primary Acts of Parliament. The output of delegated legislation in any year greatly exceeds the output of Acts of Parliament. Delegated legislation can take the form of Orders in Council, which permit the Government to make law through the Privy Council. Most delegated legislation, however, takes the form of statutory instruments, through which Government ministers exercise the powers given to them by general enabling legislation to make the particular rules which are to apply to any given

---

1 Highlighting **EU** law as a source of **UK** law demonstrates an awareness of contemporary sources. It also demonstrates an understanding of how **EU** law is incorporated into **UK** law (either automatically, called 'direct application', or through enactment by one of the UK's legislative authorities). Discussion of the impact of **EU** law is also relevant, in particular the knowledge that where **EU** and domestic sources of law conflict, **EU** law will take precedence (known as supremacy).

2 This demonstrates an understanding not only of the power of the UK Parliament as a legislator, and the relevance of statute as the main source of UK law, but also of contemporary pressures on the constitutional principle of parliamentary sovereignty.

situation within its ambit. A third type of delegated legislation is the bylaw, through which local authorities and public bodies are able to make legally binding rules within their area of competence or authority.

Any piece of delegated legislation is only valid if it is within the ambit of the powers actually delegated by Parliament. Any law made outside that restricted ambit of authority is void, as being *ultra vires*, and is open to challenge in the courts under the process of judicial review.[3]

Common Law

The next source of law that has to be considered is case law, the effective creation and refinement of law in the course of judicial decisions. It should be remembered that the UK's law is still a common law system and, even if legislation in its various guises is of ever increasing importance, the significance and effectiveness of judicial creativity should not be discounted. Judicial decisions are a source of law, through the operation of the doctrine of judicial precedent. This process depends on the established hierarchy of the courts and operates in such a way that, generally, a court is bound by the *ratio decidendi*, or rule of law implicit in the decision of a court above it in the hierarchy and usually by a court of equal standing in that hierarchy. Where statute law does not cover a particular area, or where the law is silent, it will generally be necessary for a court deciding cases relating to such an area to determine what the law is and, in so doing, that court will inescapably and unarguably be creating law. The scope for judicial creativity should not be underestimated and it should be remembered that the task of interpreting the actual meaning of legislation in particular cases also falls to the judiciary and provides it with a further important area of discretionary creativity. As the highest court in the land, the Supreme Court has particular scope for creating or extending the common law, and a relatively contemporary example of its adopting such an active stance can be seen in the way in which it overruled the long-standing presumption that a man could not be guilty of the crime of rape against his wife (see *R* (1991)). It should, of course, always be remembered that Parliament remains sovereign as regards the creation of law and any aspect of the judicially created common law is subject to direct alteration by statute.[4]

When a court is unable to locate a precise or analogous precedent, it may refer to legal textbooks for guidance and assistance. In strict terms, only certain venerable works of antiquity are actually treated as authoritative sources of law. Among the most important of these works are those by Glanvill from the twelfth century, Bracton from the thirteenth century, Coke from the seventeenth century and Blackstone from the eighteenth century. Legal works produced after *Blackstone's Commentaries of 1765* are considered to be of recent origin, and although they cannot be treated as authoritative sources, the courts on occasion will look at the most eminent works by accepted experts in particular fields in order to help determine what the law is or should be.

....

3 The discussion on delegated legislation demonstrates not only knowledge of its increasing use and importance but also an understanding of how it is enacted and its limits, as compared to statute.

4 Discussion here centres on how common law is created (i.e. it is law emanating from the courts) and its impact and importance (i.e. through the doctrine of judicial precedent). Legal authority is also provided, in support, in the form of a case example.

Custom

The final source of law that remains to be considered is custom. The romantic view of the common law is that it represented a crystallisation of common customs, distilled by the judiciary in the course of its travels around the land. Although some of the common law may have had its basis in general custom, a large proportion of these so-called customs were invented by the judges themselves and represented what they wanted the law to be, rather than what people generally thought it was.

There is, however, a second possible customary source of law and that is rules derived from specific local customs. Here, there is the possibility that the local custom might differ from the common law and thus limit its operation. Even in this respect, however, reliance on customary law as opposed to common law, although not impossible, is made unlikely by the stringent test that any appeal to it has to satisfy. Among these requirements are that the custom must have existed from 'time immemorial' (that is, since 1189) and must have been exercised continuously within that period and without opposition. The custom must also have been felt as obligatory, have been consistent with other customs and, in the final analysis, must be reasonable. Given this list of requirements, it can be seen why local custom does not loom large as an important source of law.[5]

Common Pitfalls

The temptation is to concentrate on only one source such as legislation or the common law, and to go into far more detail than is necessary for such a general question. Remember that each sub-topic in this answer can be asked as a question topic in its own right. So remember to cover most, if not all, of the potential sources.

Aim Higher

It is essential to be aware of the EU as a source of modern law and reference to the **Lisbon Treaty** will show an up-to-date awareness of that particular source. In relation to legislation, reference could be made to examples of legislation introduced by the coalition government.

QUESTION 6

Explain the emergence of the common law as a distinct historical category of legal regulation in the period following the Norman Conquest.

---

5   The discussion of custom as a source of law demonstrates an awareness that, although EU law, legislation and common law are the main sources of UK law, there are other sources. It also demonstrates an understanding that the importance of a source of law can change with time.

How to Read this Question

This question is made to look more complex than it actually is by the reference to the common law as 'a distinct historical category of legal regulation'. However, those words also suggest the way any answer should be approached: the law is to be seen and explained as a particular form of legal order which emerged from a historically specific context. Consequently the questions demands that the context, essentially the ongoing struggle to assert the Crown's authority over other sources of power, be examined in explaining how and why the early common law developed.

How to Answer this Question

A suggested plan for answering this question is as follows:

- ❖ introduction – the range of contributory factors;
- ❖ 'tradition expressed in action' (Simpson, *Legal Theory and Legal History*, 1987);
- ❖ the role of Henry II's clerics – itinerant royal justice;
- ❖ royal justice in competition with other sorts of justice;
- ❖ Pollock and Maitland's six principles (in *History of English Law*, 1911);
- ❖ conclusion – evaluating the role of an individual in legal history.

Answer Structure

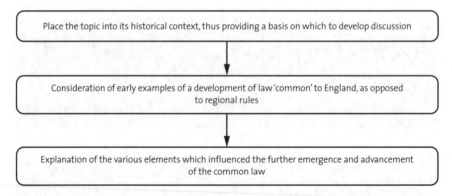

Place the topic into its historical context, thus providing a basis on which to develop discussion

Consideration of early examples of a development of law 'common' to England, as opposed to regional rules

Explanation of the various elements which influenced the further emergence and advancement of the common law

ANSWER

Unlike continental civil law, the English system does not originate from any particular set of texts or digests but from what has been described as 'tradition expressed in action'. Before the Norman Conquest in 1066, the English legal system involved a mass of oral customary rules, which varied according to region.[6] Even after the Norman invasion, there were still many different types of court apart from the royal court; most important, in their potential rivalry with the royal court in terms of power and income, were the feudal and manorial courts. The era running from the Norman invasion to the accession of Edward I in 1272 saw the struggle to administer justice between the royal judges and the

---

6   An introduction 'sets the scene' and demonstrates an understanding of what the common law developed *from*, that is, a mass of often disparate regional rules.

tribunals of feudal lords, the shires and the hundreds which had survived from Anglo-Saxon times. However, by the date of Edward I's accession to the throne the common law had been largely established. Certainly, the three courts of King's Bench, Common Pleas and Exchequer were operational by that time.

During Henry II's reign (1154–89), the clerics in his court began specialising in legal business and acting in a judicial capacity. These clerics developed a range of writs and establishing procedures which, perhaps very significantly, afforded them greater importance and provided them with a generous income.[7] These practices developed into the common law of England, the law which was available throughout the realm. Henry II may be regarded as the 'father of the common law' in that he was largely responsible for the regional and itinerant royal justice, through which (by sending his judges up and down the country) the law truly became common. Henry sent officials from the royal household to the counties and the travelling judges formed a nucleus of *iusticiarii totius Angliae* who had no local roots. It was under Henry II that judges were for the first time sent on 'circuits', hearing pleas in the major places they visited and taking over the work of the local courts. In this travelling mode, the royal representatives were *iusticiae errantes* (wandering justices) or *iusticiarii in itinere* (justices in eyre, that is, law French for journey). The judges were periodically sent on a 'general eyre', which included the whole country. Baker has argued, however, that it was the smaller circuit which was to prove 'the essence of the common law system', by bringing royal justice regularly to the counties.

The efforts of the royal judges were significantly assisted by the works of the text writers Glanvill and Bracton. Glanvill's *Tractatus de Legibus Angliae* (published under Henry II) was the first clear statement of the law, administered throughout the procedure of the royal courts. Glanvill was a senior royal judge. The writer's preface (it was probably not actually written by Glanvill, but by Hubert Walter or by Henry II's Chief Justiciary) divides the pleas into criminal and civil and the body of the work is mostly practical.

By the time of Edward I's reign, the royal judges had established the supremacy of their courts over all competing jurisdictions and the legal historians Pollock and Maitland set out six principles upon which this supremacy of the *Curia Regis* was based.

First, the King's court was a court to go to in default of justice. Under the Norman kings, the litigant who wished to proceed in the ordinary court obtained the King's 'Writ of Right Patent' which contained the threat *quod nisi feceris vicecomes meus faciet* (if you do not do this, my sheriff will). Complaints and petitions for justice were numerous and these cases formed the basis of the growth of the common law throughout the development of the Register of Writs (added to each time a judge accepted a new writ as suitable to be used again in similar cases).

Second, the Writ of Right issued by the Royal Chancery became compulsory for all pleas relating to freehold land. This was so even where the case was to be tried in the seigniorial court and so gave the King power over manorial courts.

....

7 This demonstrates an understanding of not only how but also why the 'common law' was developed.

Third was the introduction by Henry II of the Grand Assize as an alternative to trial by battle in the proceedings on the Writ of Right. As these cases were decided by impartial neighbours, it became much more popular than trial by battle and was only available in the royal court.

Fourth was Henry II's introduction of the Petty Assizes, also only obtainable in the King's court. These assizes were for trying disputes concerning *disseisin* (dispossession) of land. They did not actually infringe the feudal rights of the lord to try actions relating to the title to the freeholds of his tenants. They did, however, become very popular because of their summary nature and were frequently used by dispossessed owners to recover *seisin*, since the opponent rarely took any further action if his claim was weak.

The fifth factor was the expansion of the 'King's Peace' (the monarch's as opposed to a lord's right to deal with any local disorder, crime, etc.). Pleas of the Crown increased rapidly at this time and included many claims that would eventually evolve into torts.

Finally, Pollock and Maitland mention the important series of writs which began with the word *praecipe*, where the sheriff was commanded to investigate a matter and give any wrongdoer the right to give satisfaction, or else face the royal judges for their judgment. This was among the Pleas of the Crown and again quickly became quite popular on account of its efficiency.[8]

Kiralfy (in *English Legal History*, 1958) has advanced another factor significant in the acquisition of jurisdiction by the royal courts, namely, the construction given to the **Statute of Gloucester 1278** by the royal judges. This statute provided that no cases involving an amount of less than 40 shillings should be brought in the royal courts, but that they should be tried before local tribunals. The judges interpreted this to mean that no personal actions to recover a sum greater than 40 shillings could be commenced in the local courts, thus reserving all important legislation for themselves. It is relevant here that the judges were anxious to attract litigants because their fees varied with the amount of business done.

Apart from the advantageous nature of the remedy in the recovery of land provided by the Petty Assizes, the growth in popularity of the royal courts is connected with the progressive move towards strong, centralised government and its accompanying ability to compel attendance at court and enforce execution of its judgments. By contrast, we can look at the diminution in power of the feudal lords, their dilatory procedures and the inadequate powers to make defendants appear in their courts and to enforce judgments. Additionally, only the royal courts could give litigants the novel and desirable method of proof, the *recognitio* or jury, as it came to be called.

In conclusion, although Henry II may be seen as instrumental in making a number of important innovations which promoted the development of the common law, these policies were part of a wide and complex struggle for the power and revenue to be

8   These paragraphs provide an insight into how the common law afforded an improved system of justice and also reasons for its emerging popularity.

enjoyed by whomever controlled and administered justice. There were many other important figures involved, such as the clerics, the judges and the writers, whose own behaviour and interests it is important to appreciate in developing a proper understanding of the origins of the common law.

Common Pitfalls

Do not adopt the overly romantic, not to say misguided, approach of those who mistakenly see the progress of the judiciary round the country as a way of seeking out the existing common laws and bringing them together to establish a body of rules to be applied generally. The common law was to be common *to* all in application, but certainly was not common *from* all.

Aim Higher

The emergence of the common law has to be placed in its immediate historical context. The common law emerged as the product of a particular struggle for political power. Prior to the Norman Conquest of England in 1066, there was no unitary, national legal system. The emergence of the common law represents the imposition of such a unitary system under the auspices and control of a centralised power in the form of a sovereign king; in that respect, it represented the assertion and affirmation of that central sovereign power. The role of the legal writers, such as Glanvill and Bracton, should not be ignored in the development of the common law.

QUESTION 7

Explain how legislation is enacted and distinguish between primary and secondary legislation.

How to Read this Question

There are many possible questions that can be asked about the topic of legislation and exam candidates will have prepared for a number of such possibilities. The trick is to recognise what of the material you have prepared is necessary to answer the question actually being asked. In this case the focus of attention is on the process through which legislation is made, essentially the progress of a Bill through Parliament. This means that there are other aspects of relating to legislation that can be ignored, such as the sources of legislation or statutory interpretation, which candidates may have prepared. Unfortunately it is not uncommon for candidates to see the word 'legislation' and to regurgitate all they know about the topic, but really the key word is 'enacted'.

However, there is also a sting in the tail of this question that should not be overlooked: the requirement to differentiate between primary and secondary legislation. Although dealing with this part will not require as much as would be required in a full question on that topic, it must not be overlooked or forgotten.

How to Answer this Question

This is a wide-ranging question that requires a fairly close knowledge of the workings of Parliament. A suggested structure is as follows:

- ❖ distinguish statute law from judge-made common law;
- ❖ set out the actual process that legislation has to pass through to be enacted: this will require some detail;
- ❖ mention should be made of the role and potential conflict between the two Houses of Parliament;
- ❖ mention may be made of the Parliament Acts;
- ❖ mention the fact that enactment is not the same as implementation;
- ❖ make reference to the various types of legislation, emphasising the role of delegated legislation; mention should also be made of the potential impact of the Human Rights Act (HRA) 1998.

Answer Structure

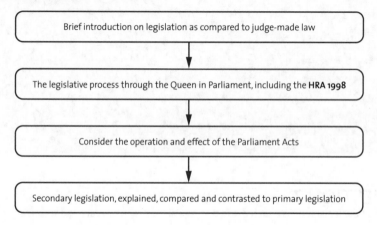

Brief introduction on legislation as compared to judge-made law

↓

The legislative process through the Queen in Parliament, including the **HRA 1998**

↓

Consider the operation and effect of the Parliament Acts

↓

Secondary legislation, explained, compared and contrasted to primary legislation

ANSWER

Although the courts retain an essential function in the interpretation of statutes, it has to be recognised that legislation is the predominant form of law making in contemporary times and is superior to the common law in that it can overrule decisions of the courts. The process through which an Act is passed by Parliament is a complicated one.[9]

The Legislative Process

Before any legislative proposal (known at that stage as a Bill) can become an Act of Parliament, it must proceed through, and be approved by, both Houses of Parliament and must receive the Royal Assent.[10] A Bill must be given three readings in both the House of Commons and the House of Lords before it can be presented for the Royal Assent. It is

---

9 A brief introduction allows legislation to be put into context and contrasted with 'judge-made' law.

10 The question specifically asks for a descriptive account of the process which must be undertaken in order to create statute. Consequently, the various stages must be clearly set out.

possible to commence the procedure in either House, although 'money Bills' (containing only financial provisions) must be placed before the Commons in the first instance.

When a Bill is introduced in the Commons, it undergoes five distinct procedures:

(a) It receives its first reading. This is purely a formal procedure in which its title is read and a date set for its second reading.

(b) After this comes the second reading; this is the time when its general principles are subject to extensive debate. The second reading is the critical point in the process of a Bill. At the end, a vote may be taken on its merits and if it is approved, it is likely that it will eventually find a place in the statute book.

(c) If the Bill passes its second reading, it is sent for consideration by a standing committee which will consider its provisions in detail. The function of the standing committee, which, if it is successfully proposed, may be replaced by a Select Committee or committee of the whole House, is to go through the Bill clause by clause and to amend it to bring it into line with the general approval given by the House at its second reading.

(d) The next stage is the report stage, at which the standing committee reports the Bill back to the House for the consideration of any amendments made by it.

(e) The final stage in the process is the third reading, during which further debate may take place, although on this occasion, it is restricted strictly to matters relating to the content; matters relating to general principles cannot be raised.

When a Bill has passed all these stages, it is passed to the House of Lords for its consideration, which is essentially similar, if less constrained by the pressures of time. After consideration by the Lords, the Bill is passed back, with any amendments, to the Commons, which must then consider such amendments. Where one House refuses to agree to the amendments made by the other, Bills can be repeatedly passed between them, but it should be remembered that Bills must complete their passage within the life of a particular parliamentary session and that a failure to reach agreement within that period might lead to the total loss of the Bill. Given the fact that the House of Lords is a non-elected institution and that the Members of the House of Commons are the democratically elected representatives of the voters, it has been apparent since 1911 that the House of Lords should not be in a position to block the clearly expressed wishes of the Commons. The **Parliament Act** of that year and of 1949 restricted the blocking power of the Lords. The situation now is that a money Bill can be enacted without the approval of the House of Lords after only one month's delay and any other Bill can only be delayed by one year by the House of Lords' recalcitrance.[11]

The most recent use of the **Parliament Acts** occurred in relation to the **Hunting Act 2004**, which in turn led to the Court of Appeal's determination of the legality of the later **Parliament Act**, which itself was introduced through the earlier **Act of 1911**. In *R (on the application of Jackson) v Attorney-General* (2005), an augmented nine-member panel of

---

11 The two Houses of Parliament (Commons and Lords) do not enjoy equal power in terms of enacting legislation, which is highlighted here.

the House of Lords concluded that the **1949 Act** was properly introduced and consequently the **Hunting Act** could not be challenged. The House of Lords, however, did differ in their assessment of the extent of the power extended to the House of Commons under the **Parliament Acts**. It is clear that a majority of the House of Lords were of the view that the House of Commons could use the powers given to it under the **Parliament Acts** to force through such legislation as it wished, but a number of the judges were of the view that the Commons could not extend its own lifetime through such a procedure, as that would be in direct contradiction to the provisions of the **Parliament Act 1911**.

No statute becomes law unless it has received the Royal Assent, and although in the unwritten constitution of the UK no specific rule expressly states that the monarch has to assent to any Act passed by Parliament, there is, by now, a convention to that effect and any monarch would place their constitutional status in extreme jeopardy by a refusal to grant the Royal Assent to legislation passed by Parliament. The procedural nature of the Royal Assent was highlighted by the **Royal Assent Act 1967**, which reduced the process of acquiring Royal Assent to a formal reading out of the short titles of any Act in both Houses of Parliament.

An Act of Parliament comes into effect on the date of the Royal Assent, unless there is any provision to the contrary in the Act itself. It is quite common for newly enacted statutes to contain commencement clauses which provide for the Act to become operational at some date in the future. Difficulty and an inevitable lack of certainty is produced, however, by the now common occurrence of passing general enabling Acts which delegate powers to a Government minister to introduce specific parts of the Acts in question at some later date, through the means of statutory instruments.[12]

Primary and Secondary Legislation

Legislation may be divided into two categories: primary legislation and secondary or delegated legislation. The former, essentially Acts of Parliament, are made by the process considered previously. On the other hand, delegated legislation is law made by some person or body to whom Parliament has delegated its general law-making power. Power to make delegated legislation is ultimately dependent upon the authority of Parliament and Parliament retains general control over the procedure for enacting such law. New regulations in the form of delegated legislation are required to be laid before Parliament. This procedure takes two forms depending on the provision of the enabling legislation. Some regulations require a positive resolution of one or both of the Houses of Parliament before they become law. Most Acts, however, simply require that regulations made under their auspices be placed before Parliament. They automatically become law after a period of 40 days unless a resolution to annul them is passed.

Delegated legislation can be challenged, through the procedure of judicial review, on the basis that the person or body to whom Parliament has delegated its authority has acted

12 This introduction to delegated or secondary legislation allows for further discussion of how primary and secondary legislation can be distinguished.

in a way that exceeds the limited powers delegated to them. It can also be declared invalid by the courts if found to be contrary to the provisions of the **HRA 1998**.

Even where a court holds that a piece of primary legislation does not comply with the provisions of the **HRA**, the court cannot declare the legislation invalid. The court can only issue a declaration of incompatibility stating that the primary legislation breaches the provisions of the Act. The actual changing of the incompatible Act remains solely the power of Parliament (*Bellinger v Bellinger* (2003)). The **HRA 1998** provides for a fast-track procedure, through secondary legislation, for changing any Act subsequently found to be in breach of the **European Convention on Human Rights**.

Common Pitfalls

❖ Answers should ensure that all aspects of the question are covered. This is a function of the essential examination skill of time management. There is so much that could be written in answering this question that the focus has to be on covering the essential materials.

❖ The question specifically refers to the enactment of legislation. It is consequently not an invitation to consider the rules of statutory interpretation (see Question 14 below).

Aim Higher

❖ Marks will be gained not just by setting legislation in contrast to the judge-made common law, but also by explaining its superiority and the source of that superiority in the democratic process.

❖ The different powers of the courts, under the **Human Rights Act 1998**, in relation to primary and secondary legislation are important and consideration of that aspect will be credited.

QUESTION 8

What do you understand by 'delegated legislation'? Consider its advantages and disadvantages and explain how it is controlled by Parliament and the courts.

How to Read this Question

Clearly the focus of this question is 'delegated' legislation so there is little scope for material about the nature of legislation generally. The question is generous to the extent that it actually reminds the candidate of the key ways in which such legislation is controlled; internally by Parliament and externally by the courts. It would be extremely careless not to take advantage of the hint provided and to ignore those aspects of the question.

How to Answer this Question

This question focuses more closely than the previous one on delegated legislation. It is suggested that the increased importance of delegated legislation makes it a likely question topic. A good answer plan will do the following:

- ❖ give an explanation of what is meant by delegated legislation;
- ❖ emphasise the large amount of delegated legislation that is produced annually;
- ❖ provide examples of the various types of delegated legislation;
- ❖ list and consider in some detail the various advantages and disadvantages;
- ❖ mention parliamentary scrutiny of delegated legislation;
- ❖ consider the powers of the courts to control delegated legislation, through judicial review and under the **HRA 1998**;
- ❖ weigh the advantages and disadvantages and offer a conclusion in favour or against its use.

Answer Structure

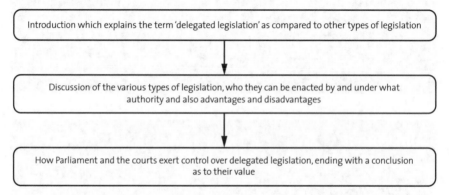

Introduction which explains the term 'delegated legislation' as compared to other types of legislation

Discussion of the various types of legislation, who they can be enacted by and under what authority and also advantages and disadvantages

How Parliament and the courts exert control over delegated legislation, ending with a conclusion as to their value

ANSWER

Generally speaking, delegated legislation is law made by some person or body to whom Parliament has delegated its general law-making power. Any piece of delegated legislation has the same legal force and effect as the Act of Parliament under which it is enacted, but equally only has effect to the extent that it is authorised by its enabling Act.

Delegated legislation can take the form of **Orders in Council** which permit the Government, through the Privy Council, to make law. The Privy Council is nominally a non-party political body of eminent parliamentarians, but in effect it is simply a means through which the Government, in the form of a committee of ministers, can introduce legislation without the need to go through the full parliamentary process. Perhaps the widest scope for Orders in Council is to be found in relation to EU law, for under **s 2(2)** of the **European Communities Act 1972**, ministers can give effect to provisions of the Community which do not have direct effect.

Statutory instruments (SIs) are the means through which Government ministers introduce particular regulations under powers delegated to them by Parliament by enabling legislation. As with Orders in Council, such provisions do not have to undergo the full

Sources of Law and Legal Reform 33

rigour of parliamentary procedure involved in the passing of Acts of Parliament. SIs tend to be of a highly specific and technical nature. One example of the way in which statutory instruments were used, if not abused, may be found in the **Limited Liability Partnership Act 2000**. Although the Act established this new form of legal entity, it stated very little about how it was to operate and be regulated. **Sections 14** and **15** of the Act simply stated that appropriate regulations would be made in the future and introduced through statutory instruments (the **Limited Liability Partnership Regulations 2001**).

Bylaws are the third type of delegated legislation, by means of which local authorities and public bodies are empowered by Parliament to make legally binding rules within their area of authority. Bylaws may be made by local authorities under such enabling legislation as the **Local Government Act 1972**.

In addition to the foregoing, the various Court Rule Committees are empowered to make the rules which govern procedure in the particular courts over which they have delegated authority, under such Acts as the **Supreme Court Act 1981**, the **County Courts Act 1984** and the **Magistrates' Courts Act 1980**.

The final source of delegated legislation is to be found in the power given to certain professional bodies to regulate the conduct of their members. An example of this type of delegated legislation is the power that the Law Society has been granted under the **Solicitors Act 1974** to control the conduct of practising solicitors.

Parliament delegates its law-making powers for a number of reasons. Among these is the fact that it simply does not have the time to consider every detail that might be required to fill out the framework of enabling legislation. A related point is the fact that given the highly specialised and extremely technical nature of many of the regulations that are introduced through delegated legislation, the majority of MPs simply do not have sufficient expertise or the technical knowledge to consider such provisions effectively.

These reasons why there has been an increased reliance on delegated legislation also suggest its potential advantages over the more traditional set-piece public Acts. For example, the fact that Parliament does not have to spend its time considering the minutiae of specific regulations permits it to focus its attention more closely, and at greater length, on the broader but no less important matters of principle in relation to the enactment of general enabling legislation. The use of delegated legislation also permits far greater flexibility in regulation, allowing rules to be changed quickly in response to changes in the situations they are aimed at regulating.

There are, however, distinct disadvantages in the prevalence of delegated legislation as a means of making legal rules. The most important of these relates to a perceived erosion in the constitutional role of Parliament, to the extent that it does not fully consider provisions made in this way. As Parliament generally is disempowered, others, notably Government ministers, are given more power than might be thought constitutionally correct. Such problems are compounded by the difficulty which ordinary MPs face in keeping abreast of the sheer mass of technically detailed legislation that is enacted in this form.

Also, the point must be raised that if parliamentarians cannot keep up with the flow of delegated legislation, how can the general public be expected to do so?

These difficulties and potential shortcomings in the use of delegated legislation are, at least to a degree, mitigated by the fact that specific controls exist in relation to it. These controls are twofold: parliamentary and judicial. Parliament exercises general control, to the extent that ministers are always responsible to Parliament for the regulations they actually make within the powers delegated to them by Parliament. Additionally, it is a usual requirement that such regulations be laid before Parliament. This procedure can take two forms, depending on the provision of the enabling legislation. The majority of Acts simply require that regulations made under their auspices be placed before Parliament and automatically become law after a period of 40 days, *unless a resolution to annul them is passed*. Other regulations require a *positive resolution* of one or both of the Houses of Parliament before they become law. Also, since 1973, there has been a Joint Select Committee on Statutory Instruments, whose function is to consider statutory instruments. It has to be remembered, however, that this committee merely scrutinises statutory instruments from a technical point of view as regards drafting, and therefore has no power as regards any question of policy in the regulation.

Previously, judicial control of delegated legislation was limited, but not unimportant. It was always possible for delegated legislation to be challenged, through the procedure of judicial review, on the basis that the person or body to whom Parliament has delegated its authority has acted in a way that exceeds the limited powers delegated to them. Any provision found to be outside this authority was *ultra vires* and consequently void. Additionally, there is a presumption that any power delegated by Parliament is to be used in a reasonable manner and the courts may, on occasion, hold particular delegated legislation to be void on the basis that it is unreasonable. The **HRA 1998** fundamentally altered the courts' power over delegated legislation. As secondary legislation, rather than primary legislation such as Acts of Parliament, delegated legislation may be declared invalid by the courts where it is found not to comply with the provisions of the **HRA 1998**, so ministers must be extremely careful to ensure that any delegated legislation is in fact compatible with the **ECHR**. An example of the courts quashing secondary legislation can be seen in *A v Secretary of State for the Home Department* (2005), in which the House of Lords quashed a derogation order wrongly made in relation to the **Anti-Terrorism Crime and Security Act 2001**. For a later example, see *HM Treasury v Mohammed Jaber Ahmed* (2010) (UKSC 2), the first substantive case heard by the Supreme Court. The court quashed fully the **Terrorism (United Nations Measures) Order 2006** and quashed parts of the **Al-Qaida and Taliban (UN Measures) Order 2006** as being *ultra vires* the powers of the Treasury extended to them under the **United Nations Act 1946**.

QUESTION 9

The English legal system can no longer be considered on its own, but has to be understood within the context of the European Union and its institutions.

What are the institutions referred to and what is their impact on the English legal system?

How to Read this Question

As with other topics the candidate will have prepared a lot of information relating to the European Union and its law and once again the task is to focus on what has been asked and to structure an answer that actually focuses on the particular aspects of the EU raised in the question. Once again the question has been posed in such a way as to invite a general answer but with a final part that challenges the candidate to go beyond the merely descriptive to offer an element of analysis as to the effect of the EU on domestic UK institutions and law. To gain top marks that final aspect cannot be ignored.

How to Answer this Question

Again, it has to be emphasised that the English legal system can only be understood in the context of the EU. This straightforward question ensures that a candidate is at least aware of that context. Such an awareness can be shown by covering the following points:

❖ a short history introductory paragraph setting out the essential institutions of the EU;

❖ a detailed description of the essential institutions of the EU and their relationships and particular roles and functions;

❖ a focus on the relationship between the CJEU and the domestic courts of the UK, with examples where possible.

Answer Structure

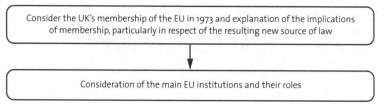

Consider the UK's membership of the EU in 1973 and explanation of the implications of membership, particularly in respect of the resulting new source of law

Consideration of the main EU institutions and their roles

ANSWER

The major institutions of the European Union are: the Council; the European Parliament; the Economic and Social Committee; the Commission; and the Court of Justice of the European Union.

The Council

The **Lisbon Treaty** established two new offices: President of the European Union, a position currently held by Herman Van Rompuy of Belgium; and High Representative for Foreign Affairs, effectively that of EU foreign minister, a position held by Baroness Ashton from the UK. However, it should be recognised that, although significant, neither of these new posts carries any real executive power as against that of the Union's main sources of political power, pre-eminently the Council of Ministers. The Council is made up of ministerial representatives of each of the 28 Member States of the Union. Thus, when considering economic matters, the various states will be represented by their finance ministers, or, if the matter relates to agriculture, the various agricultural ministers will attend. The Council of Ministers is, in essence, the supreme organ of the EU and, as such, it has the final say in deciding upon Community matters, although the **Treaty of Lisbon (2007)** has given the Parliament powers of co-determination in some areas. Although it acts on recommendations and proposals made to it by the Commission, it does have the power to instruct the Commission to undertake particular investigations and to submit detailed proposals for its consideration.

The European Parliament

The European Parliament is the directly elected European institution and, to that extent, it can be seen as the body which exercises democratic control over the operation of the EU. As in national parliaments, Members are elected to represent constituencies, the elections being held every five years. Membership is divided among the 28 Member States in proportion to the size of their various populations. The Parliament's general secretariat is based in Luxembourg and although the Parliament sits in plenary session in Strasbourg for one week in each month, its detailed and preparatory work is carried out through 18 permanent committees which usually meet in Brussels. Originally the powers of the Parliament were merely advisory and supervisory, but its powers have significantly increased since the early days of the EEC until now, following the Lisbon Treaty, it shares the EU legislative function with the Council through the process of co-decision making, now referred to as 'the ordinary legislative procedure'. In this way, the vast majority of European laws are adopted jointly and on an equal footing by the European Parliament and the Council. However, in the case of 'special legislative procedures', Parliament still retains only a consultative role. Thus, in areas such as taxation, it can only provide an advisory opinion to the Council. If such consultation is obligatory the proposal cannot acquire the force of law unless Parliament has delivered an opinion but the Council is not required to accept the opinion proffered.

The powers of the European Parliament should not be confused, however, with those of national parliaments in terms of initiating legislation. While the Parliament can reject, amend or, at its weakest, advise on proposals for legislation, it cannot, itself, make such a proposal, being dependent on the Commission putting proposals before it before anything can become law. However, it does now have a similar power to that of the Council to request the Commission to submit particular proposals to the Council.

The Commission

The Commission is the executive of the EU, but it also has a vital part to play in the legislative process. To the extent that the Council can only act on proposals put before it by the Commission, the latter institution has a duty to propose to the Council measures that will advance the achievement of the Union's general policies.

Another of the key functions of the Commission is the implementation of the policies of the Union, and to that end it controls the allocation of funds to the various common programmes within the Union. It also acts, under instructions from the Council, as negotiator between the Union and external countries.

A further executive role of the Commission is to be found in the manner in which it operates to ensure that Treaty obligations between states are met and that Community laws relating to individuals are enforced. In order to fulfil these functions, the Commission has been provided with extensive powers, both in relation to the investigation of potential breaches of Community law and the subsequent punishment of offenders. The classic area in which these powers can be seen in operation is competition law. Under **Arts 105** and **106** of the **Treaty on the Functioning of the European Union (TFEU)** (formerly **Arts 85** and **86** of the **EC Treaty**), the Commission has substantial powers to investigate and control potential monopolies and anti-competitive behaviour and it has used these powers to levy what, in the case of private individuals, would amount to huge fines where breaches of Community competition law have been discovered. For example, in 2004 Microsoft were fined €497m and in 2009 Intel were fined €1.06bn. If the individual against whom a finding has been made objects to either the result of the investigation or the penalty imposed, the course of appeal is to the ECJ.

The Court of Justice

The **ECJ** is the judicial arm of the EU and, in the field of Community law, its judgments overrule those of national courts. It consists of 28 judges, assisted by eight advocates general, and the Court sits in Luxembourg. The role of the advocates general is to investigate the matter submitted to the Court and to produce a report, together with a recommendation for the consideration of the Court. The actual court is free to accept the report, or not, as it sees fit.

The jurisdiction of the ECJ involves it in two key areas in particular:

(a) determining whether any measures adopted, or rights denied, by the Commission, Council or any national government are compatible with Treaty obligations. Such actions may be raised by any Union institution, government or individual. A Member State may fail to comply with its Treaty obligations in a number of ways. It might fail or indeed refuse to comply with a provision of the Treaty or a regulation; alternatively, it might refuse to implement a directive within the allotted time provided. Under such circumstances, the state in question will be brought before the ECJ, either by the Commission or another Member State or, indeed, individuals within the state, as being in dereliction of its responsibility;

(b) determining, at the request of national courts, the interpretation of points of Community law. This procedure can take the form of a preliminary ruling where the request precedes the actual determination of a case by the national court. The point that has to be remembered, however, is that it is the **ECJ**'s role to determine such issues and in relation to those issues, it is superior to any national court.

The General Court (Formerly the Court of First Instance)

The **Court of First Instance**, separate from the existing Court of Justice, was introduced by the **Single European Act 1986**. Under the **Treaty of Lisbon** it was renamed the General Court. It has jurisdiction in first instance cases, with appeals going to the **CJEU** on points of law.

Civil Service Tribunal

The former jurisdiction of the Court of First Instance, in relation to internal claims by EU employees, was transferred to this distinct institution in 2004.

The above three distinct courts together constitute the **Court of Justice of the European Union**.

Common Pitfalls

It is an almost unforgivable error to confuse the European Union and the European Council and their respective courts the European Court of Justice and the European Court of Human Rights. They are distinct and must always be dealt with as such.

Aim Higher

It is essential to be aware of the consequences of the **Lisbon Treaty**, but additional marks will be awarded for a thorough knowledge of those consequential changes and the ability to refer to the new Article number. Given the significance of the changes it is not impossible that full questions could be set on the consequences of the **Lisbon Treaty**.

QUESTION 10

Explain the structure and powers of the **Court of Justice of the European Union (CJEU)**, paying particular regard to its relationship with UK courts.

How to Read this Question

It should be noted that answers to this question are required to address **three** distinct elements relating to the **CJEU**:

- ❖ structure, which is straightforward;
- ❖ powers, which is less clear; and
- ❖ relationship with UK courts, which is, at least politically, contentious.

How to Answer this Question

Particular attention should be paid to the relationship of the **CJEU** to the domestic courts within the UK. In answering it, students could usefully apply the following structure:

- ❖ reference must be made to the three distinct legal forums that constitute the **CJEU** as well as the court that goes by that name;
- ❖ describe the overall structure and the interrelationship between the several individual courts within that structure;
- ❖ detail the role and powers of the **CJEU**;

❖ explain the way in which references can be made to the **CJEU** from domestic courts under **Art 267** (formerly **Art 234**);

❖ provide some examples of cases decided by the **CJEU** that have had particular impact on the UK.

Answer Structure

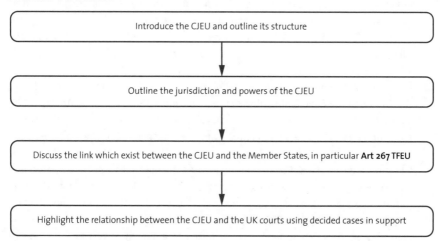

Introduce the CJEU and outline its structure

Outline the jurisdiction and powers of the CJEU

Discuss the link which exist between the CJEU and the Member States, in particular **Art 267** TFEU

Highlight the relationship between the CJEU and the UK courts using decided cases in support

ANSWER

Prior to the **Lisbon Treaty**, it was accurate to refer to European Community law, but this reference has now been replaced by European Union law. The **Court of Justice of the European Union (CJEU)** is the judicial arm of the EU and, in the field of European Union law, its judgments overrule those of national courts. Prior to the Lisbon Treaty this court was known as the **European Court of Justice (ECJ)**.

The current **CJEU** consists of 28 judges, assisted by eight advocates general, and sits in Luxembourg. The role of the advocates general is to investigate the matter submitted to the Court and to produce a report, together with a recommendation for the consideration of the Court. The actual Court is free to accept the report or not, as it sees fit.

A Court of First Instance, separate from the **CJEU**, was introduced by the **Single European Act 1986**. Under the **Treaty of Lisbon** it was renamed the **General Court**. It has jurisdiction in first instance cases, with appeals going to the **CJEU** on points of law.

The former jurisdiction of the Court of First Instance, in relation to internal claims by EU employees, was transferred to a newly created **European Union Civil Service Tribunal** in 2004. Together the three distinct courts constitute the **Court of Justice of the European Union**. The aim of introducing the two latter courts was to reduce the burden of work on the **CJEU**, but there is a right of appeal, on points of law only, to the full **CJEU**.[13]

13 This introduction provides a helpful overview of the **CJEU**, in particular its structure and composition.

The **CJEU** performs two key functions:[14]

(a) It decides whether any measures adopted, or rights denied, by the Commission, Council or any national government are compatible with Treaty obligations. Such actions may be raised by any **EU** institution, government or individual. A Member State may fail to comply with its Treaty obligations in a number of ways. It might fail or, indeed, refuse to comply with a provision of the Treaty or a regulation; alternatively, it might refuse to implement a directive within the allotted time provided for. Under such circumstances, the state in question will be brought before the **CJEU**, either by the Commission or another Member State or, indeed, individuals within the state concerned.

(b) It provides authoritative rulings, at the request of national courts under **Art 267**[15] of the **Treaty on the Functioning of the European Union (TFEU)** (formerly **Art 234** of the **EC Treaty**), on the interpretation of points of Union law. When an application is made under **Art 234**, the national proceedings are suspended until such time as the determination of the point in question is delivered by the **CJEU**. While the case is being decided by the **CJEU**, the national court is expected to provide appropriate interim relief, even if this involves going against a domestic legal provision, as in *Factortame Ltd v Secretary of State for Transport (No 1)* (1989). The Common Fishing Policy established by the EEC had placed limits on the amount of fish that any member country's fishing fleet was permitted to catch. In order to gain access to British fish stocks and quotas, Spanish fishing boat owners formed British companies and re-registered their boats as British. In order to prevent what it saw as an abuse and an encroachment on the rights of indigenous fishermen, the British Government introduced the **Merchant Shipping Act 1988**, which provided that any fishing company seeking to register as British would have to have its principal place of business in the UK and at least 75 per cent of its shareholders would have to be British nationals. This effectively debarred the Spanish boats from taking up any of the British fishing quota. Some 95 Spanish boat owners applied to the British courts for judicial review of the **Merchant Shipping Act 1988**, on the basis that it was contrary to Community law. The case went from the High Court, through the Court of Appeal, to the House of Lords, which referred the case to the **CJEU**. There, it was decided that the **EC Treaty** required domestic courts to give effect to the directly enforceable provisions of Community law and, in doing so, such courts are required to ignore any national law that runs counter to Community law.

The reference procedure can take the form of a preliminary ruling where the request precedes the actual determination of a case by the national court. **Article 267** (formerly **Art 234**) provides that:

....

14 In order to answer the question set, the jurisdiction and powers of the **CJEU** need to be carefully considered.

15 **Art 267 TFEU** provides the only direct link between the **CJEU** and courts within the Member States. As the question specifically asks for consideration of the relationship between the European Court and the UK courts, no answer would be considered complete without such discussion.

The Court of Justice shall have jurisdiction to give preliminary rulings concerning:

(a)   the interpretation of treaties;
(b)   the validity and interpretation of acts of the institutions of the Union and of the European Central Bank;
(c)   the interpretation of the statutes of bodies established by an act of the Council, where those statutes so provide.

Where such a question is raised before any court or tribunal of a member state, that court or tribunal may, if it considers that a decision on the question is necessary to enable it to give judgment, request the Court of Justice to give a ruling thereon.

Where any such question is raised in a case pending before a court or tribunal of a member state against whose decision there is no judicial remedy under national law, that court or tribunal shall bring the matter before the Court of Justice.

It is clear that it is for the national court, and not the individual parties concerned, to make the reference. Where the national court or tribunal is not the 'final' court or tribunal, the reference to the **CJEU** is discretionary. Where the national court or tribunal is the 'final' court, then reference is obligatory. However, there are circumstances under which a 'final' court need not make a reference under **Art 267** (formerly **Art 234**). These are:

(a)   where the question of Community law is not truly relevant to the decision to be made by the national court;
(b)   where there has been a previous interpretation of the provision in question by the **CJEU**, so that its meaning has been clearly determined;
(c)   where the interpretation of the provision is so obvious as to leave no scope for any reasonable doubt as to its meaning. This latter instance has to be used with caution given the nature of Union law; for example, the fact that it is expressed in several languages using legal terms which might have different connotations within different jurisdictions. However, it is apparent that where the meaning is clear, no reference need be made.

In interpreting EU provisions, a purposive and contextual approach is mainly adopted, as against the more restrictive methods of interpretation favoured in relation to UK domestic legislation. The clearest statement of this purposive/contextualist approach adopted by the **CJEU** is contained in its judgment in the *CILFIT* case:

Every provision of Community law must be placed in its context and interpreted in the light of the provisions of Community law as a whole, regard being had to the objectives thereof and to its state of evolution at the date on which the provision in question is to be applied.

CILFIT Srl v Minister of Health (No 283/81) (1982)

Another major difference between the **CJEU** and courts within the English legal system is that the former is not bound by the doctrine of precedent[16] in the same way as the latter

16   The matter of precedent is significant as, although the **CJEU** is not bound by its own decisions, its decisions are binding on national courts, including those of the UK.

are. It is always open to the **CJEU** to depart from its previous decisions where it considers it appropriate to do so. Although it will endeavour to maintain consistency, it has on occasion ignored its own previous decisions, as in *European Parliament v Council* (1990), where it recognised the right of the Parliament to institute an action against the Council.

Common Pitfalls

❖ Do not confuse the **CJEU** with the **ECtHR**.
❖ Ensure that reference is to the current titles of the courts.
❖ Ensure that references are to the current treaties.

Aim Higher

❖ It is a requirement of the question, but the functions of the three different judicial forums will be welcomed by examiners.
❖ Many textbooks will not, even yet, have been updated in time to include the new Article numbers in the two new treaties. Clearly good marks are available for anyone who knows the changes.

QUESTION 11

Critically examine the role of the Law Commission in the development of law in England.

How to Read this Question

This is a very straightforward question and has nothing to hide. It simply looks for a general coverage of how the Law Commission operates, so you can feel confident in producing an overall explanation and consideration, as long as you bear in mind the points made in the next section.

How to Answer this Question

This question requires an analysis of the role of, and the work undertaken by, the Law Commission. As is usually the case, the word 'critically' indicates that what is required is not merely a description of the Law Commission and its role, but an examination of its position, as a source of legislative proposals, within the wider constitutional framework together with an assessment of its effectiveness or any reasons for its lack of effectiveness.

Particular points to cover are:

❖ the limitations inherent in the roles of Parliament and the courts in formulating new legal proposals;
❖ the creation, structure and procedure of the Law Commission should be considered in some detail;
❖ reference should be made to the content of the current (eleventh) programme;

❖ reference should also be made to previous commission recommendations that have been implemented;

❖ rejected recommendations and as yet unimplemented recommendations should be mentioned;

❖ the provisions of the **Law Commission Act 2009** should be considered.

Answer Structure

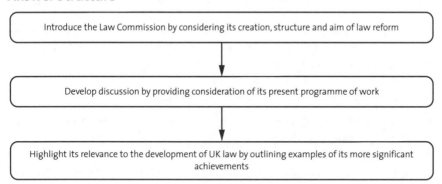

Introduce the Law Commission by considering its creation, structure and aim of law reform

Develop discussion by providing consideration of its present programme of work

Highlight its relevance to the development of UK law by outlining examples of its more significant achievements

ANSWER

According to strict legal practice, law reform is either a product of parliamentary or judicial activity. Parliament tends, however, to be concerned with particularities of law reform, and the judiciary are constitutionally and practically disbarred from reforming the law in anything other than an opportunistic and piecemeal way. Therefore, there remains a need for the question of law reform to be considered generally and a requirement that such consideration be conducted in an informed but disinterested manner.

That need is met particularly by the Law Commission.[17]

The Law Commission was established under the **Law Commission Act 1965**. It was set up under the auspices of Lord Gardiner LC, with the specific aim of improving the previous ad hoc consideration of law reform by charging it with the duty of keeping the law *as a whole* under review and making recommendations for its *systematic* reform. Under the **Act of 1965**, the Law Commission was constituted as an independent body with full-time members. It was given duties with regard to the revision and codification of the law, but its prime duty was, and remains, law reform.

The Law Commission only ever recommends reform after it has undertaken an extensive process of consultation with informed and/or interested parties. It is this process of general and disinterested consultation, as the basis for the formulation of a genuinely informed recommendation, which distinguishes the procedure of the Commission from the reforms of the judiciary and the partial reforms advocated by interested parties.

17 This introduction sets the scene for the rest of the answer by immediately clarifying the need for the Law Commission.

Although it is certainly true that it was the judiciary who altered the common law rule relating to rape within marriage (*R* (1991)), but it is perhaps worthy of mention that the Law Commission had already issued a working paper, entitled *Rape Within Marriage* in 1990, and its report of the same name was issued in 1992 (Law Com No 205). The point to be made is that judges can only change the common law with regard to the problem encapsulated in the case that comes before them; the Commission, on the other hand, is at liberty to consider all matters relating to a specific issue.

Although the scope of the Commission is limited to those areas set out in its programme of law reform, its ambit is not unduly restricted, as may be seen from the range of matters covered in its eleventh programme set out in July 2011.[18]

Among the areas to be covered in the new programme are:

❖ Charity law, examining a range of issues concerning the constitution and regulation of charities and their activities;

❖ Contempt, reviewing the law on contempt to take into account use of the internet and other technologies and to ensure courts have the powers they need to deal with contempt in the face of the court;

❖ Misconduct in a public office, simplifying and clarifying this common law offence, and ensuring the law takes into account the fact that functions traditionally considered to be public in nature are now often discharged by private individuals and volunteers;

❖ Offences against the person, restructuring the law, probably by creating a new hierarchy of offences, and modernising and simplifying the language used to define offences against the person.

In addition to these programme projects, ministers may refer matters of particular importance to the Commission for its consideration. For example, it was just such a referral by the Home Secretary, after the Macpherson Inquiry into the *Stephen Lawrence* case, that gave rise to the Law Commission's recommendation that the rule against double jeopardy be removed in particular circumstances. An extended version of that recommendation was included in the **Criminal Justice Act 2003**.[19]

Annual reports list all Commission publications. The Law Commission claims that, in the period since its establishment in 1965, over 100 of its law reports have been implemented. Examples of legislation following from Law Commission reports are: the **Contracts (Rights of Third Parties) Act 1999**, based on the recommendations of the Commission's Report No 180, *Privity of Contract*; and the **Trustee Act 2000**, based on the Commission's Report No 260. In February 2002 the **Land Registration Act** was passed, which has had a major impact on the land registration procedure. The Act implemented the draft Bill which was the outcome of the Commission's largest single project.

....

18 Consultation on the twelfth programme was initiated in spring 2014.

19 Provision of details relating to some of its noteworthy achievements again allows depth of knowledge to be demonstrated.

Current judicial review procedures are very much the consequence of a 1976 Law Commission report, and a review of their operation and proposals for reform was issued in October 1994.

In the area of criminal law, the preparatory work done by the Commission on several aspects of the criminal justice system (bail, double jeopardy and the revelation of an accused person's bad character) was incorporated into the **Criminal Justice Act 2003**.

In November 2006 the Law Commission published its final *Report on Partial Defences to Murder* setting out recommendations for reform of the law of homicide proposing the adoption of the three-tier structure, comprising first degree murder, second degree murder and manslaughter.

Although the recommendations on partial defences were implemented to a substantial extent in the **Coroners and Justice Act 2009**, as yet there has been no move to implement the Commission's wider recommendation in regard to the law relating to murder. However, such a dilatory response to Commission reports is not unusual. In its report covering 2005/06, its fortieth anniversary year, the then chairman Sir Roger Toulson expressed some regret, not to say frustration, at the limited impact that the Commission could make in the area of law making and reform. As he stated:

> The public money spent on enabling us to help provide the citizen with laws that are understandable and relevant to the 21st century can only be justified if the government is able to find time to implement those proposals it accepts.

In response to this failure to implement Law Commission reports, the former Law Lord, Lord Lloyd of Berwick, introduced the Law Commission Bill 2008–09 in the House of Lords. In support of the Bill Lord Kingsland pointed out that: 'Over the years … [the Law Commission] has been tasked with many seemingly intractable problems, has grappled with them and produced a solution, only to find that solution spurned by the political classes.'

The resultant Act[20] contains provisions that amend the **Law Commission Act 1965** so as to:

❖ require the Lord Chancellor to prepare an annual report, to be laid before Parliament, on the implementation of Law Commission proposals;

❖ require the Lord Chancellor to set out plans for dealing with any Law Commission proposals which have not been implemented and provide the reasoning behind decisions not to implement proposals;

❖ allow the Lord Chancellor and Law Commission to agree a protocol about the Law Commission's work. The protocol would be designed to provide a framework for the relationship between the UK Government and the Law Commission, and the Lord Chancellor would have to lay the protocol before Parliament.

---

20 The **Law Commission Act 2009** is important as it strengthens the influence of the Law Commission and encourages Government to look carefully at its proposals.

The Commission's annual report for 2012/13 states that currently 70 per cent of Commission reports have been accepted and implemented at least in part.

Common Pitfalls

In regard to this topic, the temptation is to undertake an answer without sufficient information. The assumption, and probably the fact, is that the writer knows something about the role and function of the Law Commission, but such general, superficial, knowledge soon runs out. It is for that very reason that a good plan/structure is necessary, to ensure that the answer will cover sufficient ground to generate good marks.

It is also essential to make sure that reference is made to the appropriate, and by definition the most up-to-date, sources of information relating to the Law Commission's programmes and its latest successes, or otherwise, in implementation.

Aim Higher

References to specific investigations, outside of the general programme, which may have been approved, should be referenced, as should any legislation introduced as a result of previous Commission recommendations.

Ensure that reference is made to the **Law Commission Act 2009**.

3

Judicial Reasoning

INTRODUCTION

This chapter examines the way in which judges reach decisions in particular cases. Central to the common law is the doctrine of judicial precedent. This means that, depending on the level of the court in the hierarchy, previous 'decisions' of one court are supposed to be binding on later courts. The implication of the traditional approach to precedent is that it is a strictly applied, highly rational and almost scientific process. However, as will be demonstrated, the mechanisms deployed by judges in deciding cases allow them a large degree of discretion in reaching decisions. This introduction of the possibility of discretion necessarily opens the question of the accountability of the judges, which will be addressed directly in Chapter 7.

While the common law is, by definition, judge made, the extent to which judges can influence the operation of statute law through interpreting it in particular ways should not be underestimated.

Checklist
You should be familiar with:
■ the nature of legal reasoning, as opposed to reasoning in general;
■ the hierarchy of the courts;
■ the doctrine of binding precedent;
■ how judges avoid the strict operation of precedent;
■ the rules of, and presumptions relating to, statutory interpretation.

QUESTION 12

Consider how the doctrine of binding precedent operates within the English court structure, having particular regard to its advantages and disadvantages.

How to Read this Question

A full answer on the nature of precedent would require no little consideration of the impact on that doctrine of European law and courts, both the **CJEU** and the **ECtHR**. Such a full-scale treatment would be beyond the scope of the relatively short examination answer, and in recognition of that fact the writer of the questions has, at least, attempted to place limits on the answer by restricting it to matters 'within' the English court structure.

How to Answer this Question

Once the scope of the question is realised, as pointed out above, it appears as a very straightforward, traditional question. It requires the following:

- ❖ define what binding precedent is in such a way as to explain how it is supposed to operate, with appropriate reference to *ratio decidendi* and *obiter dictum/ dicta*;
- ❖ emphasise the authoritative hierarchy of the court structure in the UK legal system;
- ❖ highlight the fact that the Supreme Court has now replaced the House of Lords as the highest court in the UK;
- ❖ consider the relationship between the various courts within the hierarchy, and also the extent to which they are governed by their own previous decisions;
- ❖ consider the difference between the criminal and civil law at the level of the Court of Appeal;
- ❖ refer to the process of distinguishing cases on the basis of their facts;
- ❖ consider advantages and disadvantages – it is essential to note that some of the supposed advantages are, in fact, problematic, not to say contradictory.

Answer Structure

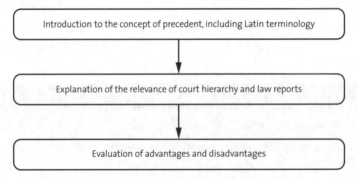

Introduction to the concept of precedent, including Latin terminology

Explanation of the relevance of court hierarchy and law reports

Evaluation of advantages and disadvantages

ANSWER

The doctrine of binding precedent, or *stare decisis*, lies at the heart of the English legal system. In essence, the doctrine refers to the fact that within the hierarchical structure of the English courts, a decision of a higher court will be binding on a court below.[1]

Since September 2009 the Supreme Court[2] has replaced the House of Lords so the Supreme Court now stands at the summit of the English court structure and its decisions are binding on all courts below it in the hierarchy (all future references to the Supreme Court will include the previous court where appropriate). As regards its own previous

---

1   An introduction allows the scene to be set and the basics of the topic to be outlined.

2   The hierarchy of the courts is a basic element of the system of binding precedent and consequently has to be discussed in detail.

decisions, up until 1966, the Supreme Court regarded itself as bound by its previous decisions. In the *Practice Statement (Judicial Precedent)* of that year, however, Lord Gardiner indicated that the Supreme Court would in future regard itself as free to depart from its previous decisions[3] where it appeared right to do so and there have been a number of cases in which it has elected to exercise this discretion (for example, *Miliangos v George Frank (Textiles) Ltd* (1976), in which it decided that damages in English court cases did not have to be awarded in sterling).

The next court in the hierarchical structure is the Court of Appeal, but in order to consider its place within the doctrine of binding precedent, it is necessary to consider its civil and criminal jurisdiction separately.

In a civil case, the situation is that the Court of Appeal is generally bound by previous decisions of the Supreme Court. Although the Court of Appeal, notably under the aegis of Lord Denning, attempted on a number of occasions to escape from what it saw as the constraints of *stare decisis*, the Supreme Court repeatedly reasserted the binding nature of its decisions on the Court of Appeal in such cases as *Broome v Cassell* (1972) and *Miliangos v George Frank (Textiles) Ltd* (1976).

The Court of Appeal is generally also bound by its own previous decisions but there are a limited number of exceptions to this general rule as set out in *Young v Bristol Aeroplane Co Ltd* (1944). These exceptions arise where:

(a)   there is a conflict between two previous decisions of the Court of Appeal, in which case the later court must decide which decision to follow and, as a corollary, which to overrule;

(b)   a previous decision of the Court of Appeal has been overruled, either expressly or impliedly, by the Supreme Court, in which case the Court of Appeal is required to follow the decision of the Supreme Court;

(c)   one of its previous decisions has been given *per incuriam* or, in other words, that previous decision was taken in ignorance of some authority, either legislative or common law, that would have led to a different conclusion, in which case the later court can ignore the previous decision in question.

Once again, there was an attempt by the Court of Appeal under Lord Denning to widen these exceptions in *Gallie v Lee* (1971), but again, the Supreme Court reaffirmed the limited nature of these exceptions and reasserted the strict operation of the doctrine of *stare decisis*.

Although, on the basis of *Spencer* (1987), it would appear that there is no difference in principle between the operation of the doctrine of *stare decisis* between the criminal and civil divisions of the Court of Appeal, it is generally accepted that, in practice, precedent is not followed as strictly in the former as it is in the latter.

....

3   Mention of the various means of departing from – or avoiding – seemingly binding precedent should not be ignored as they allow the courts discretion.

Further down the hierarchy, the Divisional Court is bound by the doctrine of *stare decisis* in the normal way and must follow decisions of the Supreme Court and of the Court of Appeal. It is also normally bound by its own previous decisions, although in civil cases it may avail itself of the exceptions open to the Court of Appeal (in *Young v Bristol Aeroplane Co Ltd* (1944)), and in criminal appeal cases the Queen's Bench Divisional Court may refuse to follow its own earlier decisions where it feels the earlier decision to have been wrongly made.

As regards the High Court, decisions by individual High Court judges are binding on courts inferior in the hierarchy. Such decisions are not binding on other High Court judges, although they are of strong persuasive authority and tend to be followed in practice. Although subject to binding precedent from superior courts, Crown Courts cannot create precedent and their decisions can never amount to more than persuasive authority. The decisions of county courts and magistrates' courts are never binding.

The operation of the doctrine of binding precedent is, of course, dependent on the existence of an extensive reporting service to provide access to judicial decisions. However, it should not be thought that the doctrine is as hard and fast as it originally appears. The technique of 'distinguishing' cases on their facts provides judges with scope for declining to follow precedents by which they would otherwise be bound. The legal decision in any case is an abstraction from the immediate facts of the case. If a judge decides, for some reason, that the facts in the case before him are so different from those of a case setting a precedent, he is at liberty to ignore the precedent and treat the case in question as not being covered by it. He can then decide the case as he thinks fit, without being bound by the otherwise binding precedent.

Scope for further uncertainty is introduced by the necessary distinction between *ratio decidendi* and *obiter dicta*.[4] The only part that is binding in any judgment previously decided is the *ratio* of the case: the actual legal reason for the decision. Anything else in the judgment is by the way, or *obiter*. Difficulty arises from the fact that judges do not label their judgments in this way. They do not actually nominate the *ratio* of the case. Additionally, their judgments may be of great length, or there may be as many as five judges delivering individual judgments on the case, and there is no requirement that all the judgments should agree on the principle of law governing the decision in the case. In any event, it is later judges who, in effect, determine what the particular *ratio* of any case was. The problem in relation to binding precedent is that it is open to later judges to avoid precedents by declaring them to be no more than *obiter* statements.

There are numerous *advantages*[5] to the doctrine of *stare decisis*. Among these are the following:

....

4   Both the *ratio* (binding element) and what is said *obiter* ('by the way') are recorded and are often difficult to differentiate, as they are not highlighted in a way which distinguishes them.

5   In order to answer the specific question set, both the advantages and disadvantages of the system of precedent must be discussed. Confusingly, the advantages and disadvantages are sometimes seen as overlapping!

(a) It saves the time of the judiciary, lawyers and their clients, since cases do not have to be re-argued – this also has the benefit of saving the money of potential litigants.
(b) It provides a measure of certainty to law – thus, lawyers and their clients are able to predict what the outcome of a particular legal question is likely to be in the light of previous judicial decisions.
(c) It provides for a measure of formal justice, to the extent that like cases are decided on a like basis.
(d) It provides an opportunity for judges to develop the common law in particular areas without waiting for Parliament to enact legislation.

There are, however, corresponding *disadvantages* in the doctrine. Among these are the following:

(a) The degree of certainty provided by the doctrine is undermined by the absolute number of cases that have been reported and can therefore be cited as authorities – this uncertainty is compounded by the ability of the judiciary to select which authority to follow, through use of the mechanism of distinguishing cases on their facts.
(b) Law may become ossified on the basis of an unjust precedent, with the consequence that previous injustices are perpetuated – an example of this is the long delay in the recognition of the possibility of rape within marriage, which has only recently been recognised.
(c) In developing law, it might be claimed that the judiciary is, in fact, overstepping its constitutional role by making law rather than simply deciding its application.

Common Pitfalls

❖ It is simply not acceptable not to be aware of the Supreme Court, nor should it be referred to as additional to the House of Lords.
❖ It is also important to explain in clear terms the meaning and difference between the *ratio decidendi* of a judgment and *obiter dicta* within that judgment.

Aim Higher

❖ Although the Supreme Court merely replaces the House of Lords and is not the same as other Supreme Courts in jurisdictions with written constitutions, it is valuable to consider the potential for future developments in the that area, especially given the increased powers of the courts under the **Human Rights Act**.
❖ It is important to be able to cite some of the decisions made by the Supreme Court since it started in 2009.
❖ A good explanation of how 'distinguishing' works is likely to be well rewarded.

QUESTION 13

How can the common law progress if judges are bound by precedent?

How to Read this Question

This apparently simple question addresses the crucial paradox that lies at the core of the English common law. The issue is that if the courts are bound to follow previous decisions, as is suggested by the accepted version of precedent, then how can the common law progress in such a way as to allow it to accommodate ever-changing social circumstances?

Implicit in this question is a critique of the traditional view of how precedent operates and clearly the examiner is looking for an explanation of the mechanisms that allow judges to avoid a strict adherence to precedent. It follows, therefore, that simply setting out the commonly accepted explanation of the doctrine of precedent will not be adequate to answer this particular question.

How to Answer this Question

A question of this type requires the following approach:

- ❖ consider what is meant by the common law;
- ❖ explain what is involved in the declaratory view of the role of the judiciary;
- ❖ analyse the operation of the system of *stare decisis* as it is supposed to operate;
- ❖ highlight some of the loopholes in the traditional version of *stare decisis*, for example, *Curry v DPP* (1994);
- ❖ provide some examples where the judges have continued to create new law;
- ❖ consider the constitutional role of the judiciary in the UK, and whether it should or should not be allowed to go on making new law.

Answer Structure

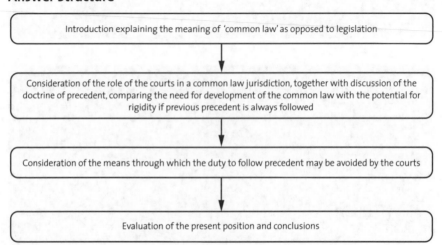

Introduction explaining the meaning of 'common law' as opposed to legislation

↓

Consideration of the role of the courts in a common law jurisdiction, together with discussion of the doctrine of precedent, comparing the need for development of the common law with the potential for rigidity if previous precedent is always followed

↓

Consideration of the means through which the duty to follow precedent may be avoided by the courts

↓

Evaluation of the present position and conclusions

ANSWER

Within the constitutional division of powers in the UK, it is the function of the legislature to make law and it is the function of the courts merely to apply that law. The declaratory view of the function of the English judiciary accepts this constitutional division of power and portrays it as not making law, but merely deciding cases in accordance with existing legal rules. The doctrine of binding precedent operates in such a way that judges, in deciding particular cases, are not merely referred to earlier decisions for guidance, but are actually bound to apply the rules of law contained in those decisions. The operation of this principle depends on the established hierarchy of the court structure: all courts standing in a definite relationship of superiority/inferiority to every other court. Usually, a court is bound by decisions of a court of equal standing or of higher authority than itself in the court structure. Allowing for the fact that the doctrine of *stare decisis* is supposed to have binding force within this hierarchical framework, two questions still arise.

It is axiomatic that legal rules cannot be subject to infinite regression; every rule of the common law must have had an origin. If one rejects as untenable the proposition of natural law – that it is possible for law to exist as an entity outside of, and distinct from, social practice – then it follows that if a particular law was not created by statute, it must have been created by a judge; even if this creative activity is no more than recognising the legitimacy, or otherwise, of the practice in question. As a matter of course, it follows that where there is no established precedent, the doctrine of *stare decisis* breaks down and the courts are faced with the alternatives of either refusing to decide a case, or stating what the law should be. Even in modern times, courts are still required on occasions to consider situations for the very first time without access to precedent. These cases, described as cases of first impression, inevitably involve judges in the establishment of new law.

In practice, flexibility is achieved through the possibility of previous decisions being either overruled or distinguished, or the possibility of a later court extending or modifying the effective ambit of a precedent. At this stage, it must be emphasised that, strictly speaking, it is wrong to speak of a decision being binding, just as it is technically incorrect to refer to a decision being overruled. It is not the actual decision in a case that sets the precedent, but the rule of law on which that decision is founded. This rule, which is an abstraction from the facts of the case, is known as the *ratio decidendi* of the case. Thus, the *ratio decidendi* of a case may be understood as the statement of the law applied in deciding the legal problem raised by the concrete facts of the case. Moreover, not every statement of law in a judgment is binding; only those which are based on the particular facts of the case, as found and upon which the decision was based, are binding. Any other statement of law is, strictly speaking, superfluous and any such statement is termed *obiter dictum*, that is, said by the way. It is significant that although *obiter dicta* do not form part of the binding precedent of the case in which they occur, and therefore do not have to be followed by judges deciding later similar cases, they do amount to persuasive authority and can be taken into consideration in later cases if the judge in the later case considers it appropriate to do so. This apparently small measure of discretion, in relationship to whether later judges are minded to accept the validity of *obiter* statements in precedent cases, opens up the possibility that judges in later cases have a much wider degree of discretion than is originally apparent in the traditional view of *stare decisis*, when it is real-ised that it is the judges in the later cases who actually determine the *ratio decidendi* of previous cases. In delivering judgments in cases, judges do not separate and highlight the *ratio decidendi* from the rest of their judgment, and this can lead to a lack of certainty in determining the *ratio decidendi*. This uncertainty is compounded by the fact that reports of decisions in cases may run to considerable length and where there are a number of separate judgments, although the judges involved may agree on the decision of a case, they may not agree on the legal basis of the decision reached. This difficulty is further compounded where there are a number of dissenting judgments. In the final analysis, it is for the judge deciding the case in which a precedent has been cited to determine the *ratio* of the authority and thus to determine whether he is bound by the precedent or not. This factor provides the courts with a considerable degree of discretion in electing whether to be bound or not by a particular authority.

It is somewhat anomalous that within the system of *stare decisis*, precedents gain increased authority with the passage of time. As a consequence, courts tend to be reluctant to overrule long-standing authorities, even though they may no longer accu-rately reflect contemporary practices or morals. Allied to the wish to maintain a high degree of certainty in the law, the main reason for judicial reluctance to overrule old deci-sions would appear to be the fact that overruling operates retrospectively. Overruling a precedent might therefore have the consequence of disturbing important financial arrangements previously settled in line with what were thought to be settled rules of law. It might also in certain circumstances lead to the imposition of criminal liability on previ-ously lawful behaviour. It has to be emphasised, however, that the courts will not shrink from overruling authorities where they see them as no longer representing an appropri-ate statement of law. The legal recognition of the possibility of rape within marriage is simply one example of this process (see *R* (1991)).

In comparison to the mechanism of overruling, which is rarely used, the main device for avoiding binding precedents is that of distinguishing. As has been previously stated, the *ratio decidendi* of any case is an abstraction from, and is based upon, the material facts of the case. This opens up the possibility that a court may regard the facts of the case before it as significantly different from the facts of a cited precedent and thus not binding. The cases have been distinguished on their facts and the court is at liberty to ignore the prece-dent in the prior case.

Judges use the device of distinguishing where, for some reason, they are unwilling to follow a particular precedent. The law reports provide many examples of strained distinc-tions, where a court has quite evidently not wanted to follow an authority that it would otherwise have been bound by. An example is *Curry v DPP* (1994), in which the Court of Appeal attempted to remove the previous presumption that children between the ages of 10 and 14 charged with a criminal offence do not know that their actions are seriously wrong and the requirement that the prosecution provide evidence to rebut the presump-tion. Mann LJ justified reversing the presumption by stating that although it had often been assumed to be the law, it had never actually been specifically considered by earlier courts. On such reasoning, he felt justified in departing from previous decisions of the Court of Appeal which otherwise would have bound him. The House of Lords, as it then was, subsequently restored the original presumption. Although their Lordships recognised the problem, they thought it was a matter more for parliamentary action than judicial intervention.

A further way in which judges have a creative impact on the law is in the way in which they adapt and extend precedent in instant cases. Judicial reasoning tends to be carried out on the basis of analogy, and judges have a large degree of discretion in selecting what are to be considered as analogous cases. They also have a tendency continuously to extend existing precedents to fit new situations, as the historical evolution of the tort of negligence will show.[6]

Common Pitfalls

It is common either to underestimate, but more likely to overestimate, the extent to which judges can manipulate the rules of precedent to develop law.

Aim Higher

It should not be lost on the good student that the various advantages and disadvantages that are usually cited in ELS textbooks are, at least to a degree, contradictory. How can the law be certain yet flexible?

QUESTION 14

To what extent and why has there been a shift away from the traditional judicial approach to statutory interpretation?

How to Read this Question

This question is tricky in that really good marks cannot be gained unless the candidate's answer actually deals with the change that has taken place in the approach to statutory interpretation, but it does at least allow for the possibility of a less well-prepared candidate picking up marks by delivering a standard answer on statutory interpretation.

How to Answer this Question

This question recognises the change that has taken place in the way judges interpret, or perhaps more correctly, justify their interpretations of, statutes. Students must know the traditional rules of statutory interpretation, but they must also show that they are fully

6 The discussion set out above provides clear evidence of both knowledge and understanding of the doctrine of precedent, together with its application and effects. Such consideration also demonstrates skills such as analysis and evaluation.

aware that there has been a shift from the literal to the purposive approach to statutory interpretation. They are not all compatible, nor do they form a clear hierarchy. Judges therefore have a measure of freedom to select which ones they wish to follow. Answers should:

- ❖ address the point that interpretation is creative by its very nature;
- ❖ note that statutes may partake of the general uncertainty inherent in language;
- ❖ set out the three rules of statutory interpretation and highlight the use of each with reference to cases;
- ❖ refer to the cases which indicate a shift towards the purposive approach to statutory interpretation;
- ❖ refer to the **Human Rights Act (HRA) 1998**, citing cases in support of the analysis.

Answer Structure

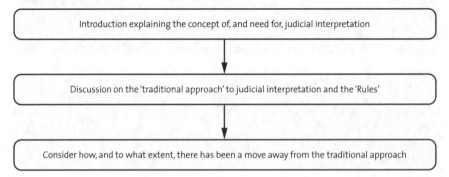

Introduction explaining the concept of, and need for, judicial interpretation

Discussion on the 'traditional approach' to judicial interpretation and the 'Rules'

Consider how, and to what extent, there has been a move away from the traditional approach

ANSWER

According to the traditional theory of the division of powers, the role of the judiciary is simply to apply the law that Parliament has created. This view is, however, simplistic in so far as it denies, or at least ignores, the extent to which the judiciary has a measure of discretion and creative power in the manner in which it interprets the legislation that comes before it.[7]

Legislation shares the general problem of uncertainty inherent in any mode of communication. The conflicting aims of legislation, however, give rise to particular problems of interpretation; these conflicting aims are the need to be clear while at the same time being general. Clarity and precision tend to be achieved only in inverse proportion to generality, but legislation must, by and large, endeavour to be of general applicability. There is therefore in all legislation a penumbra of uncertainty that can only be illuminated and made certain by judicial interpretation. That interpretation is a creative process and inevitably involves the judiciary in the process of creating law.

---

7   The introductory paragraphs 'set the scene', providing evidence of knowledge and understanding of why judicial interpretation is necessary to the appropriate application of law.

The question arises, therefore, as to how judges actually interpret legislation that comes before them and the traditional answer was that in determining the actual meaning of legislation, they make use of the three primary rules of statutory interpretation and a variety of other secondary aids to construction.[8]

The three rules of statutory interpretation are: (a) the literal rule; (b) the golden rule; and (c) the mischief rule. Before any detailed consideration of these rules of interpretation is undertaken, however, it must be emphasised that they are not really rules, but, as will be shown, they may best be considered as post hoc justifications for decisions taken in line with judicial preference.

The Literal Rule

Under this rule, the judge is required to consider what the legislation *actually* says, rather than considering what it *might mean*. In order to achieve this end, the judge should give words in legislation their literal meaning, that is, their plain, ordinary, everyday meaning, even if the effect of this is to produce what might be considered as an otherwise unjust or undesirable outcome. *Inland Revenue Commissioners v Hinchy* (1960) concerned s25(3) of the **Income Tax Act 1952**, which stated that any taxpayer who did not complete their tax return was subject to a fixed penalty of £20 plus *treble the tax which he ought to be charged under the Act*. The question that had to be decided was whether the additional element of the penalty should be based on the total amount that should have been paid, or merely the unpaid portion of that total. The House of Lords adopted a literal interpretation of the statute and held that any taxpayer in default should have to pay triple their original tax bill.

The Golden Rule

This rule is used when application of the literal rule will result in what appears to the court to be an obviously absurd result. An example of the application of the golden rule is *Adler v George* (1964). Under the **Official Secrets Act 1911** in operation at the time, it was an offence to obstruct HM Forces *in the vicinity of* a prohibited place. George had in fact been arrested while obstructing such forces *within* such a prohibited place. The court found no difficulty in applying the golden rule to extend the literal wording of the statute to cover the action committed by the defendant.

The Mischief Rule

This rule gives the court a justification for going behind the actual wording of a statute in order to consider the problem that the particular statute was aimed at remedying. At one level, the mischief rule is clearly the most flexible rule of interpretation, but it is limited by being restricted to using previous common law to determine the particular mischief the statute in question was designed to remedy. In *Heydon's Case* (1584), it was stated that in making use of the mischief rule, the court should consider the following four matters:

....

8   In order to assist the courts in ensuring that they interpreted statute in accordance with the intention of Parliament, a system of 'rules' was developed by the courts to aid them in their task. Without discussion of these 'traditional approaches' it would not be possible to evaluate whether there had been a 'shift away', in addition to the 'rules'.

(a) What was the common law before the passing of the statute?

(b) What was the mischief in the law with which the common law did not adequately deal?

(c) What remedy for that mischief had Parliament intended to provide?

(d) What was the reason for Parliament adopting that remedy?

An example of the use of the mischief rule is clearly found in *Corkery v Carpenter* (1951), where a person was arrested for being drunk in charge of a bicycle. He was subsequently charged under **s 12** of the **Licensing Act 1872** with being drunk in charge of a carriage, as the legislation made no actual reference to bicycles. It is certainly arguable that a bicycle is not a carriage, but in any case, the court elected to use the mischief rule to decide the matter. The purpose of the Act was to prevent people from using any form of transport on the public highways while in a state of intoxication. The bicycle was clearly a form of transport and therefore its user was correctly charged.

The foregoing represents the traditional approach to judicial interpretation; however, it has to be recognised that for some time there has been a move away from the over-reliance on the literal approach to statutory interpretation to a more purposive approach. As Lord Griffiths put it in *Pepper v Hart* (1993):[9]

> The days have long passed when the court adopted a strict constructionist view of interpretation which required them to adopt the literal meaning of the language. The courts now adopt a purposive approach[10] which seeks to give effect to the true purpose of legislation and are prepared to look at much extraneous material that bears on the background against which the legislation was enacted.

Such a shift has been necessitated, to no little degree, by the need for the courts to consider matters that were not within the original contemplation of Parliament at the time when the legislation was passed, but which have since been brought into play by the effect of technological advances.

Thus in *Quintavalle v Secretary of State for Health* (2003) the House of Lords held that embryos created by cell nuclear replacement (CNR), a form of human cloning involving a human egg and a cell from a donor's body, were regulated under the **Human Fertilisation and Embryology Act (HFE) 1990**, which had been passed at a time when embryos were only ever created by fertilisation of an egg by a sperm. The House of Lords held that CNR organisms were, in essence, sufficiently like other embryos to be considered as belonging to the same 'genus of facts'. Parliament could not rationally have been assumed to have intended to exclude such embryos from the regulation.

....

9   In addition to the traditional rules of interpretation, the courts have access to a number of aids which can be internal to the legislation, such as other sections of legislation, and external, such as dictionaries, the **Interpretation Act** and, since the case of *Pepper v Hart*, **Hansard** (account of parliamentary debate). These are discussed in the next question.

10   The purposive method of interpretation is the method favoured by the Court of Justice of the EU and is used by the courts, among other times, when interpreting law emanating from the EU. It is consequently a good example of the courts 'shifting away' from tradition.

In reaching his decision, Lord Bingham considered the purpose and procedure of statutory interpretation and concluded that:

> The court's task, within the permissible bounds of interpretation, is to give effect to Parliament's purpose. So the controversial provisions should be read in the context of the statute as a whole, and the statute as a whole *should be read in the historical context of the situation which led to its enactment.*[11]

QUESTION 15 --

Explain the resources and presumptions that judges may use in their interpretation of legislation.

How to Read this Question

There is nothing particularly challenging in this question, other than the fact that it covers material at the more obscure end of the ELS syllabus. Nonetheless, it is fair and syllabuses do have to be covered over a certain cycle of time. Once again the examiner has been generous in bringing together two aspects of the syllabus that could have been examined independently. So, even if you have only prepared one aspect of the question you should still be able to manage pass marks.

How to Answer this Question

This fairly narrow, knowledge-based question asks students to explain the sources, other than the statute itself, to which judges can make reference in search of the actual meaning of legislation. It also requires a consideration of the presumptions that the judges will operate under. As usual, case authorities should be cited in support of all the references made.

In addition to the three main rules of interpretation, there are a number of secondary aids to construction. These can be categorised as either intrinsic or extrinsic in nature:

In particular:

- ❖ Candidates should explain the distinction between *intrinsic* and *extrinsic* assistance.
- ❖ Reference should be made to the decision in *Pepper v Hart*, which is important for the fact that it replaced the long-standing rule denying judges the right to use parliamentary debates to decide the meaning of legislation.
- ❖ The presumptions that the judges will normally apply should then be dealt with in some detail.

....

11 The *dicta* in this case provide an excellent example of why the courts have needed to move away from more traditional methods.

Answer Structure

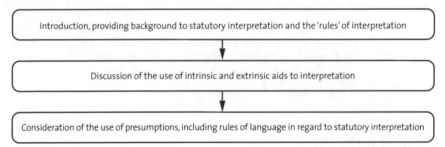

Introduction, providing background to statutory interpretation and the 'rules' of interpretation

Discussion of the use of intrinsic and extrinsic aids to interpretation

Consideration of the use of presumptions, including rules of language in regard to statutory interpretation

ANSWER

In addition to the main rules of interpretation,[12] there are a number of secondary aids to construction to which the judges will refer in an endeavour to find the meaning of particular pieces of legislation. These specifically relate to sources to which the judges may make reference, but in addition to these there are a number of presumptions that the judges will accept as normally operating.

With regard to the sources to which judges may resort, these may be divided into intrinsic and extrinsic sources of assistance as below.

Intrinsic Assistance

Intrinsic assistance is derived from the statute which is the object of interpretation; the judge uses the full statute to understand the meaning of a particular part of it. The *title*, either long or short, of the Act under consideration may be referred to for guidance (*Royal College of Nursing v DHSS* (1981)). It should be noted, however, that a general intention derived from the title cannot overrule a clear statement to the contrary in the text of the Act.

Schedules appear as additions at the end of the main body of the legislation. They are, however, an essential part of the Act and may be referred to in order to make sense of the main text.

Some statutes contain section headings and yet others contain marginal notes relating to particular sections. The extent to which either of these may be used is uncertain, although *DPP v Schildkamp* (1969) does provide authority for the use of the former as an aid to interpretation.

Finally, in regard to intrinsic aids to interpretation, it is now recognised that punctuation has an effect on the meaning of words and can be taken into account in determining the meaning of a provision.[13]

---

12   The rules of interpretation have already been discussed in the previous question. (If this had not been so, a very brief overview would have been included here.) This introduction is also helpful as it places the resources and presumptions into context, demonstrating understanding as well as knowledge.

13   This discussion on intrinsic aids to interpretation is particularly good because it clearly demonstrates that even within a statute there may be a number of different sources to consider. In addition, it provides all-important legal authorities in support of what has been proposed.

Extrinsic Assistance

Extrinsic assistance, that is, reference to sources outside of the Act itself, may on occasion be resorted to in determining the meaning of legislation; but which sources? Some external sources are unproblematic. For example, judges have always been entitled to refer to *dictionaries* in order to find the meaning of non-legal words. They also have been able to look into *textbooks* for guidance in relation to particular points of law, and in using the mischief rule, they have been able to refer to *earlier statutes* to determine the precise mischief at which the statute they are trying to construe is aimed. The **Interpretation Act 1978** is also available for consultation with regard to particular difficulties. Unfortunately, its title is somewhat misleading in that it does not give general instructions for interpreting legislation, but simply defines particular terms that are found in various statutes.

Until relatively recently *Hansard*, the verbatim record of parliamentary procedure, literally remained a closed book to the courts, but in the landmark decision in *Pepper v Hart* (1993), the House of Lords held that where the precise meaning of legislation was uncertain or ambiguous, or where the literal meaning of an Act would lead to a manifest absurdity, the courts could refer to *Hansard*'s reports of parliamentary debates and proceedings as an aid to construing the meaning of the legislation.

The operation of the principle in *Pepper v Hart* was extended in *Three Rivers DC v Bank of England (No 2)* (1996) to cover situations where the legislation under question was not in itself ambiguous, but might be ineffective in its intention to give effect to some particular EC directive. Applying the wider purposive powers of interpretation open to it in such circumstances the court held that it was permissible to refer to *Hansard* in order to determine the actual purpose of the statute.

The *Pepper v Hart* principle only applies to statements made by ministers at the time of the passage of legislation, and the courts have declined to extend it to cover situations where ministers subsequently make some statement as to what they consider the effect of a particular Act to be (*Melluish (Inspector of Taxes) v BMI (No 3) Ltd* (1995)).[14]

Presumptions

In addition to the rules of interpretation, the courts may also make use of certain presumptions. As with all presumptions, they are rebuttable. The following presumptions operate:[15]

❖   *Against the alteration of the common law.* If there is no express intention to that effect, it is assumed that statute does not make any fundamental change to the common law. (See *R (Rottman) v Commissioner of Police* (2002).)

---

14 Again, this discussion is particularly good because not only does it demonstrate in-depth knowledge, it is also very well supported by appropriate legal authority and includes reference to the important case of *Pepper v Hart* (1993).

15 This provides in-depth consideration of the presumption, again well supported by appropriate authority, and also highlighting the rebuttable nature of the presumptions.

❖ *That a mental element is required for criminal offences*. It is a general requirement of the criminal law that, in order for a person to be convicted of a crime, they are proved not only to have committed the relevant act or conduct but also to have done this with a blameworthy state of mind known as *mens rea*. However, in some areas of social concern, such as traffic offences, Parliament has seen fit to pass what are known as 'strict liability' offences. These are criminal offences for which it is *not* necessary for the prosecution to prove that the defendant had a particular attitude towards the crime in question, for example, that he intended to commit it, but merely that the relevant conduct took place. The general rule is that Parliament will be presumed not to have created a strict liability criminal offence unless it has been explicit about doing so. In *Sweet v Parsley* (1970), the accused had a house which she rented out and visited only occasionally. She was convicted of being concerned in the management of premises used for the purpose of smoking cannabis, contrary to **s 5(b)** of the **Dangerous Drugs Act 1965**; however, she had had no knowledge that the house was being used in this way. The House of Lords held that her conviction should be quashed, since it had to be proved that it was the accused's 'purpose' that the premises were used for smoking cannabis.

❖ *Against retrospective effect of new law*. The courts operate a presumption of interpretation that statutes will not operate retrospectively. As Parliament is supreme, it can pass retrospective legislation if it wishes, but it must do so using express words to achieve this end. An example of legislation which has been made expressly retrospective is the **War Crimes Act 1991**.

❖ *Presumption against deprivation of liberty*. The law courts work on the assumption that Parliament does not intend to deprive a person of his liberty unless it is explicitly making provision for such a punishment.

❖ *Against application to the Crown*. Unless the legislation contains a clear statement to the contrary, it is presumed not to apply to the Crown.

❖ *Against breaking international law*. Where possible, legislation should be interpreted in such a way as to give effect to existing international legal obligations.

❖ *In favour of words taking their meaning from the context in which they are used*.[16] This presumption appears as three distinct sub-rules, each of which carries a Latin tag:

> The *noscitur a sociis* rule is applied where statutory provisions include a list of examples of what is covered by the legislation. It is presumed that the words used have a related meaning and are to be interpreted in relation to each other. (See *IRC v Frere* (1969), in which the House of Lords decided which of two possible meanings of the word 'interest' was to be preferred by reference to the word's location within a statute.)

> The *ejusdem generis* rule applies in situations where general words are appended to the end of a list of specific examples. The presumption is that the general words have to be interpreted in line with the prior restrictive examples. Thus, a provision which referred to a list that included 'horses, cattle, sheep and

---

16 The rules of language can help make the meaning of words and phrases clear where particular sentence construction is used and this answer makes this important point.

other animals' would be unlikely to apply to domestic animals such as cats and dogs. (See *Powell v Kempton Park Racecourse* (1899).)

The *expressio unius exclusio alterius* rule simply means that where a statute seeks to establish a list of what is covered by its provisions, then anything not expressly included in that list is specifically excluded. (See *R v Inhabitants of Sedgley* (1831).)

4 The Courts and the Appellate Process

THE COURTS

A sound knowledge of the civil and criminal court structure is essential for a proper understanding of many aspects of the English legal system. You should be aware of the jurisdiction of each court (that is, which types of cases each court is competent to deal with), how its workload compares with other courts, how it is organised and what criticisms have been made of these features. The courts in question are the county courts, magistrates' courts, the Crown Court, the High Court, the Court of Appeal, the Supreme Court and the Judicial Committee of the Privy Council.

The court system of 2014 is significantly different from that of 20 years earlier. It has undergone many changes to fit in more with the interests and conveniences of litigants and less with the interests of lawyers. A charter for the civil courts now states, for example, that anyone telephoning a court between 9 am and 5 pm on a weekday will get a prompt and helpful answer. It also says that within ten working days of a court receiving a letter, the sender will get a reply by letter or telephone.

The Judicial and Court Statistics (published in June 2011 and revised in July 2011) give the following profile of court activity for 2010:

KEY FINDINGS

Appeals

A total of 80 appeals were entered, and 33 disposed of by the Judicial Committee of the Privy Council during the year, compared to 65 and 47 for 2009 respectively.
250 appeals were presented to the Supreme Court, of which 220 were disposed of: 130 of these were refused outright.

Of the 7,250 applications for leave to appeal filed with the Court of Appeal Criminal Division, 21 per cent were appeals against conviction and 76 per cent were appeals against sentence. Of these 13 per cent of the appeals against conviction were allowed and 27 per cent of the appeals against sentence were allowed.

In the Civil Division of the Court of Appeal 1,180 appeals were set down, of which 45 per cent were allowed.

In the Administrative Court (a division of the High Court Queen's Bench Division), there were 16,300 applications for permission to claim judicial review, a 24 per cent increase from 2009. Of the 460 substantive applications for judicial review disposed of in 2010, 42 per cent (194) were allowed.

County Courts

The total number of civil (non-family) cases started in 2010 was 1,617,000, a 14 per cent decrease compared with 2009.

The number of 'money' claims with specified claim amounts in 2010 was 1,041,000, a decrease of 19 per cent from 2009. 36 per cent of these claims had a claim value of up to £500, down from 38 per cent in 2009.

The total number of 'money' claims with unspecified claim amounts was 191,000 in 2010, an increase of 6 per cent compared with 2009.

The number of mortgage repossession claims issued in 2010 was 75,000, a decrease of 19 per cent from 2009. The number of landlord possession claims decreased by 1 per cent compared with 2009.

The number of defences was 8 per cent lower and the number of allocations to track 6 per cent lower than in 2009.

There were 20,000 trials, a 2 per cent rise on 2009, and 43,000 small claim hearings, a 9 per cent decrease on 2009.

Trials took place on average 50 weeks following issue, up from 48 weeks in 2009, while small claim hearings took place 31 weeks following issue, the same as in 2009.

Magistrates' Courts

An estimated 1.68 million defendants were proceeded against in criminal cases in magistrates' courts in 2010.

Magistrates' courts recorded 180,000 trials in 2010 (unchanged from 2009). Of those trials, 39 per cent were recorded as cracked (up by one percentage point from 2009), with 19 per cent recorded as ineffective (down by one percentage point from 2009).

The estimated time from offence to charge in 2010 was 85 days. Sexual offences took the second longest time between offence and charge (285 days), while drink-driving offences took the shortest (15 days).

The estimated average time taken from offence to completion in 2010 was 138 days for defendants in completed criminal cases in magistrates' courts (down from 141 days in 2009).

The estimated average time taken from charge to completion in 2010 for adult charged cases, excluding cases sent or committed to the Crown Court, was 6.7 weeks (down from 6.9 weeks in 2009).

Enforcement of financial penalties: the amount paid in England and Wales in 2010 was £281 million (a 12 per cent increase from 2009).

Crown Court

The number of cases committed/sent for trial to the Crown Court in 2010 was 97,700, the same as in 2009. The number of disposals for cases committed/sent for trial increased by 6 per cent to 100,100.

The number of cases committed to the Crown Court for sentence increased by 6 per cent to 40,800, while the number of appeals decreased by 4 per cent to 13,800. Guilty pleas as a proportion of all cases where a plea was entered fell from 71 per cent in 2009 to 70 per cent in 2010.

The cracked and ineffective trial rates both rose by one percentage point to 43 per cent and 14 per cent respectively.

The average waiting time for defendants committed for trial on bail was 15.6 weeks and 19.4 weeks for those held in custody. The average waiting time for defendants sent for trial on bail was 23 weeks and 15.5 weeks for those held in custody.

THE APPELLATE PROCESS

Checklist

You should be familiar with:

- what rights of appeal exist and what conditions, if any, apply in relation to all courts (civil and criminal);
- the findings and recommendations of the **Runciman Commission on Criminal Justice (1993)** about criminal appeals;
- appeals procedure: what powers the appellate courts have;
- the systems for references to be made to the Court of Appeal (Criminal Division) by the Home Secretary and the Attorney-General;
- how the **Criminal Appeal Act 1995** changed the system of criminal appeals, and changes made from 1998 to the work of the Court of Appeal (Civil Division) as a result of the *Bowman Report*;
- the recommendations of the Royal Commission on Criminal Justice, under the chairmanship of Viscount Runciman, which reported in July 1993. Many of its 352 recommendations address matters relating to the courts, juries and the appellate process. Wherever appropriate, the relevant proposals have been incorporated into answers here;
- the findings and recommendations of the Auld Review of the Criminal Courts of England and Wales.

QUESTION 16

State and explain in what circumstances the Supreme Court can overrule one of its own previous decisions, and illustrate your answer with an example.

How to Read this Question

This question is asking you to consider a specific issue in relation to the Supreme Court, its ability to depart from its own decisions. You should not waste time discussing the role, composition or history of the Supreme Court in any more detail than is necessary for that particular purpose, as illustrated by the answer below. The 1966 Practice Statement is central to this topic and it is worth learning the elements required. Also note that this question requires you to illustrate the answer with a single example. You will therefore need to be able to give some detail about one case. Other questions may require you to illustrate from a range of cases over the period since the Practice Statement was issued.

How to Answer this Question

A good answer will:

❖ set the historical and legal theory context, and say why the matter is important within the English legal system;
❖ explain in some detail the provisions of the 1966 Practice Statement;
❖ explain something of the meaning of the 1966 formula as given in subsequent case law like *Herrington v British Railways Board* (1972);
❖ illustrate the principle being used to change the law, for example in *Horton v Sadler* (2006);
❖ conclude with some evaluation or appraisal of the power being used in this case, perhaps revisiting the essay's opening paragraph's coverage of the finality/flexibility issue, and examining that issue in relation to the case.

Answer Structure

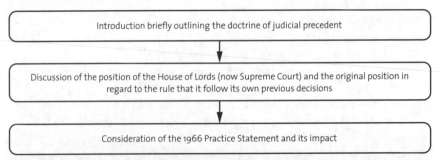

> Introduction briefly outlining the doctrine of judicial precedent

> Discussion of the position of the House of Lords (now Supreme Court) and the original position in regard to the rule that it follow its own previous decisions

> Consideration of the 1966 Practice Statement and its impact

Up for Debate

Should the Supreme Court be given more power to depart from its own decisions? If it had greater powers to be flexible, what issues would arise concerning certainty, and the relationship between the judiciary and the legislature?

ANSWER

One expected quality of the court at the apex of a pyramidal court structure is finality of judgment. What is laid down as the law by such a court will be certain and reliable because there is no court above it to which a dissatisfied side can appeal for another decision on the law. Historically, before the Supreme Court was established in 2009, the House of Lords for a long time would not overrule its earlier decisions even if they later seemed wrong. Since 1966, however, it was able to overrule its earlier rulings. It seldom did so, but did in 2006, and thereby conduced to greater justice for litigants.

House of Lords' decisions are binding on all other courts in the legal system, except, today, the Supreme Court. The House of Lords was bound by its own previous decisions until it changed this practice in 1966. The historical practice of always sticking faithfully to whatever it had earlier ruled was the law that had been established by the nineteenth century and was reaffirmed in a famous case in 1898 – *London Tramways Co Ltd v London County Council*.

However, this approach did not appear to create certainty and had become very rigid by the end of the nineteenth century. Several areas of law fossilised because rules laid down by the Lords remained fixed, while social developments rendered them archaic and Parliament did nothing to modernise them using legislation. The practice was eventually changed in July 1966 when Lord Gardiner, the Lord Chancellor, made a statement on behalf of himself and his fellow Law Lords. This Practice Statement says:

> Their Lordships regard the use of precedent as an indispensable foundation upon which to decide what is the law and its application to individual cases. It provides at least some degree of certainty upon which individuals can rely in the conduct of their affairs as well as a basis for orderly development of legal rules.

Their Lordships nevertheless recognise that too rigid adherence to precedent may lead to injustice in a particular case and also unduly restrict the proper development of the law. They propose, therefore, to modify their present practice and, while treating former decisions of this House as normally binding, to depart from a previous decision when it appears right to do so. In this connection they will bear in mind the danger of disturbing retrospectively the basis on which contracts, settlements of property, and fiscal arrangements have been entered into and also the special need for certainty as to the criminal law. This announcement is not intended to affect the use of precedent elsewhere than in this House.

[1966] 3 All ER 77

> The House of Lords 1966 Practice Statement on departure from its own previous decisions applies equally to the Supreme Court.
>
> *Austin v Mayor and Burgesses of the London Borough of Southwark* (2010)
> Lord Hope, paras [24]–[25]

The current practice enables the Supreme Court to adapt English law to meet changing social conditions. It was also regarded as important at the time (in 1966) that the House of Lords' practice be brought into line with that of superior courts in other countries, like the United States Supreme Court and state supreme courts elsewhere which are not bound by their own previous decisions.

The possibility of the Supreme Court changing its previous decisions is a recognition that law, whether expressed in statutes or cases, is a living, and therefore changing, institution which must adapt to the circumstances in which, and to which, it applies if it is to retain practical relevance.

Since 1966, the House used this power quite sparingly. Today, the Supreme Court will not refuse to follow its earlier decision merely because that decision was wrong. A material change of circumstances will usually have to be shown.

In *Herrington v British Railway Board* (1972), the House of Lords overruled *Addy and Sons v Dumbreck* (1929). In the earlier case, the House of Lords had decided that an occupier of premises was only liable for the injury to a trespassing child if that child was injured by the occupier intentionally or recklessly. In its later decision, the House of Lords changed the law in line with the changed social and physical conditions since 1929. Their Lordships felt that even a trespasser was entitled to some degree of care, which they propounded as a test of 'common humanity'. In imposing a duty of care on occupiers, and arguing for the overruling of the 1929 decision, Lord Pearson said:

> It seems to me the rule in *Addie v Dumbreck* has been rendered obsolete by changes in physical and social conditions and has become an incumbrance impeding the proper development of law. With the increase in population and the larger proportion living in cities and towns and the extensive substitution of blocks of flats for rows of houses with gardens or back yards and quiet streets, there is less playing space for children and so a greater temptation to trespass. There is less supervision of children so they are more likely to trespass … Also with the progress of technology there are more and greater dangers for them to encounter …
>
> [1972] 1 All ER 749 at 785–786

The rarely used power of the House of Lords was utilised in *Horton v Sadler* in 2006.

The claimant had been injured in a road traffic accident for which the defendant was responsible in negligence. The defendant was not insured, and so a claim was to be made against the Motor Insurance Bureau (MIB). The plaintiff issued proceedings just before the expiry of the period, but failed to give first the requisite formal notice to the MIB. He appealed against dismissal of his second set of proceedings for want of exercise of a judicial discretion to extend the limitation period. The House of Lords held that the claimant's appeal should succeed. The House was being asked to depart from its decision in *Walkley v Precision Forgings* (1979) which had created an artificial distinction between claimants who made no application within the limitation period, and those who issued, but then failed to serve and had to re-issue outside the limitation period. Several cases were referred to where the case had been distinguished and there had been a reluctance to apply it. The court did have the discretion denied to it by Walkley, to allow extension of the time for a claim. Walkley was overruled.

Lord Bingham said:

> Over the past 40 years the House has exercised its power to depart from its own precedent rarely and sparingly. It has never been thought enough to justify doing so that a later generation of Law Lords would have resolved an issue or formulated a principle differently from their predecessors.

In the result, *Walkley* was departed from as it unfairly deprived claimants of a right Parliament intended them to have; it had driven the Court of Appeal to draw distinctions which were so fine as to reflect no credit on the instant area of law; and it subverted the clear intention of Parliament.

It held that the case would be remitted to the county court for the judge to resolve the application under **s 33** of the **Limitation Act 1980**.

One of the main reasons that the House of Lords decided to overrule the legal analysis it had given in the 1979 case was that the decision had caused great unfairness ever since. To give justice to injured claimants who would otherwise fall foul of the 1979 House of Lords' decision, subsequent courts had to make all sorts of dubious distinctions. The House of Lords was right to change its mind. The authority and 'finality' of the 1979 decision created many human difficulties, and as Lord Atkin once observed (*Ras Behari Lal v King-Emperor* (1933)): 'Finality is a good thing, but justice is a better.'

Common Pitfalls

The 1966 Practice Statement is a multifactor formula. It is a common fault to omit one or more elements of the formula. Its contents should be learnt in full.

Aim Higher

High credit can be earned by demonstrating an understanding of the subtleties of what, socially or jurisprudentially, leads the highest court to regard an earlier decision as not just technically wrong but definitely requiring correction. This is best done through case illustrations such as *Walkley v Precision Forgings Ltd* (1979).

QUESTION 17

Describe the work of the coroners' courts and explain what social role this part of the legal system is expected to perform.

How to Read this Question

This question asks for a description of not only what coroners' courts do, but, crucially, the part this system plays in investigating, monitoring and recording deaths at a local and national level. Your answer should deal with this aspect throughout the essay.

How to Answer this Question

You should:

- ❖ explain the historical setting of coroners' courts;
- ❖ note current numbers and duties of coroners;
- ❖ consider verdicts and purpose of classifications;
- ❖ consider patterns of death;
- ❖ discuss the problems posed by the meaning of the word 'how' in the require-ment for inquests to decide 'how' someone died;
- ❖ ensure that the social role of coroners' courts is discussed throughout.

Answer Structure

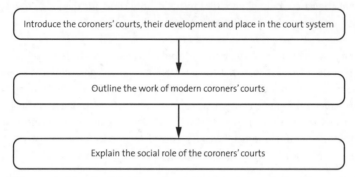

Introduce the coroners' courts, their development and place in the court system

⬇

Outline the work of modern coroners' courts

⬇

Explain the social role of the coroners' courts

ANSWER

The coroners' courts are one of the most ancient parts of the English legal system, dating back to at least 1194. They are not, in modern function, part of the criminal courts, although, for historical reasons, they have an association with that branch of the justice system.

Coroners were originally appointed as *custos placitorum coronae*, keepers of the pleas of the Crown. They had responsibility for criminal cases in which the Crown had an interest, particularly if this interest was financial. By development of their role, however, and particularly through the pioneering work of the nineteenth-century coroner Dr Thomas Wakley, the coroner became, in Wakley's phrase, 'the people's judge'. The coroner is the ultimate public safeguard in an area of unmatched import-ance: the official documenting of how people die. Marilyn Lannigan, an authority on the history of the coroner, has pointed to the fact that it was Wakley who originally campaigned for all suspicious deaths, deaths in police custody or prison and deaths attributable to neglect to be brought within the jurisdiction of the coroner. He was an energetic reformer who was also an MP and the founder of the medical journal *The Lancet*.

Today, there are 157 coroners' courts, of which 21 sit full-time. Coroners are usually lawyers (with at least a five-year qualification within **s 71** of the **Courts and Legal Services Act**

1990), although about 25 per cent are medical doctors with a legal qualification. The main jurisdiction of the coroner today concerns unnatural and violent deaths, although treasure troves are also something occasionally dealt with in these courts. However, the **Treasure Act 1996** which came into effect in 1997 introduced new rules relating to the reporting of finds and how they should be dealt with. The number of inquests into treasure troves will eventually fall away to zero.[1]

The classifying of types of death, of which there are about 500,000 each year in England and Wales, is clearly of critical importance, not just to the state, politicians and policy makers, but also to the sort of campaign groups that exist in a constitutional democracy to monitor suicides, drug-related deaths, deaths in police custody and prison, accidental deaths, deaths in hospitals and through industrial diseases. About 40 per cent of deaths each year are reported to coroners as unnatural, or violent, or as reportable from certain industries, or are from an unknown cause.

In 2009, there were 500,100 registered deaths in England and Wales. The number of these reported to coroners was 229,900, resulting in 105,400 post-mortem examinations and 31,000 inquests. Having a reliable system for charting who is dying, and in what circumstances, is of considerable social value. It is important for us to know, for example, that there were 3,800 suicides in England and Wales in 2009, as this should inform public policy related to the health service, community services, custodial policy and the emergency services.[2]

Most inquests (96 per cent) are held without juries, but the state has been insistent that certain types of case must be heard by a jury in order to promote public faith in government. When in 1926, legislation, for the first time, permitted inquests to be held without juries, certain types of death were deliberately marked off as still requiring jury scrutiny and these included deaths in police custody, deaths resulting from the actions of a police officer on duty and deaths in prison. This was seen as a very important way of fostering public trust in potentially oppressive aspects of the state. In 1971, the *Brodrick Committee Report* (Cmnd 4810) on the coronial system saw the coroner's jury as having a symbolic significance and thought that it was a useful way to legitimate the decision of the coroner.

The coroner's court is unique in using an inquisitorial process. There are no 'sides' in an inquest. There may be representation for people like the relatives of the deceased, insurance companies, prison officers, car drivers, companies (whose policies are possibly implicated in the death) and train drivers, etc., but all the witnesses are the coroner's witnesses. It is the coroner who decides who shall be summoned as witnesses and in what order they shall be called.

....

1   Introductory paragraphs provide an interesting overview of the original coroners' courts and also then moves on to place the courts into a modern-day context.

2   Rather than being a purely descriptive answer in terms of the role of the coroners' courts, the essay recognises the importance of getting to grip with the main issue of their 'social role'.

Historically, an inquest jury could decide that a deceased had been unlawfully killed and then commit a suspect for trial at the local assizes. When this power was taken away in 1926, the main bridge over to the criminal justice system was removed. There then followed, in stages, an attempt to prevent inquest verdicts from impinging on the jurisdictions of the ordinary civil and criminal courts. Now, an inquest jury is exclusively concerned with determining who the deceased was and 'how, when and where he came by his death'. The court is forbidden to make any wider comment on the death, and must not determine or appear to determine criminal liability 'on the part of a named person'. Nevertheless, the jury may still now properly decide that a death was unlawful (that is, a crime). The verdict of 'unlawful killing' is on a list of options (including 'suicide', 'accidental death' and 'open verdict') made under legislation and approved by the Home Office.

Under the **Coroners and Justice Act 2009**, the coronial system was reorganised.[3] Under the Act, a senior coroner who is made aware that the body of a deceased person is within that coroner's area must as soon as practicable conduct 'an investigation' into the person's death if there is evidence that

(a)   the deceased died a violent or unnatural death;
(b)   the cause of death is unknown; or
(c)   the deceased died while in custody or otherwise in state detention.

Some of the legal questions vexing the coronial process are quite significant when one considers the general role of the coroner system to plot national patterns of death. It is, as noted above, the purpose of an inquest to determine, among other things, how the deceased died, and 'how' in this context means, according to one view, simply by what physical cause and in what immediate circumstances. According to another proposition, however, one needs to take a much broader interpretation of the word 'how', in order to give a sufficiently thorough investigation to the issue (in some cases) of whether there was an unlawful killing.

The meaning of the word 'how' in a coroner's court was addressed in *Homberg*. Simon Brown LJ stated that although the word 'how' is to be widely interpreted, it means 'by what means' the death came about, rather than 'in what broad circumstances'. Thus, a coroner or counsel at an inquest can object to any line of inquiry which seeks to find out about 'the broad circumstances of the death'. On the other hand, unless the court knows something about the broad circumstances of a company's operations, it is impossible to determine whether there has been 'gross negligence'. Questions from counsel designed to elicit information from witnesses about the past practices of a company, its record on safety, or who in the company knew what and at what time, could thus be objected to on the basis of *Homberg*, while being perfectly defensible on the basis of testing whether the principle of 'gross negligence' manslaughter is applicable.

....

3   Including consideration of the most recent legislation demonstrates up-to-date knowledge and adds
    weight and authority to the answer.

Not all of the work of coroners is as riddled with intrigue as a day in the life of the American medical examiner, as portrayed in contemporary fiction and television. Nonetheless, the importance of the system in maintaining an open society and acting as a buttress against sinister conduct is immense.

Common Pitfalls

Under the **Coroners and Justice Act 2009**, there are clear rules governing when an inquest should be held. Ignorance of these rules is a common feature of poorer answers. Try to avoid writing a purely descriptive section about coroners' courts at the beginning of the essay and then a section on their social role – incorporate this into each point you make.

Aim Higher

High credit can be gained by demonstrating a good knowledge and understanding of the social importance of the coronial system – for example, why it is important for a society to know how many people commit suicide each year.

Notes

Under the **Coroners and Justice Act 2009**, the coronial system was reorganised. The Act establishes a Chief Coroner to lead the coroners' service, with powers to intervene in cases in specified circumstances, including presiding over an appeals process designed specifically for the coroner system. The Act establishes a senior coroner for each coroner area (previously known as coroner districts) with the possibility of appointing area coroners and assistant coroners to assist the senior coroner for the area (in place of the existing deputy coroners and assistant deputy coroners). A senior coroner who is made aware that the body of a deceased person is within that coroner's area must as soon as practicable conduct 'an investigation' into the person's death if there is evidence that

(a) the deceased died a violent or unnatural death;
(b) the cause of death is unknown; or
(c) the deceased died while in custody or otherwise in state detention.

The general rule is that an inquest must be held without a jury. There are, though, some exceptions. A jury must be summoned where the deceased died while in custody or otherwise in state detention, and the death was violent or unnatural, or of unknown cause; where the death was as a result of an act or omission of a police officer or member of a police force in the purported execution of their duties; or where the death was caused by an accident, poisoning or disease which must be reported to a government department or inspector. This includes certain deaths at work. Although a jury is not required in any other case, the coroner will be able to summon one in any case where he or she believes there is sufficient reason for doing so. Coroners sit with juries of between 7 and 11 people.

QUESTION 18

In what ways does the English legal system seek to balance interests? Using examples, discuss the challenges faced by the system in doing this effectively.

How to Read this Question

The danger of this question is that it is very general and it would be possible to write in vague terms which do not demonstrate your knowledge. Instead, distinguish between balancing interests at the substantive level (for example, freedom of speech against the right not to be defamed) and the procedural level (how the courts manage their processes to be fair to different litigants). Make sure you give concrete examples (such as the *Gillan* case in the essay which follows). Indicate the challenges which the system faces in achieving balance, in particular the wider policy considerations which lie behind many decisions.

How to Answer this Question

A good answer will:

- ❖ give some general examples (like freedom of speech) to put the question in a context;
- ❖ give an example of the English legal system itself having to balance interests, such as where, even before arguments about balancing interests over freedom of speech, it has to decide questions like who to let into court and how long litigants get to put their cases;
- ❖ show considerations of time and resources;
- ❖ explore a concrete case example, *Gillan* (2004);
- ❖ put the question into a political or 'policy' (wider) context.

Answer Structure

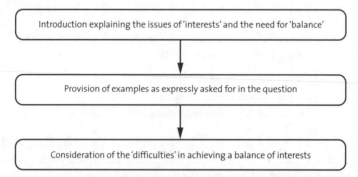

Introduction explaining the issues of 'interests' and the need for 'balance'

Provision of examples as expressly asked for in the question

Consideration of the 'difficulties' in achieving a balance of interests

Up for Debate

You can probably think of many aspects of the English legal system which involve the balancing of interests, whether they are substantive, such as privacy claims against newspapers (see e.g. the various cases involving *Mosley v News Group*

Newspapers Ltd (2008)), or procedural. Procedurally, defendants have the right to call and examine witnesses, but see the balancing issues in *Al-Khawaja & Tahery v the United Kingdom, Application No. 26766/05 and 22228/06* [2011] ECHR 2127. A recent procedural issue came up in a criminal case where Judge Peter Murphy had to decide whether a Muslim female defendant could give her evidence with her face covered. In this case, the judge had to balance the defendant's desire to follow the tenets of her religion (**Art 9, ECHR**) against the principle of open justice and the requirements of a fair trial (**Art 6, ECHR**). His decision can be found at www.judiciary.gov.uk/judgments/thequeenvd.

ANSWER

One of the important functions of the legal system is to balance interests. This it does in hundreds of different ways. One person's right to 'free speech' must be balanced against another person's right to be protected against being defamed by lies, or being attacked because of incitements to racial hatred. One person's right to play loud music or operate an airport near a residential area needs to be balanced against the rights of others not to be badly disturbed. People have the right to bring legal actions in the civil courts but it is in the interests of society that we are protected against being bothered by serial litigants who want to use the legal system in an obsessive way and, therefore, such people can be barred from the courts as 'vexatious litigants'.[4]

These issues often raise questions of fundamental social and political importance. For example, consider the question of at exactly what point we should exclude an intending litigant from the courts. Someone might have a genuine case against a part of the central or local governmental machinery. He or she might have been the real victim of repeated unfairness, or of a miscarriage of justice, or malice or prejudice. History shows that such things can happen. Such victims might then find themselves in an awful legal battle, like the case in Franz Kafka's novel *The Trial*, trying to use the law to fight parts of some huge organisation (like a governmental department, or a large telecom company, or financial institution) only to then be branded as a 'vexatious litigant' and excluded from the very processes of justice that exist to examine alleged wrongs.

The legal system can also exclude from all its own law courts a litigant who has 'habitually and persistently and without reasonable cause' instituted vexatious proceedings. In 1897, it was ruled that a court can consider the number and general character of a serial litigator's cases, and can make an exclusion order even if there may have been reasonable grounds for the proceedings in each case considered separately: *Re Chaffers, ex parte A-G* (1897). The **Supreme Court Act 1981 s 42** prevents a vexatious litigant from commencing any further proceedings without the permission of the High Court.

---

4   By providing appropriate examples, the answer immediately 'sets the scene', clearly demonstrating why the English legal system needs to balance interests. This indicates, to the examiner, an understanding of the issues and satisfies the specific instruction to provide examples contained in the question.

Similarly, the time taken in court by litigants and their lawyers needs to be controlled. It might well be that given an extra few weeks in court, a claimant or defendant might (in his or her own view) be able to make their case much more persuasively through their lawyer. If, however, they have been afforded a reasonable time, and time in line with general practice, it will commonly be seen as fair that their period for argument is curtailed. Their right to talk at inordinate length must be balanced with other considerations like that of allowing a good flow of cases through the courts. With limited resources (judges, courtrooms, court staff), a court will usually be doing better to hear, say, ten cases in a month in a time-managed way as opposed to one case in an unlimited way. Sometimes, the exceptional nature of a case will warrant the court being generous with its time. The longest opening courtroom speeches in English legal history were in the important case of *BCCI v Bank of England* (2004). This was a case where, in allowing speeches of around six months in duration, the losses of 80,000 investors and the importance of the defendant outweighed the delays to smaller and less important cases.

Another recent example[5] of the courts' balancing interests can be found in a case from the Civil Division of the Court of Appeal. In times of heightened awareness of terrorist threats, a balance must be made between civil liberty and public safety. The scales could be weighted entirely in favour of public safety by giving the police the unlimited authority to do anything they saw fit in order to counter possible terrorist threats: to arrest anyone and question him for months or years without having to give a reason for the suspect having been arrested. Tens of thousands of people could be imprisoned on the basis of suspicion as evidenced by their clothes or ethnicity or religion; traffic could be outlawed from whole sections of cities; and the population could be put under an 8 pm curfew. That might reduce the risk of terrorist acts but there would be a high price to pay in the dimension of civil liberty.

By contrast, the police could be asked to prevent and detect terrorism without being given any extra powers. That would allow a high degree of civil liberty but would arguably make life easier for terrorists. These issues were considered in the following case. The Court of Appeal decided that the disadvantage of the intrusion imposed on individuals by being stopped and searched by police officers under the **Terrorism Act 2000 s 44** was outweighed by the advantage of the possibility of a terrorist attack being avoided or deterred by use of that power.

In *R (on the application of Gillan) v (1) Commissioner of Police for the Metropolis (2) Secretary of State for the Home Department* (2004), the Court of Appeal addressed these issues. The applicants (G and Q) appealed against the dismissal of their claim for judicial review of the lawfulness of their being stopped and searched by police officers. In September 2003, G, a student, was on his way to demonstrate at an arms fair in London when he was stopped and searched under the **Terrorism Act 2000 s 44** for articles concerned in terrorism. Q was stopped and searched under the same provisions at the same event. She was at the fair to film the protests. Nothing incriminating was found on G or Q and they

---

5   The inclusion of up-to-date examples demonstrates impressive current knowledge and awareness.

later complained. The police officers relied on an authorisation made under s 44 of the 2000 Act by the Assistant Commissioner and its subsequent confirmation by the Secretary of State to justify their actions.

The authorisation ran for 28 days and had then been further authorised twice for two further periods of 28 days. G and Q stated that the evidence showed that the rolling programme of authorisations had become part of day-to-day policing, contrary to the intention of the 2000 Act. The Court of Appeal had to interpret s 44 and the way it had been applied in this case and consider the impact of the **Human Rights Act 1998 s 3**.

The Court of Appeal held that it was entirely consistent with the framework of the Act that a power to stop and search should be exercised when a senior police officer considered it advantageous for the prevention of terrorism and ss 44 and 45 could not conflict with the provisions of the European Convention. However, the court could determine the proportionality of the police action.

The disadvantage of the intrusion imposed on individuals by being stopped and searched was outweighed by the advantage of the possibility of a terrorist attack being avoided or deterred by use of the power. The rolling programme was justified in the current situation and there was nothing to support the suggestion that the powers were used for day-to-day policing.

The police commander had been entitled to decide to use the s 44 powers at the arms fair, given the particular circumstances. However, the police had not shown that there had been adequate instructions to officers on how those powers should be used. As the onus was on the police to show that the interference with G's and Q's rights was lawful and they had not discharged this, the appeal was allowed.

This case is a good illustration of the way a law court can be engaged in the evaluation of social or political issues in the process in deciding what is the appropriate balancing (or imbalance) of oppositional interests. Several cases have sought to balance the interests of the individual and those of the state, especially in respect of issues, as in the *Gillan* case above, arising from the **European Convention on Human Rights**.

In *Gillan*, the Court of Appeal makes a comparably 'political' point when it ruled that the disadvantage of individuals by being stopped and searched by police officers was outweighed by the advantage of the possibility of a terrorist attack being avoided or deterred by use of that power.

One thing that this case illustrates, along with the other issues examined in this essay, is that, ultimately, the balancing of interests is an exercise that must be carried out according to large political or social principles that are above and beyond clinical legal questions.[6]

6   The provision of a brief conclusion not only brings discussion to an end but, importantly, allows the question to be referenced and a succinct overview of the main thrust of the answer to be provided.

QUESTION 19

Explain and assess the effectiveness of cross-examination as a method of getting to the truth in court.

How to Read this Question

Remember the importance of process words. 'Explain' means more than simply describe. You should show why cross-examination is effective. 'Assess' requires you to weigh up or evaluate that effectiveness. You are also given a standard by which to measure the effectiveness. It is not, for example, whether cross-examination is a useful tool for winning a case, but rather whether it enables the court to establish the truth.

How to Answer this Question

The court case – the civil and criminal trial – is at the heart of the English legal system. Within such trials, the process of cross-examination is a key mechanism for producing the truth, or at least of producing a just result. The answer should make it clear how, in general terms, the system works and why it is used.

❖ Introduce the procedure.
❖ Explain its basic purpose.
❖ Explain the balance of power between advocate and witness.
❖ Illustrate effective use of questioning: e.g. Isaacs and Seddon.
❖ The use of sustained questioning: e.g. Cadbury's case.
❖ Conclusion – effective unless one too many questions are asked.

Answer Structure

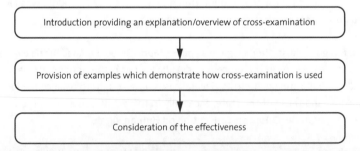

Introduction providing an explanation/overview of cross-examination

Provision of examples which demonstrate how cross-examination is used

Consideration of the effectiveness

Up for Debate

Cross-examination can be a devastating tool in the hands of the skilled advocate – is its use always justified? One difficult area is the cross-examination of rape victims, where the defence's best line of attack will often be to try to discredit the complainant by exploring her sexual history. As this can discourage complainants from coming forward, and thereby make establishing the truth more difficult, statutory provisions limit the extent to which such cross-examination may take place (**s 41 Youth Justice and Criminal Evidence Act 1999**).

ANSWER

Cross-examination is an important feature of criminal and civil trials. It has been recognised by the Court of Appeal that an unwarranted restriction of an advocate's opportunity to cross-examine a witness can render a trial unfair under Art 6 of the **European Convention on Human Rights**, and therefore be a reason for ordering a retrial: *R v John K* (2007). The simple point of significance decided in this case in the context of the English legal system is the indispensable value of cross-examination.

In court, cross-examination is where an advocate questions a witness who is part of the other side of the case. The questions cross from one side's lawyer to the other side's witness.[7]

The aim of the exercise is to weaken the opponent's case, and to help establish facts which are favourable to the side of the cross-examiner. It is an opportunity to expose any unreliability in an opposing witness's testimony. Cross-examination can be done politely and without hostility. Sir John Mortimer QC notes (*Clinging to the Wreckage*, 1982, p. 106) that his late father (also a distinguished barrister) used to say 'the art of cross-examination is not the art of examining crossly'.

When a prosecuting advocate has finished questioning (called 'examining') a witness called by the prosecution, defence counsel can cross-examine that witness. Later the prosecution has the same chance to discredit the evidence of defence witnesses. In a civil case, similarly, the claimant and the defendant (usually through advocates) can cross-examine each other, and each other's witnesses. The procedure has a long history. The noun 'cross-examination' was first recorded in a case in 1729, although the technique itself is much older, appearing in one case involving a will in Norwich at the beginning of the thirteenth century. Cross-examination is an excellent method of clarifying the facts of a disputed matter. It is a serious intellectual contest fought in the threat of grave consequences. It is people at the peak of rational truth-finding.

The advocate has many advantages over the witness, such as knowing the rules of evidence, and choosing the line of inquiry in cross-examination. But the advocate does not always get the upper hand. A barrister in Ireland once began a cross-examination of an Irish prelate with the words: 'Am I wrong in thinking you are the most influential man, and decidedly the most influential Prelate or Potentate, in the Province of Connaught?' The witness replied: 'Well, you know, they say these things, but it is in the sense that they would say that you are the very light of the Bar of Ireland: these are children's compliments.'

Cross-examination can involve counsel taking a witness through a sequence of propositions he will have to agree with until he is eventually cornered into agreeing with one final deadly point. But, equally, advocates sometimes pivot quickly to a riveting question.

---

7   Sets the scene by explaining cross-examination, what it involves and its uses.

In opening the cross-examination of Frederick Seddon (who was on trial for the murder of his lodger, Miss Eliza Barrow), Sir Rufus Isaacs, Attorney General, began thus:

> ISAACS: Miss Barrow lived with you from July 26, 1910, to September 14, 1911?
> SEDDON: Yes.
> ISAACS: Did you like her?

This flummoxed Seddon and he did not regain his composure. He could see that if he said he had liked her he would be asked why he had put her in a pauper's grave, whereas if he said he had not liked her he would tilt the case further against himself. Decidedly, this was a killer question. Seddon was eventually executed for the murder.

One masterful cross-examination was that in 1909 by Sir Edward Carson KC of the witness William Cadbury, director of the chocolate company (see Richard Du Cann, *The Art of the Advocate*, 1964, ch. 7). Between 1901 and 1908, Cadbury's chocolate obtained half their cocoa from islands off Angola which exploited forced slave labour. Cadbury's knew about the slavery and profited hugely from it for years, but did not reveal it to the public. Instead, it traded on its reputation as a model employer, and the benevolent treatment of its workers at Bournville in England. Meanwhile, people were snatched as slaves and forced to march up to a thousand miles to the plantations, and killed if they did not keep up. The *Evening Standard* published an article critical of Cadbury's, and the firm sued saying it made them look like 'a bunch of canting hypocrites'. In a brilliant cross-examination lasting five hours, Carson dismantled the case of William Cadbury and the firm. The final exchange was a dramatic dénouement. After hours of quizzing about how much slave blood and suffering was involved in the production of the chocolate, and the complicity of Cadbury, there was this question:

> CARSON: Have you formed any estimate of the number of slaves who lost their lives in preparing your cocoa from 1901 to 1908?

That is a bit like asking 'Have you stopped beating your wife?' – a question which, answered either way, condemns the quizzed person. In answer to the question whether he had quantified the suffering on which he had sold chocolate, the director replied meekly:

> CADBURY: No, no, no.

The jury found Cadbury's had been libelled but awarded damages of one farthing.[8]

Cross-examination, however, is not a useful instrument if used too casually or in a slipshod way. Sir Henry Curtis-Bennett KC (1879–1936) was famous for maintaining that in cross-questioning an advocate should never ask a question if he did not already know the answer. A modern case in point was recounted by Sir Oliver Popplewell (*Benchmark*, 2003, p. 130). As a young barrister defending a man charged with careless driving, Mr Popplewell was cross-examining a prosecution witness who had testified that the defendant had been speeding.

---

8 Provision of appropriate examples clearly demonstrates the effectiveness of carefully crafted cross-examination questions.

The witness was repeatedly pressed to estimate the speed of the car but declined. Having satisfactorily established the witness's incompetence in car-speed estimation, Mr Popplewell did not sit down but asked one final, fatal question: 'Why are you telling the court you cannot estimate the speed of my client's car?' The witness's response was calm and clear: 'Because I have never seen a car go as fast as that in all my life!'[9]

When it is used effectively, however, cross-examination is a technique at the core of forensic truth-finding. It is the apotheosis of rational and empirically based testing of any contention or argument.

QUESTION 20

What general principles (if any) can be deduced from the existing appeal structure in England and Wales?

How to Read this Question

The appeal structure is a complicated set of rules defining when, and how, someone can appeal in criminal and civil cases. This question invites you to look behind the rules and determine the wider principles of justice on which the rules are founded.

How to Answer this Question

You should include:

❖ criminal appeals;
❖ principles discussed in the Runciman Commission and the *Auld Report*;
❖ changes in civil appeals;
❖ the *Practice Direction on Civil Appeals* (2000).

Answer Structure

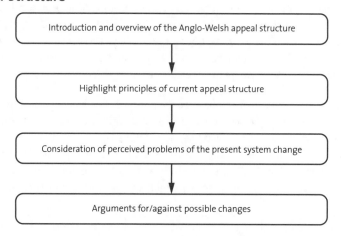

Introduction and overview of the Anglo-Welsh appeal structure

Highlight principles of current appeal structure

Consideration of perceived problems of the present system change

Arguments for/against possible changes

---

9   Once examples have been provided, it will then allow an opportunity to move on and evaluate how effective the process can be/is in ascertaining the truth, as specifically required by the question.

Up for Debate

Do you think the balance is right between allowing litigants a second, or even third, opportunity to have their case considered and the efficient use of the court system? It is also worth bearing in mind that the other side in litigation may be put under pressure by the continuation of litigation. Can you think of any other factors which should be taken into account?

ANSWER

Several general principles emerge from a study of the current appeal structure, principles which relate to the evolved purposes of the appeal process. These purposes include:

(a) the opportunity for a litigant to have more than one occasion to put his case – an idea based upon the premise that people and processes are fallible;

(b) the opportunity to reconsider a problem in the light of new evidence; and

(c) the need for an appellate body to standardise the legal response to particular sorts of problem.

Research undertaken for the **Royal Commission on Criminal Justice (1993)** revealed that of 300 appeals in 1990, just over one-third were successful. Almost two-thirds of defendants appealed against conviction on the ground that the trial judge had made a critical mistake and of these, 43 per cent succeeded in having their convictions quashed. In about 80 per cent of cases where convictions were quashed, there had been an error at the trial, usually by the judge.

In general, the Anglo-Welsh system of appeals avoids 'finality' after just one appeal hearing. There is for most cases (subject to the approval of the first appeal court or the next intended forum) more than one possible appeal hearing. An appeal from the civil jurisdiction of the magistrates' court, for example, could be taken to the Divisional Court of the Family Division and thence to the Court of Appeal Civil Division and finally, within the UK, to the Supreme Court. Additionally, both the Civil and Criminal Divisions of the Court of Appeal can order retrials where the interests of justice so require.[10]

The appeal structure puts great emphasis on the principle of extempore judicial wisdom.[11] In the USA, the appeal system relies more upon reserved, written judgments, and most appellate judges enjoy the services of 'law clerks' (accomplished graduates from law school, paid from public funds), who assist the judges with research work and discussion of complex and contentious points of law. The English system makes much use of unreserved judgments in the Court of Appeal, after listening to oral argument, again in contrast to the American

10 Provision of an overview of the present appeal system demonstrates both knowledge and understanding of an important element of the English legal system.

11 Consideration of 'principles' demonstrates that the question has been carefully analysed and its requirements recognised.

preference for appellate judges considering long, written submissions in respect of the appeals. This principle of orality was reaffirmed by Sir John Donaldson MR (as he then was) in an article in 1982: he said that 'the conduct of appeals by way of oral hearing lies at the heart of the English tradition' ((1982) 132 NLJ 959).

Another principle clearly governing the operation of the appeal system is that of carefully controlled accessibility. Probably as a deterrent against what might be regarded as overuse of the system by all convicted defendants, there are several obstacles placed in front of anyone contemplating an appeal. Leave must be obtained in all appeals, for example, from the Crown Court to the Court of Appeal (Criminal Division), unless the matter is concerned only with a point of law. The Court of Appeal also has a power to order that time spent appealing will not count towards the sentence. Shortly after this policy was introduced in 1970, the number of applications for leave to appeal in such cases was reduced by about half.

Accessibility to the appeal courts is also restricted by the poor record of trial proceedings in magistrates' and county courts.[12] Additionally, appeals can be based upon fresh evidence, but the courts have sometimes taken a very narrow view of what is within this term. In criminal cases, the Court of Appeal has discretion whether to admit new evidence if it thinks it 'necessary or expedient in the interests of justice' (**Criminal Appeal Act 1968**). The court 'shall' admit the new evidence, that is, it *must*, where it: (a) affords a ground for appeal; (b) looks credible; (c) would have been admissible at the trial; and (d) the court is satisfied of a reasonable explanation as to why the evidence was not adduced at the trial.

Similar rules apply in respect of civil appeals. If the new evidence is something that could, with 'reasonable diligence', have been obtained for use in the trial, then it will not be permitted as the foundation of an appeal. In *Linton v Ministry of Defence* (1983), the House of Lords upheld this principle and denied a fresh trial to the appellant in circumstances where it was clear that his case would be very much stronger than in the original trial. This principle also applies to points taken by counsel; if they could have been put at trial, then they cannot form the basis of an appeal. In *Maynard* (1979), Roskill LJ said that if the rule were otherwise, it would enable counsel to keep a point up their sleeve at trial and then, if the case went against them, try to raise the point for the first time on appeal, thus having a second bite at the 'forensic cherry'.

If an appellant has not succeeded in the ordinary appeal process, he cannot get around the problem indirectly by taking an action for negligence against his lawyers (*Rondel v Worsley* (1969)). Neither may a convicted person re-open the trial by suing for defamation anyone who says he was rightly convicted (**Civil Evidence Act 1968**).

Access to the final appellate court, the Supreme Court, is very limited, since it will only hear cases with leave, and in criminal appeals, there must also be a certificate from the Court of Appeal that the case involves a point of law of general public importance.

. . . .

12 Highlighting perceived problems provides a helpful link between the discussion of 'general principles' and the requirement of considering the need for change to the system.

Even when access to the appeal process has been granted to the appellant, a constellation of rules is set to prevent technical abuse of the system. Thus, the 'proviso' to **s2** of the **Criminal Appeal Act 1968** allows the court to agree with the ground for the appeal, but to keep the conviction if no substantial miscarriage of justice has occurred.

Sceptical views have been expressed about court appeal systems across the world. In 1911, in *The Devil's Dictionary*, Ambrose Bierce defined 'Appeal' as 'v.t. In law, to put the dice into the box for another throw'. The progressive refinements to the civil and criminal appeal systems over the last hundred years now ensure that all reasonable effort is dedicated to the correction of error in the trial processes of the English legal system.

QUESTION 21

'Government cuts are not fair.' Discuss how the legal system is being affected by the economic recession.

How to Read this Question

Remember that 'discuss' means to give two sides to the question, so you will need to look at this emotive issue objectively and rationally. Use evidence to support your arguments, as shown below. The issue of 'fairness' and the meaning of that term must also be explored.

How to Answer this Question

❖ Evidence of the recession on the legal system (*R v SH* [2010] EWCA Crim 193, para 5).
❖ Judge Paul Collins' comments.
❖ Cutbacks in family justice system.
❖ Tribunal Service.
❖ Crown Prosecution Service.
❖ Judges threaten industrial action.
❖ What is meant by 'fair'.
❖ Conclusion.

Answer Structure

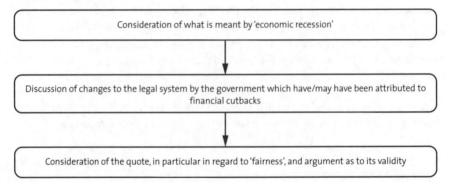

Consideration of what is meant by 'economic recession'

Discussion of changes to the legal system by the government which have/may have been attributed to financial cutbacks

Consideration of the quote, in particular in regard to 'fairness', and argument as to its validity

Up for Debate

You might also wish to consider recent action by barristers in 'striking' against legal aid cuts. Barristers are, of course, self-employed, but in January and March 2014 they staged a series of walkouts before eventually agreeing a deal with the Ministry of Justice. Is such action justified? Solicitors complained that the deal left them no better off and the damage to the system was still considerable.

It is clear that the legal system is under an economic strain. The state of the economy has even been commented upon judicially. A judge in a Crown Court trial concerning a charge of 'causing racially aggravated fear or provocation of violence' told the court we do not have the luxury of trying such cases because 'This country is next to broke.'

That was in 2010 (*R v SH* [2010] EWCA Crim 193, para 5),[13] and since then things have deteriorated. Recent governmental plans will see the Ministry of Justice's budget cut by 23 per cent. The staffing of courts is already desperately inadequate but 14,250 of these frantically demanding jobs have been ended since 2008, or are currently set not to be replaced when the incumbents go, leaving the residual workforce to toil in an awful, Sisyphean challenge.

Judge Paul Collins, London's most senior county court judge, said in 2007 that low pay and high turnover among staff meant that serious errors were commonplace and routinely led to incorrect judgments in court. He said that with further cuts looming, 'we run the risk of bringing about a real collapse in the service we're able to give to the people using the courts'.

The law is everybody's law but historic and prospective legal aid cuts have now decitizenised huge swathes of the population. Ministers now plan to cut the legal aid bill by £600 million a year, and family cases will bear the brunt, with 246,000 cases a year taken out of public funding.

In 2011, Stephen Cobb QC, chairman of the 2,500-strong Family Law Bar Association, said that the proposals going through Parliament in the **Legal Aid, Sentencing and Punishment of Offenders Bill** would have a 'serious and damaging effect'. Some 54,000 fewer people would be represented in the family courts a year, affecting some 68,000 children at the centre of family breakdowns, he said (Frances Gibb, *The Times*, 29 September 2011).

In 2010, the Tribunal Service reported an increase of 56 per cent in the number of claims in the year up to March against employers in England, Scotland and Wales. This is the highest ever: the total is 236,000, up from 151,000.

---

13 The use of appropriate, supporting legal authority is always valuable, as it can add weight to any argument and/or assist with explanation.

In 2012, it was reported that errors by Crown prosecutors are leading to about 63,000 criminal cases a year across England and Wales being wrongly dropped or unjustifiably brought to trial. It is estimated that the mistakes are being made in 7 per cent of the 900,000 Crown Court cases each year. The court performance of Crown Prosecution Service (CPS) advocates has also shown an overall decline over two years. In the bulk of cases, where defendants plead not guilty, CPS advocates are often ill-prepared and fail to challenge prejudicial evidence (see Frances Gibb, *The Times*, 30 March 2012, and Her Majesty's Crown Prosecution Service Inspectorate 2012).

In 2012, some 400 judges took an unprecedented first step towards suing the Government over changes to their pensions that effectively amounts to a pay cut (Frances Gibb, *The Times*, 9 March 2012).

The judges sent a letter to the Lord Chancellor, Kenneth Clarke, warning that if he proceeds with the controversial plans, they will challenge him in the courts.

The action by the judges, who instructed the international law firm Clifford Chance to send the 'letter before action', gave ministers 14 days to respond before legal proceedings were launched but the Government did respond in time. A Ministry of Justice spokesman added: 'These changes will see judges contribute towards their own pension for the first time, creating up to £7 million in savings for taxpayers.'

In 2011, the former Lord Chief Justice Lord Woolf warned that the Government must amend its proposals to overhaul the £2.1 billion legal aid system so as to protect access to justice. Lord Woolf said that the proposals, some of which have already been implemented, breach fundamental principles of the rule of law because people will be denied access to the courts.[14]

Can the Government's cuts be fair? There are 60 million people in the UK and most did not do anything wrong in places like Lehman Brothers to cause the near collapse of Western capitalism. So, according to one principle, it is not fair that the majority will now have to suffer painful cuts in their standard of living and reduced access to legal justice.

Unfairness can be a visceral and hard-wired feeling. Long before they hear or read anything about theories of justice, young children can say 'it's not fair' if they are the victims of inequity.

Defining what is 'fair', though, in a serious and rational way is as impossible as defining what is the best political party or the best music. Different people have different ideas about what is fair.

So, saying that the cuts to the justice system are unfair begs the question 'according to what definition of fairness?' The debate then fragments into a hundred shards of opinion.

....

14 Discussion not only highlights a number of cuts resulting from financial cutbacks but, importantly, also assesses the impact of such cuts on the legal system.

What can be shown, however, is that if the cuts are implemented, they will prevent the proper functioning of the legal system.

It is only after a society secures law and due process that it can move on to debate what is economically fair. In the phrase of the pre-eminent twentieth-century jurist Herbert Hart, we should be primarily concerned with 'social arrangements for continued existence, not with those of a suicide club'.

Law is the foundation of civilised society. The legal system has greater first-order importance than education and health in one key respect: unless you have guaranteed order and peaceful ways of settling disputes and punishing rule-breakers, there is little point in investing in classrooms and hospital wards.

The Chancellor George Osborne has said that in adjusting to the world of new hardships, the heavy burdens should fall on the broadest shoulders. If the Government is serious about that it should consider making the multi-billion-pound businesses worldwide which use the English courts as their favoured litigation forum pay much more than they do for that privilege.

Poets and philosophers might show how it is unfair that the financial acts of a reckless few have impoverished the lives of the blameless many. More urgent is the stark truth that without clemency, the axe set to fall on justice will break the legal system.

5 The Criminal Process

INTRODUCTION

The official purpose of the **criminal justice system (CJS)** is 'to deliver justice for all, by convicting and punishing the guilty and helping them to stop offending, while protecting the innocent'. It is responsible for detecting crime and bringing offenders to justice, and carrying out the orders of court, such as collecting fines and supervising community and custodial punishment.

The key goals for criminal justice were stated in 2010 as being:

❖ to improve the effectiveness and efficiency of the **CJS** in bringing offences to justice;
❖ to increase public confidence in the fairness and effectiveness of the **CJS**;
❖ to increase victim satisfaction with the police, and victim and witness satisfaction with the **CJS**;
❖ to consistently collect, analyse and use good-quality ethnicity data to identify and address race disproportionality in the **CJS**; and
❖ to increase the recovery of criminal assets by recovering £250 million of assets acquired through crime by 2009–10.

Not all parts of the **CJS** are working well. In November 2011 a **National Audit Office (NAO)** report into financial management at the Ministry of Justice (which is responsible for the **CJS**) revealed that Courts in England and Wales were owed £413 million in unpaid fines and £388 million in uncollected confiscation orders. The amount in outstanding fines has increased by 25 per cent since 2006–07. The **NAO** observed that in 2011–12 the Ministry of Justice was asked to make savings of £500 million in order to achieve the required funding cut of 23 per cent by 2014, and will therefore need to make significant efficiency savings. While finding that the financial management of the Ministry of Justice has improved since the audit in November 2010, the **NAO** nevertheless stated that in some important areas, 'the Ministry still has a great deal to do'.

The **CJS** is designed to operate as a coherent whole. It comprises: the National Criminal Justice Board, 42 Local Criminal Justice Boards across England and Wales, and the Office for Criminal Justice Reform.

The scale of activity is large. In 2012, Government statistics revealed that in the 12 months ending September 2011, there were 230,700 police cautions in England and Wales and 1.32 million offenders were convicted and sentenced.

The Ministry of Justice was created in 2007 to provide a stronger focus on the criminal justice system, and to reduce re-offending. Many changes have been made since by the **Criminal Justice and Immigration Act 2008**. Among other things, the Act:

❖ introduces a minimum tariff of two years for prisoners serving indeterminate public protection sentences;

❖ ends automatic discounts for offenders given an indeterminate sentence after the initial sentencing decision has been judged unduly lenient;

❖ gives powers for courts to make dangerous offenders given a discretionary life sentence serve a higher proportion of their tariff before being eligible for parole;

❖ creates a presumption that trials in magistrates' courts will proceed in the event the accused fails to appear;

❖ provides for non-dangerous offenders who breach the terms of their licence to be recalled to prison for a fixed 28-day period;

❖ creates a Youth Rehabilitation Order – a generic community sentence for children and young offenders – this will target the causes of offending behaviour and will simplify the current sentencing framework;

❖ creates the Youth Conditional Caution for children and young offenders;

❖ brings compensation for those wrongly convicted broadly into line with compensation for victims of crime.

Checklist

In particular, you should be familiar with the following recommendations and changes in the law:

Appeals
■ The work of the Criminal Cases Review Commission.
■ The powers for the Court of Appeal.
■ The Court of Appeal's decision in *Secretary of State for the Home Department ex p Hickey and Others* (1995).

Trial by jury
■ The provisions of the Criminal Justice Act 2003, ss 43–50 and 321.

Right to silence
■ Sections 34–37 of the Criminal Justice and Public Order Act (CJPOA) 1994, which explain what inferences may now be drawn in what circumstances from the silence of the accused.

Confessions
■ Sections 32–33 of the CJPOA 1994, which abolish the rules requiring the court to give the jury a warning about convicting the accused on the uncorroborated evidence of a person who is an accomplice or, in sexual cases, the victim.

Plea bargaining
Limited introduction was recommended by Runciman – reduced sentences for guilty pleas.

In general, you will need to know the major provisions of the Police and Criminal Evidence Act (PACE) 1984 **and other provisions relating to criminal procedure:**

- **the general powers of arrest – s 24 of** PACE;
- the general arrest conditions – s 25 of PACE;
- the common law powers of arrest;
- procedure on arrest;
- information on arrest;
- stop and search – ss 1 and 2 (and revised Code A) of PACE;
- search of arrested person – s 32 of PACE;
- search on detention – s 54 of PACE;
- search of premises – ss 17, 18 and 32 of PACE;
- search warrants – ss 8, 15 and 16 of PACE;
- interrogation, confession and admissibility of evidence;
- bail – the CJPOA 1994 changes;
- plea bargaining.

QUESTION 22

Critically evaluate the use of civil law by citizens who seek justice from it as an alternative to the criminal law.

How to Read this Question

Critical evaluation means that, using evidence, you should examine arguments on an issue from all sides and reach a conclusion. Note that the question is not a general comparison between the civil law and the criminal law, although you do need to understand the different nature and purposes of the two systems. Rather it concerns the circumstances when victims who do not feel they have received justice from the criminal justice system resort to suing in the civil courts.

How to Answer this Question

In your answer you should:

- ❖ explain the differences between the civil law and the criminal law;
- ❖ explain the basic nature of the private prosecution;
- ❖ give examples of citizens resorting to civil action where the criminal justice system has been judged by them to have failed;
- ❖ identify the legal difficulties concerning the appropriate standard of proof in civil trials about criminal matters;
- ❖ draw conclusions about the implications of the rising phenomenon for the legal system at large.

Up for Debate

Another possibility open to victims is to sue the police for failure to investigate, and thereby prevent, crime under the **Human Rights Act 1998**. The case of *DSD and NVB v The Commissioner of Police for the Metropolis* [2014] EWHC 436 (QB) is an excellent example, where the police were liable for failure to detect the 'black cab rapist'. Such cases must balance the operational priorities of the police against potential serious harm to victims.

Answer Structure

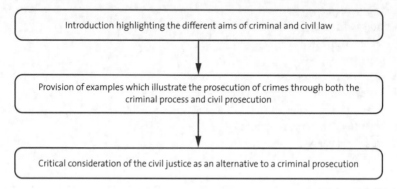

Introduction highlighting the different aims of criminal and civil law

Provision of examples which illustrate the prosecution of crimes through both the criminal process and civil prosecution

Critical consideration of the civil justice as an alternative to a criminal prosecution

ANSWER

Whereas the main purpose of the criminal law is for a start, on behalf of society, to condemn and punish serious wrongs, the purpose of civil law is to allow citizens to gain compensation or court orders if someone else has broken a civil law and caused them loss or harm. Sometimes, however, the civil law is used by citizens because the criminal law has been ineffective.

A private prosecution is a prosecution started by a private individual who is not acting on behalf of the police or any other prosecuting authority such as the Health and Safety Executive or the Inland Revenue. The right to bring private prosecutions is preserved by the **Prosecution of Offences Act 1985 s 6(1)**. There are, however, some controls: under the **Prosecution of Offences Act 1985 s 6(2)** the DPP has the power to take over private prosecutions. In some cases, the private prosecutor must seek the consent of the Attorney General or of the DPP before the commencement of proceedings.

At just after 3 pm on 15 August 1998, in a busy shopping street in Omagh, Northern Ireland, 29 people were murdered in a terrorist car-bomb atrocity. No one was convicted for this crime (Colm Murphy was sentenced to 14 years in prison in January 2002 for conspiracy to cause the explosion, but the conviction was overturned on appeal years later; as the criminal law was seen to be ineffective in condemning the guilty, relatives of the victims brought a civil action. In 2009, four men and the Real IRA were held liable in civil law for the homicides

(*Breslin & Ors v McKenna & Ors (Omagh Bombing case)* (2009)). Mr Justice Declan Morgan awarded more than £1.6 million in damages to 12 relatives of the 29 people. An appeal against the finding was rejected in 2013. The compensation is unlikely ever to be paid and, in any event, the action was not motivated by money but by a quest for court justice.

Victor Barker, whose 12-year-old son, James, was killed in the attack, noted that in 1998 the Prime Minister had pledged to convict the killers, leaving not one stone unturned, and added: 'Well, he clearly did because the families had to pick up all those stones and bring them to court' (*The Times*, 9 June, 2009).[1]

The Omagh litigation is part of a growing use of the *civil* process to pin a legal judgment of liability on culprits who have not, but arguably should have been, convicted by the criminal law. The purpose of the criminal law, according to Blackstone's elegant encapsulation, is to condemn and punish acts which 'strike at the very being of society'. He said that civil wrongs were wrongs that affected 'individuals, considered merely as individuals' whereas crimes were wrongs which struck at the whole community 'in its social aggregate capacity' (*Commentaries on the Laws of England*, IV, 1, 5).

If the civil justice system is being used in a makeshift way only because the criminal justice system has failed, the result is unsatisfactory. A civil suit does not really fit these circumstances.

An early use of the civil process to get a law court to condemn what was essentially a serious crime came in the case of Michael Brookes. In a civil case in 1991, a High Court judge ruled that Michael Brookes had killed Lynn Siddons, a 16-year-old stabbed 40 times in 1978. Her family were awarded £10,641 damages (*The Times*, 1 October, 12 December 1991). Mr Justice Rougier, however, applied the criminal standard of proof (that the case must be proven beyond a reasonable doubt) saying that a civil action for murder demanded no less (*Halford v Brookes and another* (1991)). The original police investigation and case against another defendant were found to have been completely bungled, but, after the civil case, Brookes was later convicted following a fresh criminal investigation of the murder (*The Times*, 9 October 1998).

In 1995, Linda Griffiths went to the civil courts in an action alleging that she had been raped by Arthur Williams, a former chef at the Dorchester, while working for him in 1991 as a dishwasher. The Crown Prosecution Service had decided not to prosecute Mr Williams. In the civil case against Mr Williams for trespass against the person, Ms Griffiths won and was awarded £50,000 damages (*The Times*, 5 November 1997).

In 1997, not long before OJ Simpson was found liable in a Californian civil court for the homicide of his former wife Nicole and her friend Ronald Goldman, a civil summons

----

1   The use of appropriate examples affords the opportunity to provide clear explanation of how crimes may
    be persecuted using both criminal and civil means. It also allows the answer to move on, seamlessly and
    logically, to the failings of the criminal system and the value of civil prosecutions in attaining justice.

relating to homicide was issued in London by the father of a murdered doctor, Joan Francisco. The following year, Mr Justice Alliott identified Tony Diedrick as the killer of Dr Francisco (*Francisco v Diedrick* (1998)). He awarded her family £50,000. Diedrick was later convicted of the killing and sentenced to life imprisonment.

Mr Justice Alliott decided the issue of liability (in an allegation of assault causing death) by reference to the balance of probabilities 'while bearing in mind that the allegation is of utmost gravity and can only be established by truly cogent evidence'.

He cited the decision of the House of Lords in *Re H and R (Child Sexual Abuse: Standard of Proof)* (1996), and, in particular, the speech of Lord Nicholls of Birkenhead in these terms (at p. 96B):

> The balance of probability standard means that a court is satisfied an event occurred if the court considers that, on the evidence, the occurrence of the event was more likely than not. When assessing the probabilities the court will have in mind as a factor, to whatever extent is appropriate in the particular case, that the more serious the allegation the less likely it is that the event occurred and, hence, the stronger should be the evidence before the court concludes that the allegation is established on the balance of probability. Fraud is usually less likely than negligence. Deliberate physical injury is usually less likely than accidental physical injury ...

That subtlety is important when a High Court judge comes to direct himself as to the standard of proof required in a civil case arising from an alleged crime. But, from a public perspective, put simply, the difference between the burden of proof in civil and criminal cases is that the burden of proof is lower in civil courts than in criminal courts. It is easier to prove a tort than a crime. This gives some opportunity for people successfully sued for alleged crimes to protest that just because their conduct is certified by the civil system as a civil wrong does not mean that a crime has been committed.

In some cases, prosecutors have been, are and will be absolutely justified in declining to prosecute because there is insufficient credible and admissible evidence to satisfy the Code for Crown Prosecutors criterion requiring there to be a 'realistic prospect of conviction'. There might be circumstances in which the acquisition of sufficiently good evidence to build a prosecution case is impossible. More troubling, though, are those cases in which inadequate police investigations effectively rule out a prosecution. That some police investigations are inadequate is strongly suggested where privately garnered evidence enables a civil win, and, thereafter, a public prosecution and conviction. British policing is, as you might expect from the world's earliest professionalised service, about the best in the world; but any unprosecuted serious crime leaves an enduring scar on the body politic.[2]

---

2   The provision of this conclusion provides the opportunity to highlight/emphasise the value of civil law in circumstances that would normally be dealt with under the criminal system. Re-reading the question before attempting a conclusion can often be valuable, as it allows the conclusion to be directed towards the specific question set.

Common Pitfalls

A candidate who does not exhibit a clear understanding of the different purposes and processes of civil and criminal law will make a poor impression.

Aim Higher

High ability will be demonstrated by showing a knowledge of *Shah v Gale* (2005).

Demonstrating a good knowledge of the reasoning in *Re H and R (Child Sexual Abuse: Standard of Proof)* (1996) will be highly creditable.

QUESTION 23

After a shop has been set on fire late one night, Detective Constables Whistle and Cuff, in a nearby road, hear about the incident on their car radio. They then see two youths, Gas and Spark, running down the road away from the area of the shop. The officers stop the youths, who smell of petrol, and ask them some questions. Gas and Spark are then arrested for arson and taken to the police station.

Before questioning, the officers untruthfully told Gas that his fingerprints had been discovered on a discarded bottle of petrol found in the burnt-out shop. The solicitor, unaware of the deceit, advised Gas to disclose any involvement he had had in the incident and Gas admitted having taken part.

Spark declined to accept any legal advice after the proper notices about its availability had been given to him. Spark was a drug addict and after a session of relentless questions being fired at him for over two hours, he asked whether the police would agree to bail if he admitted to being involved in the incident. The officer in the room agreed and Spark made a statement, in which he said he was at the shop at the time the fire was just becoming serious, and had gone in to see if any property could be salvaged, but he had not started the fire.

▶ Advise Gas and Spark on the admissibility of their statements.

How to Read this Question

The next six questions are problem questions and this advice applies to all problem questions. Before you begin, you should identify the issues. Here, we have listed these in 'How to Answer this Question', but if you have reading time, use this to jot down everything you can see. You need to explain and apply the law and reach a conclusion as to the likely outcome. This is often summarised as IRAC (Issue, Rule, Application, Conclusion), but remember that any one problem question may have more than one issue, so this sequence may be repeated at different points within the answer.

How to Answer this Question

Advice to Gas

In your advice to Gas, you should:

- ❖ explain the significance of s 82(1) of the **Police and Criminal Evidence Act (PACE) 1984**;
- ❖ explain the relevance of **ss 76** and **78** of **PACE**;
- ❖ explain and apply *Sang* (1980);
- ❖ explain and apply *Mason* (1988).

Advice to Spark

When advising Spark, include discussion of:

- ❖ the rule in *Zavekas* (1970);
- ❖ s **76** of **PACE**, Code C and *Sharp* (1988);
- ❖ *Goldenberg* (1988) and the drug issue;
- ❖ three possible arguments on appeal, ss **76, 78** and **82** of **PACE**;
- ❖ precedent on 'oppressive', for example, *Miller* (1986).

You should apply each rule to the facts.

Answer Structure

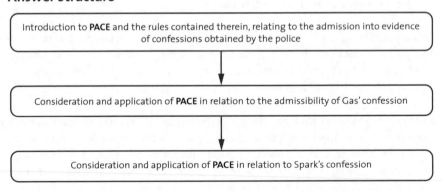

Introduction to **PACE** and the rules contained therein, relating to the admission into evidence of confessions obtained by the police

Consideration and application of **PACE** in relation to the admissibility of Gas' confession

Consideration and application of **PACE** in relation to Spark's confession

ANSWER

Advice to Gas

A confession is defined[3] in s **82(1)** of **PACE** as a statement 'wholly or partly adverse to the party who made it'. Gas, within these terms, appears to have made a confession. The admissibility of a confession is governed by several sections of **PACE**. **Section 76(2)** states that in relation to confessions which have allegedly resulted from 'oppression', or in consequence of anything said or done which was likely, in the circumstances existing at the

---

3   Always consider providing definitions of legal terminology relevant to the question. Remember that an examiner is unlikely to give you marks for such knowledge unless you specifically provide it.

time, to render unreliable any confession made, the court shall not admit the evidence unless the prosecution proves that the confession was not obtained in such a manner.

Section 78 allows a court to refuse to admit evidence if it appears, having regard to all the circumstances including the circumstances in which the evidence was obtained, that admission of the evidence would have such an adverse effect on the fairness of the proceedings that the court ought not to admit it. It was held by the Court of Appeal in *Mason* (1988) that regardless of whether the admissibility of a confession falls to be considered under s 76(2), a judge has the discretion to deal with it under s 78.

Section 82 states that 'nothing in this part of the Act [**Pt VIII**, dealing with evidence] shall prejudice any power of a court to exclude evidence'. The general view is that **s 82** preserved the whole of the common law existing prior to **PACE**, so that a confession could also be excluded under decisions like that of the House of Lords in *Sang* (1980). That case permitted exclusion of evidence where its prejudicial effect outweighs its probative value. Lord Diplock thought that a discretion only existed at common law with regard to admissions and confessions and 'generally with regard to evidence obtained from the accused after commission of the offence'. One observation of Lord Diplock's which is especially helpful to Gas (although *obiter dicta*) is that the purpose of such judicial discretion is to ensure that an accused was not induced to incriminate himself by deception.

It would be possible for Gas to argue for the exclusion of his admission on all three of the above sections (**ss 76, 78** and **82**).

In *Mason* (1988), on facts similar to those in question, the defendant was tricked into making an admission of instigating an arson attack on the car of an enemy, after a police officer had told both him and his solicitor that the defendant's fingerprints had been found on a bottle of inflammable liquid used in the attack. Following the solicitor's advice to give an explanation, the defendant then admitted his role in the arson. The Court of Appeal quashed the defendant's conviction as having such an adverse effect on the fairness of the proceedings (**s 78**) that the court should have excluded it. It is not certain, however, that this case would assist Gas. In *Mason*, the trial judge had admitted the evidence of the defendant's admission, but, in saying the trial judge wrongly exercised his discretion, the Court of Appeal said he had omitted one 'vital factor' from his considerations: that of the deceit practised on the defendant's solicitor. Evidently, a deceit practised only upon the defendant – as in our case – would not in itself warrant discretionary exclusion of the admission.[4]

Advice to Spark
Spark's admission is 'mixed', in that it contains parts which are incriminating (he was at the scene of the crime and he did go into the shop) and parts which are self-serving and

---

4　While it is important to clearly set out relevant law, don't forget that examiners will also be looking for evidence of your ability to apply the law to a given scenario. You will not necessarily be expected to come to a definite conclusion but, instead, to argue the various possibilities based largely on how the courts have dealt with cases in the past, where the material facts were sufficiently similar to the scenario provided. (Thus not only is the legislation important but case law too!)

self-exculpatory (he did not start the fire). The combination of the provisions of **PACE** and the decisions of the House of Lords in *Sharp* (1988) and *Aziz* (1996) appear to have put the law on this subject beyond doubt. Their Lordships in both *Sharp* and *Aziz* specifically approved the judgment of Lord Lane in *Duncan* (1981), which held that the simplest method and, therefore, the one most likely to produce a just result is for the jury to consider the whole statement, both the incriminating parts and the excuses and explanations, in deciding where the truth lies. **Section 82(1)** of **PACE** defines 'confession' as including 'any statement wholly or partly adverse to the person who made it'. Accordingly, statements of 'mixed' content count as confessions and are admissible in evidence, subject to s 76 of **PACE** being satisfied.

Provided that the police officer, in stating that the police would agree to bail in consequence of an admission, was answering a direct question from Spark, then the police conduct is lawful and the evidence not rendered inadmissible or vulnerable to exclusion.

The fact that Spark was a drug addict and might have been sufficiently desperate for more drugs to have admitted to anything in order to get bail would not, on current case law, appear to affect the matter, provided, of course, that his confession was not prompted by any other factor of police conduct in breach of the Act or the Codes. In *Goldenberg* (1988), the defendant, a heroin addict, requested an interview five days after his arrest and, during this interview, he allegedly gave information about someone who he claimed had supplied him with heroin. At trial, counsel for the defendant argued that the evidence of the interview might be unreliable under s 76:

(a) because the admissions were made in an attempt to get bail; and
(b) because of his addiction, it might be expected that the defendant would do or say anything – however false – to get bail and thus be able to feed his addiction.

This latter argument was rejected both at trial and on appeal. There was no argument that the interviewing officer had said or done anything improper, and the words 'in consequence of anything said or done' in s 76(2)(b) meant said or done by someone other than the suspect.

If it can be shown that the police interview with Spark was 'oppressive', then the argument for the exclusion of the confession could be run in any or all of three ways: (a) that it should be excluded by virtue of s 76(2)(a), as the police conduct was oppressive *simpliciter*, or that in conjunction with the fact of Spark's addiction and in view of the *ratio* of *Goldenberg* (where the appeal was dismissed because of no evidence of police misconduct), it was a confession gained by oppression; (b) that it should be excluded by virtue of s 78 (see advice to Gas, above); or (c) that it should be excluded by virtue of s 82, as its prejudicial effect greatly outweighs its probative value and it is within Lord Diplock's formula from *Sang* (1980) of protecting a suspect's right not to incriminate himself.

It will be difficult to show that the police interview was 'oppressive', as the courts have been very reluctant to make such findings. In *Fulling* (1987), the Court of Appeal gave 'oppression' its dictionary meaning, which involves 'the exercise of power or authority in a burdensome, harsh or wrongful manner'. *Fulling* was applied in *Emmerson* (1991). Questioning that was 'rude and discourteous', with a raised voice and some bad language and which gave the impression of 'impatience and irritation', was not considered oppressive. *Paris* (1994) produced a different result. The police were held to have behaved oppressively after shouting at a suspect what they wanted him to say over 300 times, after he had denied involvement in the offence charged. However, in *L* (1994), tactics similar to those employed in *Paris* appear to have been regarded as acceptable. The length of the interviews and the nature of the questioning are, of course, the important considerations.

Rules in Code C govern how interviews should be conducted. It is provided that breaks from interviewing shall be made at recognised meal times and that 'short breaks for refreshment shall also be provided at intervals of approximately two hours'. An officer has the discretion to delay a break, but only where there are reasonable grounds for believing that the break would:

(a)   involve a risk of harm to persons or serious loss or damage to property; or
(b)   unnecessarily delay the suspect's release from custody; or
(c)   otherwise prejudice the outcome of the investigation.

It thus seems unlikely that Spark's interview, which lasted 'for over two hours' (but, presumably, nearer to two than three hours), was oppressive, unless he can show that it was deliberately aimed at producing a state of confusion, or that it transgressed the fairly wide Code rules.

Common Pitfalls

Do not waste time repeating the facts, but instead use them to provide advice. Advice should be given in the third person (do not use 'you'). Advice should be underpinned by rigorous and accurate law, rather than vague assertions. Equally, do not just state the law – marks will be available for application. You will not have time or space in a problem question to criticise the law and should save this for essay questions, although it is important to understand the practical effects of any uncertainty in the law.

QUESTION 24

After a series of burglaries in Grimtown, Pat and Billy were arrested by police and taken to the local police station. Pat and Billy were taken to separate rooms for interrogation.

Pat asked to see a solicitor. A police officer wrote something down, went out of the room and came back saying that there would need to be a little delay, as: 'We would not want word to get out to the wrong people that you're in here.' The officer then said:

'You know the ropes, Pat, we would just like to ask you a few simple questions.' Pat then made some confessions which were admitted in court and he was convicted for offences of burglary.

In the other room, Billy also asked about a lawyer. 'We can arrange for one or you can have your own', he was told. Billy thought for a moment and then replied that it would probably be too expensive, so he would not opt for legal advice. Billy asked the police to inform the president of the Civil Freedom League of his arrest. A senior officer told Billy that would not be possible. Billy has now also confessed to certain burglaries and has been tried and convicted.

▶ Advise Pat and Billy on the possibility of appealing against their convictions.

How to Read this Question
See Question 23 for general advice on reading problem questions.

How to Answer this Question
Advice to Pat
In your advice to Pat, you should:

- ❖ give the meaning of **s 58** of the **Police and Criminal Evidence Act (PACE) 1984**;
- ❖ explain the significance of **s 116**, 'serious arrestable offence';
- ❖ state whether burglary falls within this category – see **s 24(1)(b)**;
- ❖ explain and apply *McIvor* (1987);
- ❖ explain and apply *Smith (Eric)* (1987), *Samuel* (1988) and *Parris* (1989);
- ❖ explain and apply Code C, Annex B, Note B4.

Advice to Billy
In your advice to Billy, you should examine (and apply):

- ❖ his entitlement to free advice: revised Code C, para 3.1;
- ❖ the meaning of 'friend or relative' (**s 56(6)**);
- ❖ the application of *Beycan* (1990);
- ❖ the relevance of **s 76(2)(b)**.

Answer Structure

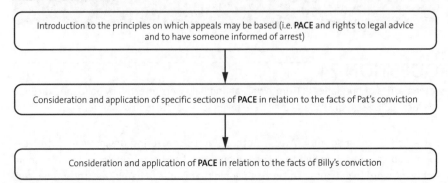

Introduction to the principles on which appeals may be based (i.e. **PACE** and rights to legal advice and to have someone informed of arrest)

Consideration and application of specific sections of **PACE** in relation to the facts of Pat's conviction

Consideration and application of **PACE** in relation to the facts of Billy's conviction

ANSWER

Advice to Pat

PACE came into effect in 1986 and, since that time, the access a suspect in a police station has to a lawyer has been governed by the Act. **Section 58(1)** of **PACE** states that a person arrested and held in custody in a police station shall be entitled, if he so requests, to consult a solicitor at any time. The request must be recorded in the custody record and the request must be granted 'as soon as is practicable', except to the extent that delay is permitted by the section. Delay in compliance with Pat's request is only permitted by the section if he is being held in connection with a 'serious arrestable offence' and an officer of at least the rank of superintendent authorises it. 'Serious arrestable offences' are defined in **s 116** and **Sched 5**. The term includes named offences such as murder and rape and also any arrestable offence which has, *inter alia*, led to 'substantial financial gain to any person' (**s 116(6)(e)**) or 'serious financial loss to any person' (**s 116(6)(f)**).

Burglary is an 'arrestable offence' by virtue of **s 24(1)(b)** of **PACE** as someone over 21 (without previous convictions) could, upon conviction for it, be sentenced to a term of imprisonment of five years. It is arguable whether Pat has been arrested in connection with a 'serious arrestable offence'.[5] It would depend on the value of the stolen goods and on the respective financial positions of:

(a) those who were burgled; and
(b) Pat.

It was held in *McIvor* (1987)[6] that the theft of 28 beagles worth £880 from a hunt was not a serious arrestable offence. The theft of the dogs, which were owned collectively by the hunt, did not cause 'serious financial loss'. In *Smith (Eric)* (1987), a robbery from Woolworths involving two video recorders (valued at £800) plus cash of £116 was regarded by the trial judge as probably not a serious arrestable offence: the loss to such a large national store would be small and the gain to the robbers would not necessarily be substantial.

Under Code C, Annex B, Note C1, an officer of at least the rank of superintendent may only delay Pat's access to a solicitor on the grounds stated in **s 58** of **PACE**. He must have 'reasonable grounds' for believing that such access will:

(a) lead to interference with, or harm to, evidence connected with a serious arrestable offence, or interference with, or physical injury to, other persons; or
(b) lead to the alerting of other persons involved in the offence but not yet arrested; or
(c) hinder the recovery of any property obtained as a result of the offence.

5 Relevant law is stated before any conclusions can be drawn as to whether Pat has grounds for appeal. Once stated, the law can then be applied to the facts of the scenario and possible outcomes considered.
6 Discussion of relevant case law such as this is important, as it is through decided cases that the courts provide their interpretation of legislation.

The words used by the officer to Pat, 'We would not want word to get out to the wrong people that you're in here', are consistent with any of the statutory reasons in (a) to (c) above. The Act says, however, that if the delay is authorised, then the suspect must be told the reason for the delay and the reasons must be recorded on the custody sheet. The officer's words here are quite vague, so neither of the requirements (the explanation to Pat and the recording of the reason) appear to have been complied with.

Moreover, it was held in *Samuel* (1988) that it was insufficient for an officer simply to believe that giving a suspect access to a solicitor might lead to the alerting of accomplices: the defendant was being questioned about offences of burglary and robbery. His request to see a solicitor was refused, on the grounds that the offences were serious and that there was a risk of accomplices being inadvertently alerted. The defendant subsequently made confessions which were admitted at trial. The Court of Appeal quashed his conviction, stating that access to a solicitor was a 'fundamental right' of a citizen and that a police officer who sought to refuse access had to justify the refusal by reference to the specific circumstances of the case. The court noted that 'solicitors are intelligent professional people', whereas most suspects were 'not very clever', so the likelihood of the latter being able to hoodwink the former into inadvertently passing on a coded message to fellow criminals was very low. This would probably only be a sustainable point in very few cases.

In *Parris* (1989), it was held that where the lawyer called was the duty solicitor, there would usually be no grounds for the police fearing that he would alert other parties to the crime. Here, the court quashed a conviction for armed robbery because of breaches of s58. In *Davidson* (1988), it was held by the Court of Appeal that the police had to be 'nearly certain' that a solicitor granted access to the suspect would warn another criminal or get rid of the proceeds of the crime. The power to delay access to a solicitor could not be exercised until the suspect had nominated an actual solicitor. This was not the case here; the court excluded the confessions given by the suspect without legal advice and, as a result, the prosecution's case collapsed.

The revised Code of Practice (Code C, Annex B, Note B4) clarifies the position further. This says that the officer may only authorise a delay if he has reasonable grounds to believe that the specific solicitor in question will, inadvertently or otherwise, pass on a message from the detained person which will lead to the alerting of accomplices, or interference with evidence. It is uncertain from the question whether Pat is asking to see a specific solicitor. Unless this is the case and the officer has reasonable grounds for the relevant suspicions, then he will be in breach of the Code and s58. Such a breach, though, does not entail automatic exclusion by the court of any resulting statement made by the suspect. The court will evaluate all the circumstances.

In *Dunford* (1990)[7] the defendant had a record and was aware of his right not to answer any questions put by the police. Before reaching the police station, he had refused to

---

7   Once more discussion of relevant case law is appropriate as, where the material facts of the decided case are sufficiently similar to the facts of the scenario, this will provide a strong indication/argument as to how the courts are likely to apply the law in Pat's situation.

answer questions and had, thereafter, answered several questions with the phrase 'no comment'. In such circumstances, the Court of Appeal ruled that the judge had been entitled to allow the confession made in the police station. Moreover, the Court of Appeal ruled in *Walsh* (1990) that an 'adverse effect on the fairness of proceedings' within the meaning of s78 would no doubt follow from a 'significant and substantial breach' of s58, but that did not necessarily mean that the evidence thus obtained had to be excluded. The court had to decide not simply whether there had been an adverse effect on the fairness of proceedings, but whether it had been such an adverse effect that justice required the evidence to be excluded.

In sum, Pat's appeal could succeed if he could persuade the Court of Appeal that s78 should have been used to exclude evidence of his confessions because of significant breaches of s58 and Code C, which had such an adverse effect on the fairness of proceedings that justice requires they be excluded. Pat's access to a lawyer is delayed, but was s58 of **PACE** complied with? The officer 'wrote something down', but was this the required entry on the custody sheet? He went out of the room, but was it to get the required permission of the superintendent? Was the vague reason given to Pat for the delay sufficient to exclude Pat's 'fundamental right'? There are also significant doubts about whether the offence was a 'serious arrestable offence' and whether, if so, the police had reasonable grounds to believe that any of the criteria in s58(8) were applicable. Overall, this gives a strong case to Pat, only slightly counterposed by virtue of Pat's possible criminal record (that is, '... you know the ropes, Pat ...') by the decisions in *Dunford* and *Walsh*.

Advice to Billy
The duty solicitor schemes at police stations, set up under **PACE**, are run by the Legal Aid Board. The provision of legal advice to suspects at police stations is not means-tested; it is paid for by the state. Research has shown that many suspects who previously did not take up the opportunity for legal advice abstained because they were unaware that it was free. The revised Code of Practice (April 1995) dealt with this problem by requiring the police to inform the suspect that the advice is free (Code C, para 3.1(ii)). The Code also requires (para 6.3) that a poster advertising the right to have free legal advice must be displayed prominently in the charging area of every police station.

We are not told whether there is a poster for Billy to see, but in not informing Billy that advice is free, the officer is in breach of the Code.

Under s56 of **PACE**, an arrested person held in custody, like Billy, has the right to have someone informed of his arrest. The person to be informed must be a 'friend or relative or other person who is known to him or who is likely to take an interest in his welfare'. Whether the president of the Civil Freedom League is within this category is a moot point. He would be if he was a friend or associate of Billy's and even, possibly, in his capacity as someone publicly concerned with civil liberties but, if the only link was the latter one, it is uncertain whether this would be sufficient. A circular issued to police to assist them with the operation of s56's forerunner (s62 of the **Criminal Law Act 1977**) excluded public figures, like pop stars and football players, from the sorts of person who could be notified. Those groups, however, are of course not related to civil liberties.

The only other reasons given in the Act to justify a delay in notifying a specified person are when, in a case of a serious arrestable offence (see under advice to Pat), an officer of at least the rank of superintendent authorises it for any of the reasons in s56(5), which are the same as those dealt with in Pat's case under s58(8). Section 56(6) states that the suspect must be told of the reason for the delay and it must be recorded on the custody sheet, neither of which appear to have been done in this case.

It seems more likely that there has been a breach of Code C (in respect of the notification of free legal advice) than of s56, but, even if there were only such a breach of the Code, it is quite possible that the Court of Appeal would quash Billy's conviction, as he was deprived of his fundamental right to legal advice as a result of the breach. In *Beycan* (1990), the Court of Appeal quashed a conviction based on a confession when the suspect had been arrested, taken to the station and asked: 'Are you happy to be interviewed in the normal way we conduct these interviews without a solicitor, friend or representative?' Billy's case is arguably stronger, as he has actually expressed a desire for advice and only proceeded reluctantly without it.

It may be possible to construe these events, in respect of Billy, in a way which shows him 'changing his mind' about taking legal advice. Thus, there could also be a possible breach of Code C, para 6.6(d):

> When the person who wanted legal advice changes his mind, the interview may be started without further delay provided the person has given his agreement in writing or on tape to being interviewed without receiving legal advice and that an officer of the rank of inspector or above has given agreement ...

In *Wadman* (1996), the defendant, having initially declined legal advice, changed his mind and then, while arrangements were being made, reverted to saying that he did not wish to have a solicitor. The police failed to comply with para 6.6(d) of Code C. The judge held that the Code was not 'mandatory' and admitted the evidence. On appeal, the conviction was quashed. The court ruled that the judge's approach to the Code was flawed; he confused the discretion he had on the voir dire – whether to admit the evidence – with the absence of discretion for police officers when complying with the Code: it was a disciplinary offence not to do so. It was not a case where the court should exercise its own discretion.

The appeals of both Pat and Billy could also be argued under s76(2)(b), which permits the court not to allow the confession if it was gained in consequence of:

> anything said or done which was likely, in the circumstances existing at the time, to render unreliable any confession which might be made by him in consequence thereof.

The basis of the argument would be the same as for s78.

QUESTION 25

After a serious assault on an old woman by a group of youths, PCs East and Wood stopped Peter in the street late at night. He had blood on his hands. When asked some simple routine questions, Peter became abusive and very hostile to the officers. He told the officers that his name was 'Mickey Mouse' and refused to answer any questions.

The following day, Mary and Paul are arrested for taking part in the assault. During questioning by police, Mary sat with her boyfriend, who is a law student. Before being cautioned, she answered some questions, but not others, and, at her trial, the judge suggested to the jury that she 'might have remained silent to avoid incriminating herself'.

Paul remained silent after being cautioned, refusing to answer police questions and, at trial, the judge invited the jury to consider whether an innocent man would have behaved in such a manner.

Peter has been convicted of obstructing the police officers in the execution of their duty. Mary and Paul have now been convicted of the assault. Advise Peter, Mary and Paul about their possible grounds of appeal.

How to Read this Question

See Question 23 for general advice on reading problem questions.

How to Answer this Question

Advice to Peter

When advising Peter:

- ❖ apply *Rice v Connolly* (1966) – consider what constitutes 'obstruction';
- ❖ apply *Ricketts v Cox* (1982) – 'the manner of a person together with his silence';
- ❖ consider whether the decisions are distinguishable.

Advice to Mary

When advising Mary:

- ❖ apply *Davis* (1959) – improper directions to a jury;
- ❖ consider the rule in *Parkes* (1976), where people are speaking on equal terms;
- ❖ discuss the decision in *Chandler* (1976);
- ❖ evaluate which case is closer to the facts of the problem.

Advice to Paul

Your advice to Paul should include:

- ❖ the basis for an appeal – the **Criminal Appeal Act 1968**;
- ❖ application of *Chandler* (1976).

Answer Structure

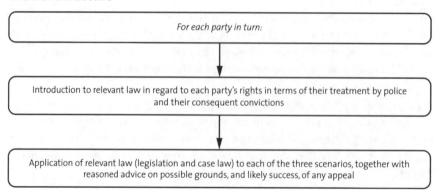

> For each party in turn:

> Introduction to relevant law in regard to each party's rights in terms of their treatment by police and their consequent convictions

> Application of relevant law (legislation and case law) to each of the three scenarios, together with reasoned advice on possible grounds, and likely success, of any appeal

ANSWER

Advice to Peter

Peter might have an appeal against his conviction for obstructing the police officers in the execution of their duty if he was not legally obliged to answer the questions put to him by the officers. Normally, the citizen is entitled to remain silent in the face of police questions, without this either being the subject of a charge of obstructing the police in the execution of their duties, or being commented on adversely by the prosecution or judge at trial.

This rule is established by the important Divisional Court decision in *Rice v Connolly* (1966). The appellant was seen by officers at night in an area where burglaries had been committed. He refused to tell the police where he had come from or where he was going. He identified himself only by his surname and a street name where he said he lived. He refused to accompany the police to a police box to further verify his identity. His conviction for an offence under **s 51(3)** of the **Police Act 1964** (resisting or wilfully obstructing a police officer in the execution of his duty) was quashed, as the Divisional Court said he had the right not to answer the questions. Lord Parker CJ stated that a proper conviction would require proof that the action was 'wilful', which means not only done intentionally, but also done without lawful excuse. Citizens, he said, had a moral duty and perhaps a social one to help the police with their inquiries, but there was no such legal duty.[8]

The decision in *Rice v Connolly* was unanimous, but James J noted that he would not go so far as to say that silence combined with conduct could not amount to an obstruction. It would be a matter for the courts to decide on the facts of any particular case. In *Ricketts v Cox* (1982), on facts similar to those in question here, the defendant's appeal against a conviction under **s 51(3)** was dismissed. Two police officers questioned the defendant and

---

8 This discussion demonstrates knowledge of relevant legislation, together with an understanding of the manner in which it has been applied by the courts in a decided case, both of which are equally important when providing advice relevant to a particular scenario.

another man in the early hours of the morning, following a serious assault. The defendant was uncooperative and shouted in obscene language at the officers, and then tried to walk away without answering any questions. The court found that this was an instance where 'the manner of a person together with his silence' could amount to obstruction. This decision probably accounts for Peter's conviction, in view of his obstreperous conduct coupled with the evidently false name he gave.

The decision in *Ricketts v Cox* has been widely criticised (Glanville Williams; Smith and Hogan; and Bailey, Harris and Jones) as flawed and at odds with *Rice v Connolly*. If a refusal to answer questions is lawful, which it clearly is, then how can this important constitutional right be cancelled merely because the questioned party is abusive? Peter's appeal could be based upon this point, inviting the Court of Appeal to deal with the confusion promoted by the two Divisional Court decisions by overruling *Ricketts v Cox*. Peter could possibly be acquitted if the facts of his case were governed simply by the decision in *Rice v Connolly*. Even though, unlike the appellant in the 1966 case, Peter had gone beyond simple reticence and told the officers his name was 'Mickey Mouse', this could perhaps be argued to be so self-evidently false as tantamount to saying, 'I shall not tell you my name'. The court agreed, in *Rice v Connolly*, that to tell a 'cock and bull' story to the police would obviously be an obstruction. This would clearly cover Peter had he said his name was Tom Smith and misled the police as to his true identity, but his sarcastic reference to a cartoon character could be regarded as not seriously misleading, and lawful, as he is not legally obliged to reveal his name.[9] It does not look like Peter was under caution when he refused to answer police questions. If he was, then his failure to answer could be made the subject of comment (see below, under 'Advice to Mary') by the trial judge under s 34 of the **Criminal Justice and Public Order Act (CJPOA) 1994.**

Advice to Mary

Mary's conviction could be quashed if it can be shown that the trial judge's words to the jury amounted to a misdirection. Before the **CJPOA 1994**, the 'right to silence' was regarded as a well-entrenched principle of law. The common law position is that everyone still has the right to remain silent in the same circumstances as they did before the **1994 Act**; what has changed is the entitlement of the judge or prosecuting counsel to make adverse comment on such a silence. There are many reasons why a suspect might remain silent when questioned (for example, fear, confusion, reluctance to incriminate another person) and, generally, failure or refusal to answer questions does not amount to evidence against the person concerned, unless it can be said that the defendant was on 'equal terms' with the questioner. In *Parkes* (1976), the Privy Council ruled that a judge could invite the jury to consider the possibility of drawing adverse inferences from silence from a tenant who had been accused by a landlady of murdering her daughter. The landlady and tenant, for this encounter, were regarded as having parity of status, unlike a person faced with questions from the police. Failure to answer questions put by a police officer, or someone in a similar position, is unlikely to lead to adverse inferences being drawn at

9   This is an excellent example of how case law can be used to illustrate a variety of possible outcomes, of how to argue different perspectives and how to provided reasoned advice.

any trial. In *Chandler* (1976), the suspect, in the company of his solicitor, refused to answer some questions asked by a police officer before the caution. The judge told the jury that they should decide whether the defendant's silence was attributable to his wish to exercise his common law right, or because he might incriminate himself. The Court of Appeal thought the presence of Chandler's solicitor meant that the parties were on 'even terms' but, on the facts, quashed Chandler's conviction, since the judge had gone too far in suggesting that silence before a caution could be evidence of guilt.

The alleged advantage of the change of law[10] is that **ss 34–38** of the **CJPOA 1994** help convict criminals who, under the old law, used to be acquitted because they took advantage of the right to keep quiet when questioned, without the court or prosecution being able to comment adversely upon that silence. However, the dangers entailed in undermining the right of silence are most acute in respect of police questioning scenarios. In *R v Condron* (1997), the Court of Appeal said that the guidelines set out in *R v Cowan* (1996), regarding the drawing of adverse inferences where the accused fails to testify, are equally applicable where the accused fails to answer questions when being interviewed by the police. More detailed guidance was given in *R v Argent* (1997), where the Court of Appeal set out the conditions which have to be satisfied before adverse inferences can be drawn from a person's failure to answer police questions (**s 34** of the **CJPOA 1994**). The conditions include:

(a)   the failure to answer has to occur before a defendant was charged;
(b)   the alleged failure must occur during questioning under caution;
(c)   the questioning must be directed at trying to discover whether and by whom the offence has been committed;
(d)   the failure must be a failure to mention any fact relied on in the person's defence; and
(e)   the fact that the defendant failed to mention has to be one which this particular defendant could reasonably be expected to have mentioned when being questioned, taking account of all the circumstances existing at that time (for example, the time of day, the defendant's age, experience, mental capacity, state of health, sobriety, personality and access to legal advice).

Therefore, **s 34(1)** only applies in respect of questioning under caution. If no caution is administered, no inference can be drawn from the failure to mention a fact in response to such questioning. A person must be cautioned where there are grounds to suspect him of an offence, before any questions are put to him regarding involvement or suspected involvement in that offence (Code C, para 10.1 of the **Police and Criminal Evidence Act (PACE) 1984**) and a person must normally be cautioned on being arrested (Code D, para 10.3). A caution need not be administered if the questions are put for other purposes. **Section 34** permits adverse inferences to be drawn from silence in situations that do not

---

10 Where law is about to be, or has recently been, amended, consideration of both positions can provide an opportunity to gain extra marks. (However, do not spend too much time on this unless it is specifically required by the question.)

amount to 'interviews', as defined by Code C of PACE, and thus which are not subject to the safeguards of access to legal advice and of contemporaneous recording, which exist where a suspect is interviewed at a police station. An 'interview' is defined by Code C, para 11.1(a) as being:

> the questioning of a person regarding his involvement or suspected involvement in a criminal offence or offences which by virtue of para 10.1 of Code C is required to be carried out under caution.

Sections 36 and **37** of the **CJPOA 1994** permit inferences to be drawn from the failure of an arrested person to account for an object, substance or mark, etc., or to account for his presence at a particular place where he is found. The main differences between s 34 and ss 36 and 37 are that s 34 applies where the suspect has been cautioned, but ss 36 and 37 only apply where the suspect has been arrested; ss 36 and 37 apply whether or not a fact is relied upon in a person's defence, whereas s 34 applies only in respect of failure to mention a fact relied upon in a person's defence.

Mary could appeal against her conviction if prosecution evidence is obtained as a result of unfair or unlawful police conduct under ss 76 and 78 of **PACE**. The questioning of Mary at the station prior to a caution being given may be in contravention of s 34 of the **CJPOA 1994** and the Codes of Practice in **PACE** (Code C, para 10 and Code D).[11] Cautions need not be given if the questions put did not constitute an 'interview' and were 'questions put for other purposes', but these considerations would not be applicable here, as Mary was already arrested at the material time of being questioned. If Mary failed to answer questions subsequently, under caution or on being charged, s 34 applies only to facts which she later relies on in her defence. The section has no function if she makes no attempt to put previously undisclosed facts forward at trial.

The common law position continues to apply where the new statutory provisions do not apply. Mary could appeal against her conviction on the grounds that she was not on 'equal terms' with the officer who interviewed her as, unlike the defendant in *Chandler*, she was accompanied not by a lawyer, but merely a law student.

Advice to Paul

Prior to 1996, the Court of Appeal would allow an appeal if they thought that: (a) the conviction was unsafe and unsatisfactory; (b) the judgment of the court trial should be set aside on a wrong decision on any question of law; and (c) there had been a material irregularity in the course of the trial. The **Criminal Appeal Act 1995** abolishes the three grounds of appeal, replacing them with a single test: namely, that the court thinks the conviction is unsafe. The Act does not contain any definition of the word 'unsafe'. Much of the former law will therefore be relevant in deciding what is liable to render a conviction

---

11 Don't worry that you always have to come to a definite conclusion. If the law were that certain, there would be no need for trials: where the outcome is unclear, embrace the opportunity to demonstrate your knowledge by considering all possibilities.

unsafe. In particular, the court may still apply the 'lurking doubt' test enunciated in *R v Cooper* (1969):

> whether we are content to let the matter stand as it is, or whether there is not some lurking doubt in our minds which makes us wonder whether an injustice has been done.

As noted above, ss 34–38 of the **CJPOA 1994** constitute a major curtailment of the 'right of silence'. Thus, although Paul retains his 'right' to remain silent both at the trial and the interrogation, 'proper' inferences may be drawn from his failure to mention certain facts when questioned under caution or on being charged (s 34).

Paul's appeal could succeed if he can show that s 78 of **PACE** should have been used to exclude adverse inferences of his silence because of significant breaches of s 34 of the **CJPOA 1994**. If he simply contends that there is no case to answer, that he has no fact which he could have contributed and he does not rely on a particular defence, s 34 can have no effect. There can be no conviction on silence alone. **Section 38** applies to all four provisions of the **1994 Act** which operate to permit the drawing of inferences, and stipulates that a defendant cannot be convicted or have a case to answer solely on the basis of an inference drawn from silence. There must, therefore, be some other evidence in addition to any inference to be drawn.

QUESTION 26

After an armed robbery at the Upland Bank in Oldcastle, the police arrested Karl for his involvement in the crime. An hour later, having interviewed Karl at the police station, the police went to his parents' home to remove for forensic examination a car parked in the driveway. Tony, Karl's father, resisted the police attempts to remove the vehicle and punched PC Grit. Tony was eventually overpowered and PC Grit then searched the garage and found a collection of plastic bank cards with different names and a pile of correspondence about crimes, including some letters bearing advice from Karl's solicitor.

Karl has been charged with involvement in the bank robbery and crimes relating to the stolen bank cards. Tony has been charged with assaulting an officer in the execution of his duty. Advise Karl and Tony.

How to Read this Question

See Question 23 for general advice on reading problem questions.

How to Answer this Question

Advice to Karl
You should include:

❖   an explanation and application of s 78 of the **Police and Criminal Evidence Act (PACE) 1984**;
❖   an explanation and application of s 18 of **PACE**;

❖ an explanation and application of **s 32** of **PACE**;
❖ an application of *Badham* (1987);
❖ consideration of Code B (revised) on searches and **s 67(11)** on exclusions;
❖ discussion of the ambit of **s 19** of **PACE**.

Advice to Tony
Include:

❖ an explanation of the effect of **s 117** of **PACE** in the context of the legality of the searches under **s 18** or **s 20**;
❖ discussion of **s 51** of the **Police Act 1964**.

Answer Structure

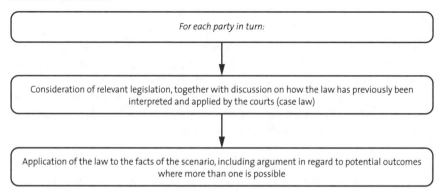

For each party in turn:

Consideration of relevant legislation, together with discussion on how the law has previously been interpreted and applied by the courts (case law)

Application of the law to the facts of the scenario, including argument in regard to potential outcomes where more than one is possible

ANSWER

Advice to Karl

The police appear to have had sufficient evidence on which to arrest Karl before any examination of the car in his driveway. Nevertheless, the car seems to be very significant evidence as the police went back to get it. It is important to discover, therefore, whether the police were legally entitled to act as they did. If not, then the evidence obtained might be excluded under **s 78** of **PACE**, if it is likely to have, in all of the circumstances, an adverse effect on the trial.

The answer to this particular question – whether the police search was lawful – will also determine whether Tony was legally justified in acting as he did, so this matter shall be returned to again later.

Karl has been arrested for robbery, which is an arrestable offence by virtue of the fact that Karl, if he was over 21 (even without previous convictions), could be sentenced to a term of imprisonment for five years or more upon conviction (**s 24** of **PACE**). **Section 18** of **PACE** empowers an officer to enter premises 'occupied or controlled by a person arrested for an arrestable offence' to search for evidence related to that or connected offences. He must, however, have 'reasonable grounds' for believing that there is evidence on the premises that relates to the offence in question or to some offence 'which is connected with or similar to that offence'. Searching for the vehicle suspected of being used in the armed robbery would be within the section's ambit, provided that Karl was an occupant of the address in the sense that he lived or stayed there. We know that letters to Karl from his solicitor were found in his father's garage, which suggests that Karl lived at that address. The search of the garage, which results in the discovery of the cards and letters, would also be within the section's scope, if crimes relating to stolen bank cards can be regarded as 'similar to' the crime of bank robbery. The element of violence or its threat involved in robbery would probably, however, put it in a different class from matters of deception and fraud.

The section also states that any officer making such a search must have prior authorisation in writing from a fellow officer of at least the rank of inspector, or subsequent approval, if such is necessary for the 'effective investigation of the offence'. The authorising officer must make a record of the search and, if the search was authorised in advance, it must show the nature of the evidence that was sought, in order to avoid 'fishing expeditions'. Failure to conform to these rules courts the risk that evidence, thus obtained, will not be admissible in court. Many searches of this type are conducted some time after arrest, so the lapse of an hour before the police come to search Tony's premises and take the evidence does not appear to affect the lawfulness of the conduct.

It may be[12] that Karl did not live with or stay with his parents, in which case the search would not be lawful under s 18. There is, however, the possibility that the search could have been lawful under s 32, which authorises the search, *inter alia*, of any premises on which the arrest took place. The search can be for anything relating to the offence for which a person has been arrested. If the search was made under this power, then it would be lawful in respect of the car (allegedly used in the robbery), but not in respect of the bank cards or letters. We do not know where Karl was arrested, but, if he was arrested at his parents' home, then s 32 would legitimise the police search. The delay, however, might be more significant here. According to the decision in *Badham* (1987), a search of the home where the defendant lived with his father, which took place three hours after the defendant's arrest, was not lawful. The Act gave no time limit, but the section was headed 'Search upon arrest' and the power was an immediate one. The Crown Court held that it would be wrong to permit an open-ended right to go back to the premises where the arrest had taken place. Here, PC Grit goes to Tony's house only an hour after Karl's arrest, but the *ratio decidendi* of *Badham* would apply just as much to this shorter, but still considerable, delay. **Section 32** might perhaps permit an officer escorting an arrested suspect back to the station to turn around after two minutes' walking and return to search the premises where the arrest was made, but not after an hour.

....

12 Evidence that a thoughtful approach has been taken. More than just the obvious has been considered – but take care not to go too far in this respect, as you will not impress an examiner by making up your own facts to suit your argument.

It is a requirement of the revised Code B that when conducting a search, the police shall give to the occupier a written notice of powers and rights showing which powers have been exercised. This applies to searches made under several powers, including those under **ss 18** and **32**. The notice must specify under which power the search is being made. The notice must also explain the rights of the occupier and the owner of any property seized. The Codes of Practice are not technically 'law'. If Karl can show that evidence (that is, relating to the car) has been obtained in breach of the Code, then the trial judge or Appeal Court can be invited to exclude that evidence (**s 67(11)**).

There is no common law power to enter and search premises after an arrest, so any search not lawful under **ss 18** or **32** would be unlawful.

Under **s 19**, an officer who is lawfully searching any premises is authorised to seize any article (if it is not covered by legal professional privilege) if he reasonably believes that it is evidence relating to the offence which he is investigating, or 'any other offence', and that it is necessary to seize it in order to prevent it from being 'concealed, lost, damaged, altered or destroyed'. It would be possible for the police to make a convincing case for the car (if there was evidence connecting it to the robbery) and the bank cards to be seized. It seems likely, however, that the solicitor's letters would be protected within the status of professional legal privilege, as **s 10(1)(a)** defines items 'subject to legal privilege' as including 'communications between a professional legal adviser and his client made in connection with giving legal advice to the client'.

In sum, Karl might be able to show that any evidence obtained relating to the car should be excluded by **s 78**. The search might not be lawful under **s 18** if:

(a) Karl was not an occupant of his father's house; or
(b) the search was not properly authorised in writing by an inspector; or
(c) there were no reasonable grounds to believe that there was evidence at Tony's address which related to the robbery.

Additionally, the search might not be lawful under **s 32** if it was not the site of Karl's arrest.

Advice to Tony

If the search of Tony's premises is lawful under either **s 18** or **s 32**, then **s 117** of **PACE** confers power on the police to use force in order to carry out their search, provided that the force used is reasonable and necessary. In such circumstances, PC Grit would have been acting in the execution of his duty and Tony would be guilty of an assault under **s 51** of the **Police Act 1964**. If, however, PC Grit's search was unlawful, so that he was not acting in the execution of his duty, then Tony would be entitled to use force to resist the intrusion onto his premises. There are many decisions to vindicate Tony's actions if the search was unlawful. The convictions of *Badham* (1987) and *Churchill* (1989), for obstructing a police officer in the execution of his duty and assault occasioning actual bodily harm, respectively, were quashed on appeal, because the searches in both cases were not justifiable within the provisions of **PACE**. If the search was unlawful for the reasons discussed in the advice to Karl, then the prosecution of Tony for the assault might fail.

QUESTION 27

Ben was walking home in the early hours of the morning. He was approached by two constables, PC Blue and PC Green, and asked to stop. He then, reluctantly, answered some questions about who he was and where he had been. By now fed up, he started to walk away as PC Blue was checking his details over the radio. PC Green tried to stop Ben and was punched in the face.

Later, but before dawn, PC Blue saw Dodger, who appeared scruffy and panicked and whom he suspected was carrying a set of 'skeleton keys' to fit various types of household door. He stopped Dodger and asked, 'Okay if we have a look at what you have got on you?' and then, receiving no reply, searched him very thoroughly. Dodger then protested and PC Blue replied: 'Look, this is quite legal, I am PC Blue of Fenwick Street station and I think you are up to no good.' PC Blue found 'skeleton keys' on Dodger, who has, as a result, now been convicted of 'going equipped to steal'.

Ben has been charged with assaulting a constable in the execution of his duty and Dodger wishes to appeal against his conviction. Advise Ben and Dodger.

How to Read this Question

See Question 23 for general advice on reading problem questions.

How to Answer this Question

Advice to Ben

Consider:

- ❖ whether PC Green was acting in the course of his duty;
- ❖ the *de minimis* rule;
- ❖ any application of *Bentley v Brudzinski* (1982).

Advice to Dodger

You should:

- ❖ explain the statutory setting: **ss 1, 67** and **78** of the **Police and Criminal Evidence Act (PACE) 1984** and revised Code A;
- ❖ apply this to the facts;
- ❖ discuss **s 2** of **PACE** and the legality of the search;
- ❖ apply *Fennelley* (1989).

Answer Structure

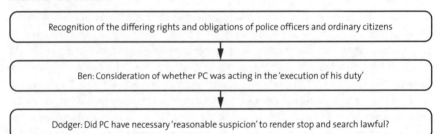

Recognition of the differing rights and obligations of police officers and ordinary citizens

Ben: Consideration of whether PC was acting in the 'execution of his duty'

Dodger: Did PC have necessary 'reasonable suspicion' to render stop and search lawful?

ANSWER

Advice to Ben

In order to discover whether Ben has assaulted the constable in the execution of his duty, we need to determine whether PC Blue was acting 'in the course of his duty'.[13] If not, then Ben cannot be convicted of the crime charged, although it is worthy of note that had he been charged with common assault,[14] he could have been found guilty, according to *obiter dicta* of Donaldson LJ in *Bentley v Brudzinski* (1982).

In *Kenlin v Gardiner* (1967), a police officer took hold of the arm of a boy whom he wanted to question about the latter's suspicious conduct. The boy did not believe the man was a policeman, despite having been shown a warrant card; he punched the officer in order to escape. Another boy whom he was with behaved similarly and their convictions for assaulting an officer in the execution of his duty were quashed by the Divisional Court. The court held that the boys were entitled to act as they did in self-defence, as the officer's conduct in trying to physically apprehend them had not been legal. There is no legal power of detention short of arrest. As Lawton LJ observed in *Lemsatef* (1977), the police do not have any powers to detain somebody 'for the purposes of getting them to help with their enquiries'. This reasoning would assist Ben, assuming that PC Green was not in fact trying to stop Ben in order to arrest him.

It is important, however, to examine the precise circumstances of the detaining officer's conduct, because there are cases to suggest that if what the officer does amounts to only a *de minimis* interference with the citizen's liberty, then forceful 'self-defence' by the citizen will not be justified. In *Donnelly v Jackman* (1970), an officer approached a suspect to ask some questions. The suspect ignored the request and walked away from the officer. The officer followed and made further requests for the suspect to stop and talk. He tapped the suspect on the shoulder and the suspect reciprocated by tapping the officer on the shoulder and saying, 'Now we are even, copper'. The officer tapped the suspect on the shoulder again, which was replied to with a forceful punch. Mr Donnelly's conviction was upheld and the decision in *Kenlin v Gardiner* was distinguished as, in the earlier case, the officers had actually taken hold of the boys and detained them. The court stated that:

> it is not every trivial interference with a citizen's liberty that amounts to a course of conduct sufficient to take the officer out of the course of his duties.

In *Bentley v Brudzinski*, the facts were very close to those in question.[15] A constable stopped two men who had been running barefoot down a street in the early hours. He

---

13 In typical 'problem' style, the answer immediately moves to the heart of the question. (Compare this to 'essay' type questions, where a more general approach may be appropriate, with the provision of an introduction which places the topic(s) into context before specific issues are directly addressed.)

14 Mention of the potential alternative charge demonstrates knowledge and is therefore likely to gain a candidate a few extra marks. It is, however, worth noting that the question does not require discussion of any alternative and any more than a mention would be excessive and rather a waste of time.

15 This is important as, where material facts of a scenario are sufficiently similar to the material facts of a decided case (precedent), this provides a strong indication of how the court would be likely to decide the issue in the scenario.

questioned them about a stolen vehicle, as they fitted the description of suspects in an earlier incident. They waited for about ten minutes while the officer checked their details over a radio and then they began to leave. Another constable, who had just arrived on the scene, then said, 'Just a minute', and put his hand on the defendant's shoulder. The defendant then punched that officer in the face. Unlike the decision in *Donnelly v Jackman*, the Divisional Court held here that the officer's conduct was more than a trivial interference with the citizen's liberty and amounted to an unlawful attempt to stop and detain him. The respondent was thus not guilty of assaulting an officer in the execution of his duty. We know that PC Green 'tried to stop Ben'. If this attempt involved physical restraint, then the authorities suggest that Ben's resistance would not have amounted to the crime of assaulting an officer in the execution of his duty, because the officer would not have been acting within his powers. Conversely, if the attempt amounted to nothing more than a tap on the shoulder, Ben would probably be guilty as charged.[16]

Advice to Dodger

Under **s1** of **PACE**, PC Blue is entitled to stop and search someone whom he reasonably suspects of carrying certain items, including an article 'made or adapted for use in the course of or in connection with …' (**s1(7)(b)(i)**) '… burglary' (**s1(8)(a)**). 'Skeleton keys' would fall within such a category. It might be, however, that PC Blue is in breach of the rules in the Codes of Practice, in particular, Code A for the exercise by police officers of statutory powers of stop and search. The Codes are not technically law[17] although they were mistakenly labelled as having 'statutory authority' by Russell LJ in *McCay* (1991). A judge may, however, exclude evidence which has been obtained in breach of the rules and an appeal court may quash a conviction where the judge failed to do so (**s67(11)**). Additionally, **s78** of **PACE** allows the exclusion of evidence which has been obtained in breach of the Act. The court, after considering all the circumstances, including the circumstances in which the evidence was obtained, will not admit evidence which would have 'an adverse effect on the fairness of the proceedings that the court ought not to admit it'.

What, if anything, has PC Blue done wrong? Did he have reasonable grounds for suspecting that Dodger was carrying 'skeleton keys'?[18] Reasonable suspicion requires an objective basis. In favour of PC Blue's case is the fact that it was in the early hours and Dodger was 'panicked'. Code A states that reasonable suspicion may exist where 'a person is seen acting covertly or warily'. It would perhaps be difficult to bring 'panic' within the categories cited by the Code. The Code specifically states that 'hairstyle', 'manner of dress' and knowledge of 'previous convictions' cannot alone or in combination give grounds for suspicion.

The current Code A (May 1997) was amended to provide some clarification of police powers in relation to groups and gangs. The additional sections (Code A, para 1.6(a) and

---

16 Thoughtful approach taken with alternative arguments effectively considered. Demonstrates strong evaluative and analytical skills.

17 A good point to make, as it demonstrates an understanding of the difference between 'law' and other 'rules' and adds to the general feeling of confidence in the answer provided.

18 Clear indication that the question has been well analysed and that the issue at the very heart of the question has been recognised.

Code A, para 1.7(aa)) state that where there is reliable information that members of a group or gang who habitually carry knives, weapons or controlled drugs and wear a distinctive item of clothing or other means of identification to indicate membership of it, then police officers may use that identifying item as the basis of their suspicion.

We are not informed as to what basis PC Blue thinks he has for his suspicions, but as he suspects Dodger to be carrying 'skeleton keys', in particular, we might infer that PC Blue knows Dodger from a previous encounter, perhaps one which resulted in Dodger's arrest and subsequent conviction. Even this, coupled with Dodger's scruffiness, would not suffice as a reasonable ground.[19] 'Time and place' and 'behaviour' are factors which can constitute the necessary reasonable grounds and it is just possible that the panic of Dodger in the early hours in the street would lend support to the officer's case, but he would still have to address the question of why he suspected Dodger of carrying 'skeleton keys'.

Under s 2 of **PACE**, the police officer who proposes to carry out a search must state his name and police station (which PC Blue does, but only after the search has begun), the purpose of the search and the grounds for the search. PC Blue fails to comply with these latter rules. A failure to give grounds, as required by s 2(3)(c), will render the search unlawful (*Fennelley* (1989)) and, in view of the very generalised explanation given by PC Blue, 'I think you are up to no good', it seems that the officer is in breach of the Act. The *Fennelley* decision shows that the courts are prepared to be quite strict in their interpretation of the rules. The defendant (F), a heroin addict, was seen by plain clothes police officers in the street. They believed they witnessed him selling drugs on the street. F was stopped, questioned and asked what he had in his pockets. He was searched and no drugs were found but, during a later strip search at the police station, some heroin was found in his underpants. F was charged with possession with intent to supply the drug, but the Crown Court decided that the evidence found by the police officers during the search should be excluded, using s 78 of **PACE**, as the police officers had failed to abide by the Act and the Codes in a number of respects. Significantly for our concerns here, they had failed to comply with the mandatory requirements of s 2(3), in that they had not informed F about their grounds for suspicion, nor about the purpose of their search. It was argued that these breaches affected the fairness of the trial, because F had not been given the chance to answer the suspicions of the police at the earliest opportunity. If he had, he might have been able to give an explanation which would have resulted in his being charged with mere possession, rather than possession with intent to supply.

The Act also requires that a search in the street must be limited to outer clothing and gloves (s 2(9)). We know that Dodger has been searched 'very thoroughly' and if that has entailed the removal of more than a coat, jacket or gloves in the street, then the rule has been broken.

....

19 Discussion of the 'rules' followed by application of the rules to the facts of the scenario has produced sound, logical argument.

The Act, however, does not apply to voluntary searches. If Dodger 'consents' to be stopped and searched, then PC Blue is not exercising any power. Dodger's protests come only towards the end of the search, so his acquiescence at the outset could be construed as consent. The revised Code A now states that juveniles or mentally handicapped people should not be subject to voluntary searches. If Dodger was in either category, then even a voluntary search would be in breach of the rules.

Thus, Dodger might be able to succeed on appeal if he can show that key evidence leading to his conviction should have been excluded as having been obtained in breach of the Act or the Codes and in a way that had an adverse effect on the proceedings. The weak grounds for his original suspicions, the failures properly to inform Dodger about the grounds for, and the purpose of, the search and the nature of the search itself are all in question and could separately, or together, form the basis of an appeal. This is provided that the search was not by consent.[20]

QUESTION 28

Dozy went shopping at his local supermarket. He picked an apple from the shelf and ate it while doing his other shopping in the store. Dozy then paid for the items in his trolley and walked towards the exit. Before he left, Dozy was apprehended by Peter, a store detective, who said, 'You cannot leave this store.' Dozy asked why not and was informed that he was not being arrested, but that the store manager wished to see him. Dozy was then taken by force to the manager's office where he was made to wait for an hour until the manager returned from his lunch. When the manager arrived, he told Dozy that the store's policy was to always prosecute shoplifters and that the police would now be called to take Dozy away.

Dozy has now been acquitted on a charge of stealing the apple and he wishes to sue the supermarket. Advise Dozy.

How to Read this Question
See Question 23 for general advice on reading problem questions.

How to Answer this Question
You should consider:

❖ grounds for Dozy's civil action;
❖ the legal definition of an 'arrest';
❖ the lawfulness of the arrest;
❖ *Walters v WH Smith & Son Ltd* (1914);
❖ *Self* (1992);
❖ *John Lewis & Co Ltd v Tims* (1952).

----

20 Strong conclusion which helpfully sums up the various arguments put forward in the main body of the answer. (Note that a conclusion should not introduce new information or be repetitive: it should be brief and no more than a quick reminder of what has been argued in the main body.)

Answer Structure

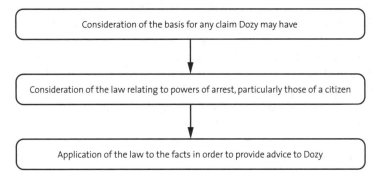

Consideration of the basis for any claim Dozy may have

↓

Consideration of the law relating to powers of arrest, particularly those of a citizen

↓

Application of the law to the facts in order to provide advice to Dozy

ANSWER

Dozy might have an action for damages against Peter or the store (if vicarious liability applies) for false imprisonment. The answer to this question would largely depend upon whether the action of Peter was lawful.[21]

There is no legal power to detain a suspect without arrest. 'Arrest', however, is a matter of fact, not a legal concept. In *Spicer v Holt* (1977), Lord Dilhorne said that:

> Whether or not a person has been arrested depends not on the legality of the arrest, but on whether he has been deprived of his liberty to go where he pleases.

Thus, Dozy may have been arrested if he was prevented from leaving (the use of force on him to take him back to the manager's office helps support such an argument), but whether the arrest was lawful will depend on other matters, namely, the conditions specified in s 24 of the **Police and Criminal Evidence Act (PACE) 1984**.[22] Aside from the technicalities of whether there has been an arrest, there seems clear *prima facie* evidence of false imprisonment. Having been forcibly taken to the manager's room, it seems likely that force or its threat was used to keep Dozy there, but, even if not, an action for false imprisonment would still exist. The claimant need not even know he has been restrained. In *Meering v Grahame White Aviation Co Ltd* (1919), Lord Atkin stated that a person could be 'imprisoned' within the terms of the tort, even if they were asleep or drunk at the time and thus remain unaware of their captivity.

Peter, though, may have arrested Dozy. If this was so, the question remains whether the arrest was lawful.

Dozy was evidently not informed of why he was being arrested. **Section 28(3)** of **PACE** states that an arrest is not lawful unless the person arrested is informed of the ground for the arrest at the time of, or as soon as practicable after, the arrest. It was, however,

21 Immediately gets to the heart of the issue, demonstrating good analysis of question.
22 Demonstrates appropriate knowledge by directly referring to relevant legislation.

recognised in *Christie v Leachinsky* (1947), and remains good law today, that the rule does not apply where the arrest is by a private citizen and the ground of arrest is obvious.[23] If Peter's actions, despite his words, do amount to an arrest, then it could be regarded as having taken place in circumstances which made it obvious why it was being carried out. Even if the arrest is regarded as unlawful for failure to inform of the relevant ground, the illegality will not operate retrospectively to vitiate the whole arrest. It will, according to the Divisional Court in *DPP v Hawkins* (1988), render the arrest unlawful, as from the moment when it would have been practicable for the arrestor to have given a reason. Thus, any damages which Dozy could claim would be limited to those reflecting his experience during the time in the office, from when he should have been informed about why he had been arrested, until the time he was told of the reason for his arrest by the police.[24]

An arrestable offence is one for which the sentence is fixed by law or for which a person over 21 may be sentenced on the first occasion to at least five years' imprisonment (s 24 of **PACE**). Theft, fitting in the second category, is an arrestable offence and ss 24 and 25 of **PACE** give a general power of arrest without warrant for 'arrestable offences'. The Act, however, preserves an old common law distinction in respect of the powers of constables and private individuals when making such arrests. Where an arrest is being made *after* an offence is thought to have been committed, then **PACE** confers narrower rights upon the private individual than on the police officer.

In *Walters v WH Smith & Son Ltd* (1914), the defendants had reasonably suspected that Walters had stolen books from a station bookstall. At his trial, Walters was acquitted as the jury believed his statement that he had intended to pay for the books. No crime had therefore been committed in respect of any of the books. Walters sued the defendants, *inter alia*, for false imprisonment, a tort which involves the wrongful deprivation of personal liberty in any form, as he had been arrested for a crime which had not in fact been committed. The Court of Appeal held that to justify the arrest, a private individual had to show not only reasonable suspicion, but also that the offence for which the arrested person was given over into custody had in fact been committed, even if by someone else. A police officer making an arrest in the same circumstances could legally justify the arrest by showing 'reasonable suspicion' alone, without having to show that an offence was in fact committed.

This principle is now incorporated into **PACE** and Peter appears to have fallen foul of the provision, because the de facto arrest takes place after the alleged crime of shoplifting but, as events fall, the criminal courts have acquitted Dozy of any crime. If there was no crime, then Peter could not rely on s 24(5), which only allows an individual to arrest a suspect who he has reasonable grounds to believe has committed the offence 'where an arrestable crime has been committed'.

....

23 Importantly, the differing rights of police officers and citizens in regard to the power of arrest have been recognised.

24 Good use of case law, demonstrating knowledge and supporting arguments put forward.

It is worthy of note that the less prudent arrestor who acts against a suspect when the latter is suspected of being in the act of committing an arrestable offence (s 24(4)) can justify his conduct simply by showing that there were 'reasonable grounds' on which to base the suspicion. He need not show that an offence was in fact being committed.

This analysis is supported by the decision in *Self* (1992), on facts very similar to the question's.[25] The defendant was seen by a store detective in Woolworths to pick up a bar of chocolate and leave the store without paying. The detective followed him out into the street and, with the assistance of a member of the public, she arrested the suspect under the powers of s 24(5) of **PACE**. The suspect resisted the arrest and assaulted both his arrestors. He was subsequently charged with theft of the chocolate and with offences of assault with intent to resist lawful apprehension or detainer, contrary to s 38 of the **Offences Against the Person Act 1861**. At his trial, he was acquitted of theft (apparently, for lack of *mens rea*), but convicted of the assaults. These convictions were quashed by the Court of Appeal on the grounds that as the arrest had not been lawful, he was entitled to resist it. The power of arrest conferred upon a citizen (s 24(5)) in circumstances where an offence is thought to *have been committed* only applies when an offence *has* been committed and, as the jury decided that Mr Self had not committed any offence, there was no power to arrest him.

We know that Dozy has been acquitted of any crime, so it looks as if any arrest made by Peter (de facto and, therefore, in law) would be invalidated by virtue of s 24(5) of **PACE**, which provides that the offence must have 'been committed'. However, despite Dozy's acquittal, it might be possible to contend that a crime had still 'been committed'. Such a contention was not possible in *Walters v WH Smith*, because there Mr Walters had denied the *mens rea* of the offence of theft, a vital ingredient of the crime, and the jury had accepted this version, thus denying that a crime had taken place. In different circumstances, perhaps, than those in the question, it might be that the defendant in any criminal proceedings (Dozy) was acquitted by way of a successful 'excusatory defence', for example, insanity, which would not deny that a crime had occurred, simply that the defendant could not be legally responsible. In such circumstances, the arrest would be lawful, as a crime would have 'been committed'.

A question would then arise as to the period of detention for over an hour. In *John Lewis & Co v Tims* (1952), Mrs Tims and her daughter were arrested by store detectives for shoplifting four calendars from the appellant's Oxford Street store. It was a regulation of the store that only a managing director or a general manager was authorised to institute any prosecution. After being arrested, Mrs Tims and her daughter were taken to the office of the chief store detective. They were detained there until a chief detective and a manager arrived to give instructions whether to prosecute. They were, eventually, handed over to police custody within an hour of arrest. In a claim by Mrs Tims for false imprisonment, she alleged that the detectives were obliged to give her into the custody of the police

----

25 Good use made of decided case (precedent) with sufficiently similar material facts for those of the scenario.

immediately upon arrest. The House of Lords held that the delay was reasonable in the circumstances, as there were advantages in refusing to give private detectives a 'free hand' and leaving to a superior official the determination of such an important question as whether to prosecute.

Dozy's case may be distinguishable (although the distinction is not a compelling one) as here, the reason for the delay is concerned with the comfort the manager will enjoy by not interrupting his lunch, rather than any matter of company business.[26] The evidence in the *John Lewis* case was that the manager came without any delay and listened to the evidence; any delay (which was evidentially in doubt) occurred while the accounts of the store detectives were being given in the presence of the suspects.

It is true that Dozy has not suffered any real damage to his person but, as Lord Porter observed in the *John Lewis* case, when 'the liberty of the subject is at stake, questions of the damage sustained become of little importance'.

QUESTION 29

On the one hand, English law rightly presumes that everyone is innocent until proven guilty, so it would be wrong to keep anyone in custody (normally a punishment) unless they have been convicted. On the other hand, some of those charged with serious crimes are likely to try to abscond or interfere with witnesses or evidence unless they are kept secure until trial. Framing rules to govern this conflict is a question of balance.

Discuss whether the law of bail in the English legal system has the balance right between the interests of the suspect and the interest of the general public.

How to Read this Question

The question helpfully gives you the two sides of the bail issue, and you should examine both of these, working towards a conclusion.

How to Answer this Question

Answers should incorporate:

- ❖ explanation of the current legal framework;
- ❖ s 27 of the **Criminal Justice and Public Order Act (CJPOA)**;
- ❖ the **Bail Act 1976** and the presumption of bail;
- ❖ s 25 of the **CJPOA 1994** and the denial of bail where there has been earlier conviction for murder, etc.;
- ❖ the social and political concerns that the law has to balance the **Bail (Amendment) Act 1993**;
- ❖ conclusions.

---

26 Importantly, the possibility that the facts of the decided case are distinguishable from those of the scenario has been highlighted, demonstrating strength in terms of application of the law.

Answer Structure

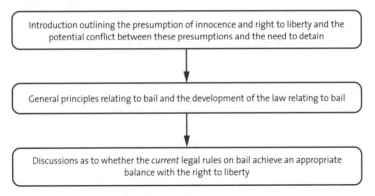

Introduction outlining the presumption of innocence and right to liberty and the potential conflict between these presumptions and the need to detain

General principles relating to bail and the development of the law relating to bail

Discussions as to whether the *current* legal rules on bail achieve an appropriate balance with the right to liberty

ANSWER

There is in most circumstances a strong legal presumption that for an unconvicted suspect, liberty must prevail over incarceration. In *Hurnam v State of Mauritius* (2005), the Privy Council held that the seriousness of an offence cannot be treated as a conclusive reason for refusing bail to an unconvicted suspect. The right to personal liberty is an important constitutional right, and a suspect should remain at large unless it is necessary to refuse bail in order to serve one of the ends for which detention before trial was permissible.[27]

In the early 1990s, the UK Government took the view that bail was too easily granted and that too many crimes were being committed by those on bail who deserved to be in custody while awaiting trial. The **Bail (Amendment) Act 1993** and the **CJPOA 1994 (ss 25–30)** emanate from that philosophy, their aim being to restrict the granting of bail.

In some respects, the statistics available demonstrate features of great concern to both legal experts and the general public. In 2012, it was revealed that at least 37 criminals were convicted of murder while on bail for another offence in 2011 – around three every month. Between 2000 and 2012, 436 murders were committed by people granted their freedom while under investigation for a variety of crimes in England and Wales. Overall, about 10 per cent of all annual crime is committed by people on bail. In 2009, there were 1,426,082 offences committed, 146,681 (10.3 per cent) of which were committed by people on bail. In 2010, there were 1,329,343 offences committed of which 142,537 (10.7 per cent) were committed by people on bail.

If a person is arrested on a warrant, this will indicate whether he is to be held in custody or released on bail. If the suspect is arrested without a warrant, then the police will have to decide whether to release the suspect after he has been charged. After a person has been charged, **s 38(1)(a)** of the **Police and Criminal Evidence Act (PACE) 1984** states that a

27 Introduction demonstrates a sound understanding of why liberty should normally prevail over incarceration.

person must be released unless: (a) his name and address are not known; or (b) the custody officer reasonably thinks that his detention is necessary for his own protection, or to prevent him from injuring someone or damaging property; or (c) because he might abscond or interfere with the course of justice. Most arrested people are bailed by the police.

This system is not working in a way that is beyond criticism because the police have such tight resources, and in many cases a technically innocent person languishes on bail (sometimes with restrictions on their life) for months. In May 2013 the BBC published data on police bail in England, Wales and Northern Ireland received following a Freedom of Information request. The data show that at least 57,428 people were on bail at that time. Of those, 3,172 had been waiting for more than six months for a decision on charges. In one case a person arrested three-and-a-half years earlier was still on bail.

The **Bail Act 1976** created a statutory presumption of bail. It states (**s 4**) that subject to **Sched 1** and amendments made by **s 25** of the **1994 Act** about murder, manslaughter, etc., bail shall be granted to a person accused of an offence in a magistrates' court or a Crown Court and to convicted people who are being remanded for reports to be made. The court must therefore grant bail (unless one of the exceptions applies), even if the defendant does not make an application. **Schedule 1** provides that a court need not grant bail to a person charged with an offence punishable with imprisonment if it is satisfied that there are substantial grounds for believing that if released on bail, the defendant would:

(a) fail to surrender to custody;
(b) commit an offence while on bail; or
(c) interfere with witnesses, or otherwise obstruct the course of justice.

The court can also refuse bail if it believes that the defendant ought to stay in custody for his own protection, or if it has not been practicable 'for want of time to obtain sufficient information to enable the court to make its decision on bail'.

The **Criminal Justice Act 2003** made a number of changes to the law in respect of bail. It enables action to be taken to reduce breaches of bail by introducing a new presumption against bail in certain circumstances. The Act enables the immediate grant of bail at the scene of arrest ('street bail') if there is no immediate need to deal with the arrested person at a police station. It gives police the discretion to decide when and where an arrested person should attend a police station for interview. It also enables reviews of the continuing need for detention without charge to be conducted over the telephone rather than in person at the police station as was previously the case.

If the court decides not to grant the defendant bail, then **s 154** provides that it is the court's duty to consider whether the defendant ought to be granted bail at each subsequent hearing. At the first hearing after the one at which bail was first refused, he may support an application for bail with any arguments, but at subsequent hearings, the court need not hear arguments as to fact or law which it has heard before. The **Criminal Justice**

Act 1982 enables a court to remand an accused in his absence for up to three successive one-week remand hearings, provided that he consents and is legally represented. Such repeated visits are costly to the state and can be unsettling for the accused, especially if he has to spend most of the day in a police cell only to be told the case has been adjourned again without bail. If someone does not consent, they are prevented from applying for bail on each successive visit if the only supporting arguments are those that have been heard by the court before (*R v Nottingham Justices ex p Davies* (1980)).

The interests of the accused are also served by the variety of appeals he may make if bail has been refused. If bail has been refused by magistrates, then, in limited circumstances, an application may be made to another bench of magistrates. Applications for reconsideration can also be made to a judge in chambers (through a legal representative) or to the Official Solicitor (in writing). Appeal can also be made to the Crown Court in respect of bail for both pre-committal remands and where a defendant has been committed for trial or sentence at the Crown Court.

Although this area of law was subject to a comprehensive revision after a Home Office special working party reported in 1974, and has been legislatively debated and modified five times since the **1976 Act**, it is still a matter of great importance, both to those civil libertarians who consider the law too tilted against the accused, and to the police and some commentators who believe criticism of the law from both sides to the debate might indicate a desirable state of balance reached by the current regulatory framework.[28]

QUESTION 30

What difficulties are involved in designing rules to govern plea bargaining and how successful is the English system in this respect?

How to Read this Question

The first part of this question looks at the underlying problems in allowing or encouraging defendants to plead guilty in return for a sentencing discount. The second part requires an evaluation of the success, or otherwise, of the English system in resolving those problems.

How to Answer this Question

Any answer on this theme should take account of the research findings presented to the Royal Commission on Criminal Justice and the recommendations made by the Commission:

- ❖ definition of terms;
- ❖ explanation of the guidelines in *Turner* (1970);
- ❖ difficulties in applying the *Practice Direction (Turner Rules)* (1976);
- ❖ discussion of the points in *Pitman* (1991);

---

28 Recognises the importance of providing a conclusion which 'sums up' and succinctly answers the specific question set.

- ❖ whether the Court of Appeal can attract proper guilty pleas while not engaging in injudicious disclosure of the possible sentence;
- ❖ Attorney General's Guidelines;
- ❖ *R v Goodyear (Karl)* [2005] EWCA 888 – normally speaking, an indication of sentence should not be given until the basis of the plea has been agreed or the judge has concluded that he or she can properly deal with the case without the need for a trial of the issue;
- ❖ conclusion.

Up for Debate

Recent guidelines on plea bargaining have introduced the idea that the interests of victims and their families should also be considered by prosecutors during these negotiations. This represents a wider shift in the criminal justice system towards giving victims a 'voice'. To what extent could this potentially limit agreements such as those described below?

Answer Structure

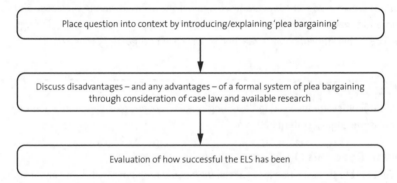

Place question into context by introducing/explaining 'plea bargaining'

Discuss disadvantages – and any advantages – of a formal system of plea bargaining through consideration of case law and available research

Evaluation of how successful the ELS has been

ANSWER

'Plea bargaining' has been defined as 'the practice whereby the accused enters a plea of guilty in return for which he will be given some consideration that results in a sentence concession' (Baldwin and McConville, *Negotiated Justice*, 1977). In practice, this can refer to a situation either where there has been a plea arrangement for the accused to plead guilty to a lesser charge than the one with which he is charged (charge bargaining), or where there is simply a sentencing discount available on a plea of guilty by the accused (sentence bargaining).

For a guilty defendant and for the prosecution, such a negotiated settlement represents a mutually valuable compromise, because the prosecution has gained a guilty plea and the defendant a sentence concession. Additionally, there will have been a significant saving to the state in the cost of a trial. Such bargains, however, are fraught with legal difficulties, chiefly because they can be construed as circumstances where undue pressure has been put on the accused to plead guilty. Many convictions have been quashed for just such a reason.[29]

A plea of guilty by the accused must be made freely. He must only be advised to plead guilty if he has committed the crime in question. In *Turner* (1970), Lord Parker CJ set out guidelines on plea bargaining. He stated that:

(a) it may sometimes be the duty of counsel to give strong advice to the accused that a plea of guilty with remorse is a mitigating factor which might enable the court to give a lesser sentence;

(b) the accused must ultimately make up his own mind as to how to plead;

(c) there should be open access to the trial judge and counsel for both sides should attend each meeting, preferably in open court; and

(d) the judge should never indicate the sentence which he is minded to impose, nor should he ever indicate that on a plea of guilty, he would impose one sentence, but that on a conviction following a plea of not guilty, he would impose a more severe sentence. The judge could say what sentence he would impose on a plea of guilty (where, for example, he has read the depositions and antecedents), but without mentioning what he would do if the accused were convicted after pleading not guilty. Even this would be wrong, however, since the accused might take the judge to be intimating that a more severe sentence would follow upon conviction after a guilty plea. The only exception to this rule is where a judge says that the sentence will take a particular form, following conviction, whether there has been a plea of guilty or not guilty.

Guidelines on 'the acceptance of pleas and the prosecutor's role in the sentencing exercise' from the Attorney General (most recently revised in 2009) create a clear framework. The guidelines note that prosecutors have an important role in protecting the victim's interests in the criminal justice process, not least in the acceptance of pleas and the sentencing exercise. The guidelines highlight the importance of transparency in the conduct of justice. The basis of plea agreed by the parties in a criminal trial is central to the sentencing process. An illogical or unsupported basis of plea can lead to an unduly lenient sentence being passed, and has a consequential effect where consideration arises as to whether to refer the sentence to the Court of Appeal under **s 36** of the **Criminal Justice Act 1988**. The guidelines take account of important cases such as *R v Underwood* [2005] 1 Cr. App.R 178.

The guidelines say that when a case is listed for trial and the prosecution form the view that the appropriate course is to accept a plea of guilty from the defendant to a relevant charge *before* the proceedings commence or continue, the prosecution should whenever practicable speak to the victim or the victim's family, so that the position can be explained. The views of the victim or the family may assist in informing the prosecutor's

---

29 Introductory paragraphs provide helpful clarification of 'plea bargaining' and its value.

decision as to whether it is in the public interest, as defined by the Code for Crown Prosecutors, to accept or reject the plea. The guidelines note that 'the appropriate disposal of a criminal case after conviction is as much a part of the criminal justice process as the trial of guilt or innocence'.

There will be cases where a defendant seeks to mitigate on the basis of assertions of fact which are outside the scope of the prosecution's knowledge. A typical example concerns the defendant's state of mind. If a defendant wishes to be sentenced on this basis, the prosecution advocate should invite the judge not to accept the defendant's version unless he or she gives evidence on oath to be tested in cross-examination. Paragraph IV.45.14 of the Consolidated Criminal Practice Direction states that in such circumstances the defence advocate should be prepared to call the defendant and, if the defendant is not willing to testify, subject to any explanation that may be given, the judge may draw such inferences as appear appropriate.

If there is no final agreement about the plea to the indictment, or the basis of plea, and the defence nevertheless proceeds to seek an indication of sentence, which the judge appears minded to give, the prosecution advocate should remind him or her of the guidance given in *R v Goodyear (Karl)* [2005] EWCA 888 that, normally speaking, an indication of sentence should not be given until the basis of the plea has been agreed or the judge has concluded that he or she can properly deal with the case without the need for a trial of the issue.

There have been calls for an even more open system than the current one but such a change would create other challenges. In one Home Office study (1992), Hedderman and Moxon found that 65 per cent of those pleading guilty in Crown Court cases said that their decision had been influenced by the prospect of receiving a discount in sentence. Even the Royal Commission recognised that not all those pleading guilty are, in fact, guilty; some may have just capitulated to the pressure of taking the reduced sentence, rather than run the risk of the full sentence. As Sanders and Young contend, this issue goes to the heart of constitutional principles. Only if the state acts properly in collecting and presenting evidence can punishment be justified, according to commonly accepted principles. Even the guilty are entitled to due process of law. A system of plea bargaining may undermine such principles, since it allows the state to secure convictions based on unproven allegations.[30]

QUESTION 31
How far should the law allow witnesses to be prepared by the advocates who will examine them in criminal courts?

How to Read this Question
Note that the question starts 'How far...'. At issue is the nature of the preparation in question. The question refers to criminal courts and any reference to the civil courts should be kept to a minimum.

---

30 Conclusion demonstrates thoughtfulness.

How to Answer this Question

Your answer should:

❖ explain the importance of witnesses to the court process;
❖ introduce the important case of *Momodou* (2005), and the Bar Code provisions;
❖ differentiate lawful 'witness familiarisation' from improper 'witness coaching';
❖ explain the dangers of witness coaching to the legal process;
❖ explain the Court of Appeal's test to distinguish the acceptable forms of witness preparation from the unacceptable forms;
❖ explain the Attorney General's 2005 proposals for change;
❖ explain the objections to his proposals.

Answer Structure

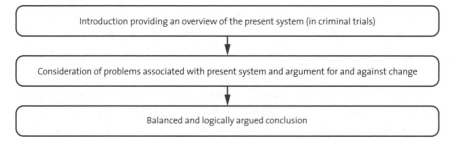

Introduction providing an overview of the present system (in criminal trials)

⬇

Consideration of problems associated with present system and argument for and against change

⬇

Balanced and logically argued conclusion

ANSWER

This question concerns matters central to the way the English legal system deals with evidence. Witnesses are integral parts of criminal and civil cases in the English legal system. They are arguably the most important feature of the process by which courts aim to get to the truth in a dispute. Can and should court witnesses be prepared by their advocate before giving their testimony?

These issues were addressed by the Court of Appeal in *R v Momodou* (2005). The legal background to this case is in a rule of the Bar Code of Conduct: Part VII – Conduct of Work.[31] It explains (rule 705) that:

A barrister must not:

(a) rehearse, practise or coach a witness in relation to his evidence;
(b) encourage a witness to give evidence which is untruthful or which is not the whole truth.

In civil cases a barrister can 'give general advice to a witness about giving evidence, for example, speak up, speak slowly, answer the question, keep answers as short as possible, ask if a question is not understood, say if you cannot remember and do not guess or speculate …' (Miscellaneous Guidance, Part F, para 9). In criminal cases a barrister can

---

31 Helpful and knowledgeable introduction which sets the scene in terms of the extent of 'witness preparation', well supported by case law and professional code.

have contact with a witness before the case 'with a view to introducing himself to the witness, explaining the court's procedure ... and answering any questions on procedure which the witness may have'. Barristers are also permitted to put a witness through some questions before the case in order to test his recollection and the quality of his evidence.

In *Momodou*, the Court of Appeal Criminal Division clearly defines the difference, in a *criminal case* context, between the proper process of 'witness familiarisation' and the improper use of 'witness training or coaching'. The case concerned defendants who had been convicted of violent disorder during a serious disturbance at the Yarls Wood Detention Centre, in Bedfordshire, in 2002. The Court rejected claims that unlawful pre-trial coaching of security guard prosecution witnesses had led to the wrongful conviction of two asylum-seekers involved in the riot at the detention centre.

The Court of Appeal held that, although two key security guard witnesses had attended a programme operated by a legal training firm, the safety of the convictions had not been undermined.

Lord Justice Judge observed that the dangers[32] in witness coaching included that a dishonest witnesses might learn, during a rehearsal, how to 'improve' his testimony. The danger augmented if the coaching was not one-to-one but conducted collectively because prospective witnesses might 'bring their respective accounts into what they believe to be better alignment with others'. Pre-trial arrangements to familiarise a witness with the layout of the court, court processes and the way evidence should be given will be fine provided the trainers, preferably lawyers, have no knowledge of the actual issues in the forthcoming trial. Lord Justice Judge explained the core of the reasoning of the Court of Appeal on this issue. He said there is a dramatic distinction between witness training or coaching, and witness familiarisation. Training or coaching for witnesses in criminal proceedings (whether for prosecution or defence) is not permitted. This is the logical consequence of the well-known principle that discussions between witnesses should not take place, and that the statements and proofs of one witness should not be disclosed to any other witness. He noted: 'The witness should give his or her own evidence, so far as practicable uninfluenced by what anyone else has said, whether in formal discussions or informal conversations' (para 61).

The rule reduces, indeed hopefully avoids, any possibility that one witness may tailor his evidence in the light of what anyone else said, and equally, avoids any unfounded perception that he may have done so. These risks are inherent in witness training.

Lord Justice Judge also said:

> An honest witness may alter the emphasis of his evidence to accommodate what he thinks may be a different, more accurate, or simply better remembered perception of events. A dishonest witness will very rapidly calculate how his testimony may be 'improved'. (para 61)

---

32 Discussing such 'dangers' highlights the problem of 'witness coaching'.

The Court ruled that this familiarisation process should normally be supervised or conducted by a solicitor or barrister, or someone who is responsible to a solicitor or barrister with experience of the criminal justice process, and preferably by an organisation accredited for the purpose by the Bar Council and Law Society. None of those involved should have any personal knowledge of the matters in issue. Records should be maintained of all those present and the identity of those responsible for the familiarisation process, whenever it takes place. The programme should be retained, together with all the written material (or appropriate copies) used during the familiarisation sessions. None of the material should bear any similarity whatever to the issues in the criminal proceedings to be attended by the witnesses, and nothing in it should play on or trigger the witness's recollection of events.

In December 2004, not long before the Court of Appeal's February 2005 decision, the Attorney-General, Lord Goldsmith QC, issued a statement in which he advocated the case for prosecutors being able to speak with witnesses privately, and off the record, before the trial.[33] This is an utterance not in perfect harmony with the views expressed by the Court of Appeal in *Momodou*.

The Attorney-General said that many people would be surprised to learn that prosecutors in England and Wales are not entitled to interview witnesses before trial, even when they are key prosecution witnesses whose credibility may be critical to whether a prosecution should go ahead or not. He said the practice should change, arguing that: 'It is striking that it is only in England and Wales that prosecutors do not have direct access to witnesses even in order to assess their credibility and reliability.'

The conclusions reached by the Attorney-General included that prosecutors should be permitted to speak to witnesses – including children and vulnerable witnesses – about matters of evidence. He said prosecution witness interviews should be conducted for the purpose and the extent that, in the view of the prosecutor, such an interview is necessary in order to assess the reliability of or clarify a witness's evidence.

Where possible, he argued, an interview should generally take place once the prosecutor considers that he/she has sufficient information and evidence for an interview to be of value, but before the prosecutor reaches a decision to proceed.

However, prosecutors should, he said, be permitted to hold witness interviews *at any stage of the proceedings* including, therefore, just before trial. He argued that this was particularly so if further evidence or material, casting doubt on the reliability of a witness's evidence, came to light at a later stage in the proceedings or if further witnesses came to light after a decision to prosecute has been reached.

The Attorney-General contended that interviews should be conducted informally with the prosecutor, the witness, where possible a police officer, and independent support if the witness so wishes. He suggested that interviews should be conducted in the absence of the defence, and that police officers should be permitted to be present at interviews.

....

33 By providing consideration of the arguments for 'witness preparation', a more balanced argument can be provided.

One sharply expressed objection to this came during a House of Lords debate. The eminent lawyer Lord Thomas of Gresham said (Lords' *Hansard* text for 17 January 2005 (250117–22) Col 626):

> In subtle ways, the complainant in a criminal case is beginning to be treated as the client of the prosecutor. The essential impartiality of prosecuting counsel is, in my view, being undermined. He is being asked to take sides and to become involved in the emotions and personalities of complainants and their families. Achieving justice, objectively, between the state and the individual should be at the heart of the criminal justice system – not, as the Government so often states, victims and witnesses.[34]

He argued that justice cannot be done if a witness is so intimidated that he does not come forward or if his account is incomplete. But that, he said, is a matter for the police to investigate and not counsel. Similarly, the voluntary witness service does a great deal to ease the fears of complainants and witnesses where the court proceedings are in themselves intimidating. The prosecutor should not be involved at all in some kind of calming and comforting role.

He contended that, generally, the American experience shows how undesirable witness coaching is. Prosecutors have the ability, consciously or unconsciously, to strengthen the case by questions and suggestions that cause the witness to fill gaps in memory, eliminate ambiguities or contradictions, sharpen language, create emphasis and alter demeanour. He asked 'Do we in this country really want to get involved in suspicions of horse shedding?'

The expression 'horse shedding' is a nineteenth-century American expression and refers to the practice whereby lawyers would coach witnesses in the horse sheds near the court houses in rural parts of the United States.

How far we do now go down that road is a political decision to be taken in the legislature on behalf of society at large, and it is clear that this apparently technical legal issue is in fact quite a contentious political issue of balancing the interests of the state and the individual.

Common Pitfalls

A failure to differentiate clearly between (i) advice related to the presentation of evidence and (ii) coaching about the content of testimony is a common feature of poor answers.

Aim Higher

High credit can be gained by exhibiting a good knowledge of the 2005 governmental reform proposals and their rationale: Lords' *Hansard* text for 17 January 2005 (250117–22) Col 626.

---

34 An important point which demonstrates an understanding of matters at the very heart of the debate on this issue.

6 Civil Process and Legal Services

INTRODUCTION

The purpose of the Civil Justice Council is that of 'ensuring that this country retains a fair and effective justice system'. How far that system is fair and effective is the key theme of this chapter.

The county courts are the main platform on which the civil law rights and duties of British citizens are played out. If something goes badly wrong here, as the evidence suggests is happening now, then the rights of British citizens are prejudiced on a significant scale.

There are 216 county courts in England and Wales, dealing with claims for matters such as personal injury, debt, house repossessions and breaches of contract. All but the most complicated and momentous civil cases are dealt with by the county courts.

In February 2007, Judge Paul Collins, London's most senior county court judge, told BBC Radio 4's *Law in Action* programme that low pay and high turnover among administrative staff mean that serious errors are commonplace and routinely lead to incorrect judgments in court. Judge Collins said:

> We are operating on the margins of effectiveness and with further cuts looming we run the risk of bringing about a real collapse in the service we're able to give to people using the courts.

According to Judge Collins, the lack of resources is causing mistakes. A common problem is one in which someone who is being sued files a defence but the papers are not passed on to the judge by overburdened court staff. The judge will automatically award damages to the person who brought the claim, assuming that the person being sued does not want to defend it. According to Judge Collins:

> This happens on a regular basis and although these errors can be put right it takes work to put them right, producing more to do for already hard pressed court staff and judges.

Staff in the court service are among the poorest paid of all Government departments. In Judge Collins' own court in Central London, the number of people employed had been cut from 125 in 1992 to just 80 at the time he spoke out. The quantity of work, however, had not diminished. Roughly speaking, therefore, the remaining staff were having to cover between them about a third more work than when there were 125 staff. It is no wonder that county court staff are becoming stressed and losing files.

The position had not improved by 2010. Judge Monty Trent, President of the Association of District Judges, noted that:

> Many of our courts are old, many are dilapidated. We can expect more court closures, impeding access to local justice.

The Times, 1 April 2010

County courts are no longer subsidised through general taxation. Instead, they are expected to generate all their income from fees charged to court users. This was intended to protect the courts from having to compete with other public services for Government funds.

Problems in the administration of the courts have, in Judge Collins' experience, been further exacerbated by cuts in the availability of legal aid. He stated that:

> There is plenty of anecdotal evidence that this has led to an increase in the number of people representing themselves without the help of a qualified lawyer. These cases inevitably take up more time and as a result court proceedings last longer to the detriment of others using the courts.

One clear way in which the system has improved in recent times has been in respect of the accessibility of its information. The website of the Ministry of Justice contains links to all the most recent judgments of the court and to the relevant **Civil Procedure Rules (CPR)**. Another useful website is that of the Civil Division of the Court of Appeal, where details on case progression, available advice and support and contact details are provided: www. justice.gov.uk/courts/rcj-rolls-building/court-of-appeal/civil-division.

Since 1999, the civil process and the provision of legal services have undergone a major change. The **Civil Procedure Rules (CPR)**, the most fundamental changes in civil process for over a century, have radically altered the operation of civil justice. Part of the rationale of the rules was to expedite the way cases were dealt with and to allow more cases to be settled early, through negotiation between the parties or alternative dispute resolution (ADR). In this respect, there is some evidence of success.

The overriding objective of the **CPR** is to enable the court to deal justly with cases. The first rule reads:

> 1.1(1) These rules are a new procedural code with the overriding objective of enabling the court to deal with cases justly.

This objective will include ensuring that the parties are on an equal footing and saving expense. When exercising any discretion given by the **CPR**, the court must, according to **r1.2**, have regard to the overriding objective and a checklist of factors, including the amount of money involved, the complexity of the issue, the parties' financial positions, how the case can be dealt with expeditiously and by allotting an appropriate share of the court's resources, while taking into account the needs of others. As a result, as Judge John

Frenkel observes ('On the road to reform' (1998)): 'The decisions of the Court of Appeal are more likely to illustrate the application of the new rules to the facts of a particular case, as opposed to being interpretative authorities that define the meaning of the rules.'

Another area of change concerns conditional fee arrangements (CFAs). In the first version of CFAs, only people who expected to win money from their case could benefit from conditional fees. This was the only way that most people could afford to pay the success fee, but it meant that a successful litigant would not receive all the money he had been awarded. So, in 2000, the Government took the power, in the **Access to Justice Act 1999**, to make it possible for the winning party to recover the success fee and any insurance premium from the losing party. This ensures that it is the person or organisation that has committed the legal wrong who pays, and it will allow defendants and claimants (other than in family law cases), whose case is not about money, to use CFAs. From April 2013, new rules came into force and clients who enter into a CFA since then have to pay the success fee of their lawyer and any after-the-event (ATE) premium from their damages. The changes were brought about by **ss 44** and **46** of the **Legal Aid, Sentencing and Punishment of Offenders Act 2012** and the **Conditional Fee Agreements Order 2013**.

Legal services have also undergone very significant change in recent times. Expanded rights of advocacy for solicitors and others (including patent agents) have changed the traditional picture of the courts as the domain of barristers. There are currently approximately 4,000 qualified solicitor-advocates. The introduction of the **Legal Services Commission (LSC)** and the **Community Legal Service (CLS)** marked a sea-change in the delivery of publicly funded law and the impending change, to a public defender system, carrying the potential for far-reaching implications for both the legal system and for the public, as consumers of its services. The cuts to the public funding of these bodies will present even greater challenges to their provision of services going forward.

Checklist

You should be familiar with:

- the main provisions of the 1996 *Woolf Report on Civil Justice*;
- the purpose and main provisions of the new CPR;
- the arguments both for and against the proposition that the reforms can work and have worked well in practice;
- the main provisions of the Legal Services Act 2007;
- the main provisions of the Access to Justice Act 1999;
- the role and purpose of the LSC and the CLS;
- CFAs;
- the nature and purpose of the Salaried Defence Service and critical commentary on this system;
- changes concerning rights of audience and legal liability of the legal professions.

QUESTION 32

Explain the process of judicial review, and state how the process is different from an appeal.

How to Read this Question

This question is looking for a thorough understanding of judicial review, together with the ability to compare the process to that of appeal.

How to Answer this Question

Set the structure of the answer by outlining the basic difference between a judicial review and an appeal.

❖ Turn to an example of a judicial review case and expound it: *The Queen on the Application of Greenpeace Ltd v Secretary of State for Trade and Industry* (2007).

❖ Explain the basic mechanics (prerogative remedies) of the judicial review.

❖ Cite and explain *Associated Provincial Picture Houses Ltd v Wednesbury Corporation* (1948).

❖ Explain the case's significance in respect of the 'reasonableness' principle.

Up for Debate

Judicial review has come under attack in recent years from Government and media sources who are concerned that judges are 'second-guessing' the executive and that there were too many 'frivolous' claims. The **Criminal Justice and Courts Bill 2013–14 to 2014–15**, Part 4, Clauses 70–78, which was going through Parliament at the time of writing, will substantially restrict access to judicial review, both for individual litigants where the review would not make a substantial difference to the outcome of the administrative action and for interveners who fund judicial review.

Answer Structure

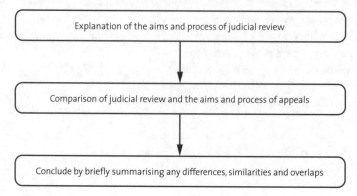

Explanation of the aims and process of judicial review

Comparison of judicial review and the aims and process of appeals

Conclude by briefly summarising any differences, similarities and overlaps

ANSWER

The process of judicial review is a part of the civil process categorised as administrative law. It is the process whereby the High Court can check that public bodies make their decisions using only legal and fair procedures. This process is different from an appeal, because the bodies that the High Court finds are in violation of the requirements of legal and fair decision making cannot be ordered to come to *different* decisions, but merely to reconsider the issue in question acting within the legal rules and fairly. Unlike a successful appeal, a successful judicial review does not result in the original decision being reversed, but merely invalidated.[1]

A recent example can be found in the decision *The Queen on the Application of Greenpeace Ltd v Secretary of State for Trade and Industry* (2007).[2] The High Court decided that a consultation process carried out by the Government on the future production of electricity was inadequate. Mr Justice Sullivan ruled that in attempting to canvass public opinion about the use of nuclear power plants, having said in a White Paper (a governmental proposal and discussion document) that it would allow 'the fullest public consultation', the Government's subsequent consultation exercise was procedurally unfair. There was a breach of the 'legitimate expectation' that there would be a full public consultation. The exercise was too rushed and confined by a tight deadline. The Government had later stated that as a result of its consultation, 'The Government believes that nuclear has a role to play in the future UK generating mix alongside other low carbon generating options.' The judicial review was brought by Greenpeace Ltd, which wanted to make a considered response to the consultation. The court did not rule that the Government's decision to build another nuclear power plant was 'wrong as a matter of policy'; it ruled simply that a political decision that condoned the development of further nuclear plants had not been made in an appropriate way. Mr Justice Sullivan held that (para 120):

> [T]here was a breach of the claimant's legitimate expectation to fullest public consultation; that the consultation process was procedurally unfair; and that therefore the decision in the Energy Review that nuclear new build 'has a role to play ...' was unlawful.

The essence of successful judicial review like this is not that a court says that a public body made a *wrong* decision but that it made a decision in a *wrong way*. Here, the Government had, in July 2006, come out in favour of new nuclear power stations without fulfilling its earlier documented promise to carry out 'the fullest consultation'. Whether the UK opts for new nuclear power stations is a *political* decision which the people (via our Government), not the law courts, will make. But in making the decision, proper process must be followed, so even mighty politicians must obey the rules of decision making. If they promise to consult fully then they must do just that.

---

1 Answer immediately demonstrates knowledge by highlighting the differences between judicial review and appeals.

2 The use of examples demonstrates deeper knowledge, aids explanation and provides support and legal authority.

Consulting the public is an important governmental activity. The people are an intrinsic part of government in the modern European setting. The European Court of Justice in 1980 referred to 'the fundamental democratic principle that the peoples [of democratic countries in Europe] should take part in the exercise of power' (Case 138/79, *SA Roquette Frères v Council* (1980) ECR 3333, 3360, para 33).[3]

Judicial review is the procedure by which *prerogative* remedies (coming from the inherent power of the court) have been obtainable in the High Court against lower courts, tribunals and administrative authorities from which there is no formal appeal process. So, where there is no procedure for an appeal to reconsider the merits of a decision (like the decision to approve new nuclear power stations), it is very important that the decision-making panel's approach to its task is impeccably fair. The primary purpose of judicial review is to control any actions of public authorities that might be made in excess of their proper powers (*ultra vires*) or on the basis of some unreasonable way of coming to a decision.

Judicial review, part of administrative law, has expanded dramatically as a part of law in recent history. In 1981, 552 applications for judicial review were made at the High Court, whereas in 2008, a total of 7,169 applications were made. We have come a long way since 1935 when Lord Chief Justice Hewart dismissed administrative law as worthless 'Continental jargon'.

The foundational precedent for modern cases of judicial review is *Associated Provincial Picture Houses Ltd v Wednesbury Corporation* (1948).[4] This concerned a local authority, in Wednesbury, central England, which had, under the **Sunday Entertainments Act 1932**, granted a licence to a company for it to open its Gaumont cinema on Sundays. The Act allowed for a licence to be granted with 'such conditions as the authority thinks fit'. The authority imposed the condition that children under 15 were not to be allowed into cinemas on Sundays. The company argued that the provision was 'unreasonable' and therefore *ultra vires*, that is, 'beyond the powers' of the local authority. It argued that the court should be the arbiter of whether a condition was reasonable.

In the Court of Appeal, the reasoning of Lord Greene, the Master of the Rolls, soon crystallised into a hallowed legal proposition. He said that where Parliament had entrusted discretionary powers to another body, like a local authority, the courts could declare that some decisions were 'unreasonable', and therefore beyond what the authority was authorised to do.

In a key passage of his judgment, the Master of the Rolls said:

The court is entitled to investigate the action of the local authority with a view to seeing whether they have taken into account matters which they ought not to take into account,

---

3   In addition to demonstrating broad knowledge, reference to this European Union case assists in illustrating the importance of the availability of judicial review.

4   Use of older cases provides background and demonstrates understanding of the development of the action.

or, conversely, have refused to take into account or neglected to take into account matters which they ought to take into account. Once that question is answered in favour of the local authority, it may be still possible to say that, although the local authority have kept within the four corners of the matters which they ought to consider, they have nevertheless come to a conclusion so unreasonable that no reasonable authority could ever have come to it. In such a case, again, I think the court can interfere. The power of the court to interfere in each case is not as an appellate authority to override a decision of the local authority, but as a judicial authority which is concerned, and concerned only, to see whether the local authority have contravened the law by acting in excess of the powers which Parliament has confided in them.

The courts, though, could not simply substitute their own opinion for that of the public body.[5] To be unreasonable, the decision would have to be one where an authority had 'taken into account matters which it ought not to take into account, or, conversely, has refused to take into account or neglected to take into account matters which it ought to take into account'. Applying the principles in this case, the court held that the local authority had not acted unreasonably or *ultra vires* in imposing the condition that those under 15 could not attend the cinema on a Sunday.

Even if the way a decision was made passes that test, the decision could still be challenged in the courts if it was one which 'no reasonable body could have come to'. In other words, if it is a patently mad decision. An example given in an earlier case was if a teacher had been dismissed 'because she had red hair, or for some equally frivolous and foolish reason'.

The principles have since become the touchstone of the courts when deciding judicial review cases, and the legal phrase '*Wednesbury* unreasonable' is shorthand for a decision of a public body or official that violates the criterion of necessary reasonableness established in this case. The judicial control of governmental power is an essential element of democracy.

Common Pitfalls

❖ The definition of 'reasonableness' according to the *Wednesbury* case decision is subtle and multifaceted. It is a common among poor answers for the definition to be inadequately recounted, so learn it well.

❖ Another common pitfall is the failure to explain the legal consequence of a successful judicial review, i.e. that the matter is remitted to the original decision maker to look at again in a legally proper way.

....

5   Demonstrates an appreciation of the fact that judicial review is not about *what* was decided by the public body but, instead, *how* the decision was reached.

Aim Higher

❖ It is highly creditable to include some European context or cases, for example: *SA Roquette Frères v Council* (1980).

❖ The demonstration of an appreciation of the political context of judicial review is also highly creditable. This can be done, for example, by reference to cases in which the tension between judicial and governmental power is manifest; see, e.g., *The Queen on the Application of Greenpeace Ltd v Secretary of State for Trade and Industry* (2007).

QUESTION 33

What pressures have been found to encourage litigants to settle claims, even against their best interests, and what approach to this issue is taken by the **CPR**?

How to Read this Question

This question requires you to analyse the reasons why parties settle and then look at how the civil justice system has tackled the question of settlement. The answer needs to be evidence driven.

How to Answer this Question

You should consider the following:

❖ the nature of settlement;
❖ fear of costs and uncertainty of outcome;
❖ Part 36 payments;
❖ the **Civil Procedure Rules (CPR)** and limiting costs;
❖ active case management.

Up for Debate

You might like to consider the increasing role of mediation in encouraging settlement. This is becoming particularly important in the field of family law, following the **Children and Families Act 2014**, which introduces compulsory mediation.

Answer Structure

Introduction explaining how civil claims can be settled both in and out of court and of the problems commonly associated with civil legal action

↓

Consideration of the Woolf Report and resulting changes introduced by the **CPR**

↓

Conclusion summarising the impact of **CPR** on reaching a settlement

ANSWER

A settlement is a compromise. In the context of litigation, it involves the parties deciding to resolve their dispute out of court, rather than go to a full hearing and have the matter decided by a judge, or even a civil jury. If a litigant is being pushed into giving in when he has a sound legal case and his rights should be vindicated, then a compromise is undesirable. Where, however, a dispute is evenly balanced and would involve a great deal of time, anxiety and resources to resolve in a full trial, then a compromise might well represent a trilateral relief: relief for both sides and the taxpayers who support the legal system.

Most civil disputes are settled out of court.[6] Less than 10 per cent of cases where a claim form is issued actually go to court and, even of those which do go to trial, many are settled before judgment.

In 2014, the judicial statistics showed that about 1.4 million civil claims and petitions are brought to the county courts each year. Typically, only about 3–4 per cent of these require a hearing. In the vast majority of cases, either the defendant does nothing so the claimant can ask the court to order the defendant to pay the amount claimed, or the disputes are settled without a court hearing being needed.

The largest study of this sort was conducted by the Oxford Centre for Socio-Legal Studies (Harris *et al.*, *Compensation and Support for Illness and Injury*, 1984), which examined a random sample of 1,711 accident victims who had been incapacitated for a minimum of two weeks.[7] Of this group, only 26 per cent had considered claiming damages, only 14 per cent had consulted a solicitor and only 12 per cent were awarded damages.

Many factors combine to persuade disputants to settle out of court[8] and the fear of prohibitive costs can be a serious deterrent to bringing proceedings. This is particularly so when it is remembered that the basic rule is that 'costs follow the event'; that is, the successful party can expect the judge to order the loser to pay some or all of his solicitor's bill. Costs,[9] however, are a discretionary matter, so the whole process is beset with uncertainties. Another gamble the claimant is faced with is the procedure of 'payment into court' (now known as a 'Part 36 payment') where, at any stage after the commencement of proceedings, the defendant may make a payment into court in satisfaction of the claimant's claim. The claimant may accept the payment or continue the action. If the claimant chooses to continue and the damages obtained are not greater than the amount paid in by the defendant, the claimant will be liable for the defendant's taxed costs (that is, costs which are authorised by a court official – a taxing master) from the time of payment in,

---

6   Such discussion demonstrates understanding of the fact that civil disputes, unlike criminal prosecutions, may – and are – settled without reference to the courts.

7   Reference to reliable research such as this demonstrates knowledge and understanding and strengthens argument. Where possible, provide a balanced argument by considering opposing or more contemporary research findings.

8   This introduces thoughtful consideration of *why* claimants settle out of court.

9   Fear of the costs is one of the main barriers to accessing justice.

even though he has won the action. When the judge makes an award of damages, he will not know the amount of any payment into court, so he cannot influence the matter of whether the claimant has to suffer under the rule.

Another factor putting pressure on litigants to settle is that of the risks and uncertainties entailed in the claim. If the case goes to trial, then the claimant will, to succeed, have to prove his case on the balance of probabilities. The process is beset with legal uncertainties. Is the defendant liable at law for the claimant's loss or injury? Even where the law is clear, there may be evidential difficulties. Genn has presented material to suggest that in many cases, a claimant's solicitor either does not have sufficient resources to undertake proper factual investigations, or does not seek out all available reports. It is also very difficult to contact all relevant witnesses and to assess how persuasive their courtroom evidence would be. Defendants, including or assisted by insurance companies, will often have resources which place them in a good position to fully investigate the circumstances of accidents. Assessing the quantum of damages is another very problematic part of litigation. In an American experiment, 20 pairs of practising lawyers were given identical information about a case and were instructed to negotiate a settlement. Their resultant settlements ranged from the highest of US$95,000 to the lowest of US$15,000, with an average of just over US$47,000.

Under the **CPR**, there is a greater incentive for parties to settle their differences. The court now takes into account any pre-action offers to settle when making an order for costs. Thus, a side which has refused a reasonable offer to settle will be treated less generously in the issue of how far the court will order their costs to be paid by the other side. For this to happen, the offer, however, must be one which is made to be open to the other side for at least 21 days after receipt (to stop any undue pressure being put on someone with the phrase: 'Take it or leave it, it is only open for one day, then I shall withdraw the offer'). Also, if the offer is made by the defendant, it must be an offer to pay compensation and to pay the claimant's costs.

Several aspects of the rules encourage litigants to settle rather than take risks in order (as a claimant) to hold out for unreasonably large sums of compensation, or to try to get away (as a defendant) with paying nothing, rather than some compensation. The system of Part 36 payments or offers does not apply to small claims, but, for other cases, it seems bound to have a significant effect. Thus, if at the trial, a claimant does not get more damages than a sum offered by the defendant in what is called a Part 36 payment (that is, an offer to settle or a payment into the court), or obtain a judgment more favourable than a Part 36 offer, the court will order the claimant to pay any costs incurred by the defendant after the latest date for accepting the payment or offer. The court now has a discretion to make a different order for costs from the normal order.

Active case management imposes a duty on the courts to help parties settle their disputes. A 'stay' is a temporary halt in proceedings and an opportunity for the court to order such a pause arises at the stage when the defence to a claim has been filed. Parties can indicate that they have agreed on a stay to attempt to settle the case and, provided the court agrees, can have an initial period of one month to try to do this. In order to avoid the stay being used as a delaying tactic, the order granting the stay will require the parties to report back to the court within 14 days of the end of the period of the stay to:

(a) inform the court if the matter has been settled either wholly or partly; or

(b) ask for more time for settlement; or

(c) report that the attempt to settle has failed, so that the process of allocation of court track can take place.

Overall, it seems likely that as a result of the **CPR**,[10] fewer of the annually settled cases will have been settled for the 'wrong reasons' (that is, because parties are frightened of the possible delays, costs and uncertainties of proceeding to a full judgment) and more disputants will settle in the truer spirit of compromise, facilitated by an improved legal system.

Note

Inordinate delay also raises questions of human rights. Consider this case from the European Court of Human Rights. In *Jose da Conceicao Guerreiro v Portugal* (2002) App No 00045560/99 (G Ress P), 31 January, the applicant complained of a violation of **Art 6(1)** of the **European Convention on Human Rights**, on the basis that civil proceedings to which he was a party had lasted 14 years and two months and had therefore exceeded the 'reasonable time' requirement of the Article. The Court held unanimously that there had been a violation of **Art 6(1)** and the applicant was awarded €5,500 (about £3,500) for non-pecuniary and pecuniary damages. Most civil cases in the UK do not last that long, but a great many do endure for longer than five years, with all the attendant cost and the stress that such a period of uncertainty entails.

QUESTION 34

The **Civil Procedure Rules (CPR)** introduced in 1999 have been an unqualified success in changing the legal system.

▶ **Discuss.**

How to Read this Question

The key word here is 'unqualified'. Can you identify qualifications to the success of the CPR? An understanding of recent changes is also necessary.

How to Answer this Question

You will need to consider the following:

❖ the background to the rules;

❖ reduction in cases;

❖ case control;

❖ court allocation and tracking;

10 Always try to access up-to-date research which will allow you to support any conclusions reached (see the suggested answer to the next question).

❖   documentation and procedures;
❖   Dame Hazel Genn's critique of Lord Woolf's reforms;
❖   Lord Dyson's speech on the CPR.

Up for Debate

Research recent reaction to changes to the CPR using either Westlaw or LexisNexis. What pitfalls can you identify in the changed regime?

Answer Structure

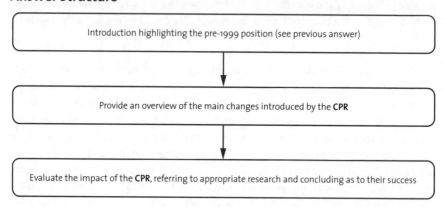

Introduction highlighting the pre-1999 position (see previous answer)

Provide an overview of the main changes introduced by the **CPR**

Evaluate the impact of the **CPR**, referring to appropriate research and concluding as to their success

ANSWER

The **Civil Procedure Rules (CPR)** (most recently updated in 2014), when introduced in 1999, wrought the most fundamental changes in civil process for over 100 years, and have radically altered the operation of civil justice.

Part of the rationale of the rules was to expedite the way cases were dealt with and to allow more cases to be settled early through negotiation between the parties or **alternative dispute resolution (ADR)**. In this respect, there is some evidence of success. Between May and August 1999, there was a 25 per cent reduction in the number of cases issued in the county courts, compared with the same period the previous year. The trend has continued, with some ups and downs, ever since. Nearly 60,000 small claims hearings were issued in 2001, whereas the number had fallen to under 37,000 by 2011.

Around 31 per cent of cases allocated to track reached a trial or small claim hearing in 2011, with most settling or being withdrawn. In total, there were 52,660 trials and small claims hearings, 13 per cent less than in 2010 and lower than in any year from 2006 onwards.

One of the main features of the civil process is case control. The progress of cases is monitored by using a computerised diary monitoring system. Parties are encouraged to co-operate with each other in the conduct of the proceedings; which issues need full investigation and trial are decided promptly and others disposed of summarily.

Another feature of the rules is court allocation and tracking. The county courts retain an almost unlimited jurisdiction for handling contract and tort claims. Where a matter involves a claim for damages or other remedy for libel or slander, or a claim where the title to any toll, fair, market or franchise is in question, then the proceedings cannot start in the county court unless the parties agree otherwise. In 2012, the Ministry of Justice announced that non-personal injury claims under £100,000 cannot be heard in the High Court.

Issuing proceedings in the High Court is now limited to personal injury claims with a value of £50,000 or more; other claims with a value of more than £100,000 and equity claims where the property is worth at least £350,000; claims where an Act of Parliament requires a claim to start in the High Court; or specialist High Court claims.

Cases are allocated to one of three tracks for a hearing, that is, small claims, fast track or multi-track, depending on the value and complexity of the claim.

The documentation and procedures of the civil system have been designed to create a smooth and flexible process. Most claims will be begun by a multipurpose form and the provision of a response pack, and the requirement that an allocation questionnaire is completed is intended to simplify and expedite matters.

The **CPR** are the same for the county court and the High Court. The vocabulary is more user-friendly, so, for example, what used to be called a 'writ' is a 'claim form' and a *guardian ad litem* is a 'litigation friend'.

The overriding objective of the **CPR** is to enable the court to deal justly with cases. It applies to all of the rules, and the parties to a case are required to assist the court in pursuing the overriding objective. Further, when the courts exercise any powers given to them under the **CPR**, or in interpreting any rules, they must consider and apply the overriding objective. The first rule reads:

> 1.1(1) These rules are a new procedural code with the overriding objective of enabling the court to deal with cases justly.

This objective includes ensuring that the parties are on an equal footing and saving expense. When exercising any discretion given by the **CPR**, the court must, according to **r1.2**, have regard to the overriding objective and a checklist of factors, including the amount of money involved, the complexity of the issue, the parties' financial positions, and how the case can be dealt with expeditiously and fairly, and allot an appropriate share of the court's resources while taking into account the needs of others.

Although in some ways all the fuss about the new **CPR** being so far-reaching creates the impression that the future will see a sharp rise in litigation, the truth may be different. The Queen's Bench Division of the High Court is the court that deals with all substantial claims in personal injury, breach of contract and negligence actions. According to official figures (*Judicial and Court Statistics 2011*, Ministry of Justice, 28 June 2012), 153,624 writs and originating summonses were issued by the court in 1995. By 2012, however, the number of annual actions issued was down to 14,454 (HM Government website of quarterly court statistics). The number of claims issued in the county courts (which deal with less substantial civil disputes in the law of negligence) has also fallen. In 1998, the number of claims issued nationally was 2,245,324 but in quarter 2 (April to June) of 2013 it was 351,000 with 11,000 hearings or trials.

The Woolf reforms have been criticised by Dame Hazel Genn in her 2009 Hamlyn lectures. Dame Hazel argued that the civil justice reforms were not primarily about greater access to law or greater justice for society but arose rather as a way to divert litigants from the courts and instead direct them to mediation. Part of the rationale, she argued, was due to the self-financing of the civil court system and the Government's lack of commitment to civil justice in favour of the criminal justice system.

Whatever was the main origin of the **CRP**, the need for their universally strict application was well made by Lord Dyson. In a speech to judges in 2013, Lord Dyson quoted Lord Esher's remark in *Coles v Ravenshear* (1907) that

> the relation of rules of practice to the work of justice is intended to be that of hand-maid rather than mistress, and the court ought not to be so far bound and tied by rules, which are after all only intended as general rules of procedure.

Lord Dyson then moved on to say that 'these words must be treated with great caution in the 21st century' and that no indulgence can be given where parties fail to comply with their procedural obligations. The key to success in the civil enterprise is that the rules (that must be rigidly applied) should sensibly facilitate justice. Updated for the 73rd time in 2014, the CPR are arguably well-designed to facilitate justice in civil disputes.

Note
The 73rd Update to the Civil Procedure Rules came into force on 5 June 2014:

Part 3 The Court's Case Management Powers
Rule 3.8 is amended to provide that parties may agree, in writing, to an extension of time, up to a maximum of 28 days without an application to the court. The parties may not make such an agreement, if the court has ordered that such an agreement cannot be made, or if any extension of time agreed puts the hearing date at risk.

QUESTION 35
What is meant by legal professional privilege, and what purpose does it serve in the English legal system?

How to Read this Question
The question calls for an explanation of the doctrine, and then a description of why the privilege is a part of the system. The part of the answer dealing with the purpose of the privilege can be enhanced by an evaluative element.

How to Answer this Question

- ❖ Introduce the theme with an example.
- ❖ Explain the principle and its origin.
- ❖ Provide some case law support for the doctrine.
- ❖ Explain the social benefits of client–lawyer confidentiality.
- ❖ Illustrate the limitation of the privilege *R v Cox and Railton* (1884).
- ❖ Conclusion – evaluation of doctrine.

Up for Debate

A 2013 Supreme Court decision (*R (on the application of Prudential Plc) v Special Commissioner of Income Tax* [2013] UKSC 1; [2013] 2 WLR 325 (SC)) held that legal professional privilege only applies to lawyers and not to other professionals giving legal advice in the course of their professional activities – in this case accountants. The Supreme Court was split 5:2 on this issue and the reasoning of the majority varied as to whether the basis of the privilege was or was not principled. Those who thought it was principled based it chiefly on the close relationship between lawyers and the courts. Should legal professional privilege be extended to other professionals who give advice related to the law?

Answer Structure

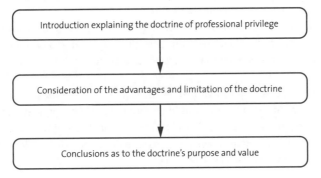

Introduction explaining the doctrine of professional privilege

⬇

Consideration of the advantages and limitation of the doctrine

⬇

Conclusions as to the doctrine's purpose and value

ANSWER

A special set of rules controls the confidentiality of communications between lawyers and their clients. It is a very important part of the legal system.

The issue of secretly recorded conversations between the lawyer Simon Creighton and his imprisoned client (*The Times*, 5 February 2008) raised for public debate the question: Why do we have the principle of 'professional privilege' that protects the lawyer–client relationship?

In essence, the privilege means that communications between a lawyer and client are confidential, and can only be revealed to a law court or the police at the option of the client. The same protection of confidentiality does not extend to doctor–patient, priest–penitent or accountant–client relationships so it is easier for the legal system to acquire information from those professional communications.[11]

The word 'privilege' comes from the Latin (*privilegium*) for 'private law': a law applying to an individual or small group. Under general law, what citizens say to each other can be used in evidence in law courts. A 'private law', though, applies to lawyers, and gives lawyer–client communications a specially guarded confidentiality.

The justification is simple and compelling. Citizens do not want to live in anarchy, they want to live in a society of laws and rules. As there are hundreds of thousands of laws, citizens do not want to have to become expert themselves on them all, any more than they want to learn medicine just so they can be their own doctor. People want experts on the laws: lawyers. So, a society should encourage citizens to go to its lawyers for advice whenever they are in difficulties. To ensure the lawyer–client relationship works well, there must be complete trust, and, in order for that to happen, the client must feel assured that client–lawyer communications are completely private and confidential.[12]

It might be argued that 'if a client has done nothing wrong, they've got nothing to worry about if their chats with their lawyer are recorded and later played to a court'. That, though, misses an important point. To be full and frank with lawyers in criminal, family, civil and commercial cases, many clients have to mention secret, embarrassing or compromising things that are incidental to their main stories, but more social good is served by those things remaining confidential, and the law taking its proper course guided by lawyers, than if clients were deterred from telling the bigger truths of their situations to lawyers for fear of the incidental compromising facts being open to be made public.

The rule of privilege is long established. In *Greenough v Gaskell* (1833), Lord Chancellor Brougham said (at 621) that the rule was important to uphold 'the interests of justice'. He said if the rule did not exist, people would be mistrustful of consulting legal experts, and so would end up worsening their own positions with do-it-yourself law. He said 'every one would be thrown upon his own legal resources'.

More recently, in 2003, the Privy Council (the highest appeal court for many Commonwealth countries) ruled that lawyer–client privilege is fundamental to the operation of justice and should not be overridden unless the law has specifically said so in a particular circumstance: *B v Auckland District Law Society* (2003). The Privy Council held that the power of a district law society in New Zealand to require the production of documents by legal practitioners when investigating complaints against them under **s101(3)(d)** of the **Law Practitioners Act 1982** did not override legal professional privilege, and privilege was

----

11 Clear and succinct explanation of the doctrine of legal professional privilege sets the scene and provides a helpful introduction.

12 Highlights the rationale behind the doctrine allowing, and encouraging, in-depth consideration of its value and limitations.

not waived by voluntarily making the documents available for limited purposes. The privilege is also protected under European law: Case 155/79 *AM&S Europe Ltd v EC Commission* (1983), and European human rights law: *Campbell v UK* (1992).[13]

The privilege against disclosure does not, however, cover all communications. In a case in 1884, an English appeal confirmed that if a client asks a lawyer for information in order to be guided on how to commit a crime, the lawyer can testify about that to a court despite the client's protests: *R v Cox and Railton* (1884).

Henry Muster, who had been libelled in *The Brightonian*, was awarded damages. But the publisher of the paper, Richard Railton, conspired with a business partner to make a property transaction in order to avoid paying the damages. Railton had asked his solicitor some questions in preparation to do something unlawful. Informed by his solicitor, for example, that he was not allowed to sell property to his own business partner, Railton asked the solicitor 'Does anyone know about the partnership except for you?' After the scam was exposed, the solicitor was called as a prosecution witness and Railton and his partner were convicted.

Allowing client–lawyer privilege does not, as is sometimes said, amount to allowing criminals to thrive. Legally, a lawyer must not assist in the commission of a crime or say to a court anything he knows is untrue – those are very serious offences. Moreover, it is a lawyer's positive duty to disclose information that he knows or suspects relates to particular crimes such as terrorism (under the **Terrorism Act 2000**) or money laundering (under the **Proceeds of Crime Act 2002**).

Sometimes, of course, deciding whether the obligation to report something wrongful to a court puts lawyers in a difficult position. The barrister Rayner Goddard (who became Lord Chief Justice in 1946) asked his first client, during their initial cell interview at the Old Bailey: 'Now, my man, what is your story?' The client replied 'Well, that's rather up to you, guv'nor.'

It might be that the privilege rule means that lawyers get to hear of some immoral or shocking non-criminal aspects of the lives of certain clients, and that those remain secret. That, though, is a small price to pay for a population knowing that the state does not have its eye and an ear in the very offices to which its citizens go when they need help.

QUESTION 36

Explain the circumstances in which an advocate can be held liable for courtroom negligence and assess the public policy arguments in this area.

How to Read this Question

The examiner will be looking for an explanation of the law on the immunity of advocates and an evaluation of the underlying policy.

13   The provision of appropriate, supporting legislation and case law aids explanation, demonstrates knowledge and also adds credibility to the discussion.

How to Answer this Question

Look at:

❖   the decision in *Arthur JS Hall & Co v Simons* (2000);
❖   the brief historical background;
❖   the advocate's divided loyalty;
❖   the 'cab rank' rule;
❖   the witness analogy;
❖   collateral attack;
❖   the need for public confidence in the system.

Up for Debate

If you are studying tort at the same time as this module, you may wish to look at the links between the developing law on negligent advice and the decision in *Arthur JS Hall & Co v Simons* (2000). It is also an interesting example of the power of the House of Lords, and now the Supreme Court, to depart from their own decisions under the 1966 Practice Statement.

Answer Structure

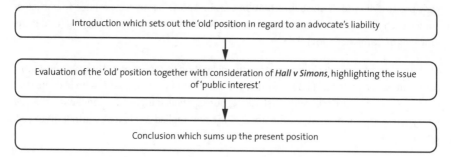

Introduction which sets out the 'old' position in regard to an advocate's liability

Evaluation of the 'old' position together with consideration of *Hall v Simons*, highlighting the issue of 'public interest'

Conclusion which sums up the present position

ANSWER

In *Arthur JS Hall & Co v Simons* (2000), the House of Lords made a bold change in this area of law. It imposed a duty of care upon courtroom advocates that had not been previously supported in law.

Lawyers are, for the general public, the most central and prominent part of the English legal system. They are, arguably, to the legal system what doctors are to the health system. For many decades, a debate has grown about why a patient injured by the negligence of a surgeon in the operating theatre can sue for damages, whereas a litigant whose case is lost because of the negligence of his advocate cannot sue. It all seemed very unfair. Even the most glaringly obvious courtroom negligence was protected against legal action by a special advocates' immunity. The claim that this protection was made by lawyers (and judges who were lawyers) for lawyers was difficult to refute. In this House of Lords' decision, the historic immunity has been abolished in respect of both barristers and solicitor-advocates (of whom there are now over 2,000 with higher courts' rights of audience) and for both civil and criminal proceedings.[14]

In three cases, all conjoined on appeal, a claimant raised a claim of negligence against a firm of solicitors and, in each case, the firms relied on the immunity attaching to barristers and other advocates from actions in negligence. The House of Lords held (Lord Hope, Lord Hutton and Lord Hobhouse dissenting in part) that in the light of modern conditions, it was now clear that it was no longer in the public interest in the administration of justice that advocates should have immunity from suit for negligence for acts concerned with the conduct of either civil or criminal litigation.

The point of departure was that, in general, English law provided a remedy in damages for a person who had suffered injury as a result of professional negligence. It followed that any exception which denied such a remedy required a sound justification. The arguments relied on by the court in *Rondel v Worsley* as justifying the immunity had to be considered. One by one, these arguments were evaluated and rejected.

Advocate's Divided Loyalty

There were two distinct versions of the divided loyalty argument.[15] The first was that the possibility of being sued for negligence would actually inhibit the lawyer, consciously or unconsciously, from giving his duty to the court priority over his duty to his client. The second was that the divided loyalty was a special factor that made the conduct of litigation a very difficult art and could lead to the advocate being exposed to vexatious claims by difficult clients. The argument was pressed, most strongly, in connection with advocacy in criminal proceedings, where the clients were said to be more than usually likely to be vexatious.

There had been developments in the civil justice system designed to reduce the incidence of vexatious litigation. The first was **r 24.2** of the **CPR**, which provided that a court could give summary judgment in favour of a defendant if it considered that 'the claimant had no real prospect of succeeding on the claim'. The second was the changes to the funding of civil litigation introduced by the **Access to Justice Act 1999**, which would make it much more difficult than it had been in the past to obtain legal help for negligence actions which had little prospect of success.

There was no doubt that the advocate's duty to the court was extremely important in the English justice system. The question was whether removing the immunity would have a significantly adverse effect. If the possibility of being held liable in negligence was calculated to have an adverse effect on the behaviour of advocates in court, one might have expected that to have followed, at least in some degree, from the introduction of wasted costs orders (where a court disallows a lawyer from being able to claim part of a fee for work which is regarded as unnecessary and wasteful). Although the liability of a negligent advocate to a wasted costs order was not the same as a liability to pay general damages, the experience of the wasted costs jurisdiction was the only empirical evidence available

---

14 Highlights the basis of the debate.
15 Knowledge of the arguments both for and against is central to the question.

in England to test the proposition that such liability would have an adverse effect upon the way advocates performed their duty to the court, and there was no suggestion that it had changed standards of advocacy for the worse.

The 'Cab Rank'

The 'cab rank' rule provided that a barrister could not refuse to act for a client on the ground that he disapproved of him or his case. The argument was that a barrister, who was obliged to accept any client, would be unfairly exposed to vexatious actions by clients whom any sensible lawyer with freedom of action would have refused to act for. Such a claim, however, was in the nature of things intuitive, incapable of empirical verification and did not have any real substance.

Collateral Attack

The most substantial argument was that it might be contrary to the public interest for a court to retry a case which had been decided by another court. However, actions for negligence against lawyers were not the only cases that gave rise to a possibility of the same issue being tried twice. The law had to deal with the problem in numerous other contexts.

Having regard to the power of the court to strike out actions which had no real prospect of success, the doctrine was unlikely, in that context, to be invoked very often. The first step in any application to strike out an action alleging negligence in the conduct of a previous action had to be to ask whether it had a real prospect of success.

Lord Hope, Lord Hutton and Lord Hobhouse delivered judgments in which they agreed that the immunity from suit was no longer required in relation to civil proceedings, but dissented to the extent of saying that the immunity was still required in the public interest in the administration of justice in relation to criminal proceedings.

This decision is of major and historic importance in the English legal system for several reasons. It can be seen as a bold attempt by the senior judiciary to drag the legal profession (often a metonym for the whole legal system) into the twenty-first-century world of accountability and fair business practice.

The case raises and explores many key issues of the legal system, including the proper relationship between lawyers and the courts, the proper relationship between lawyers and clients, the differences between criminal and civil actions, professional ethics, the nature of dispute resolution and the circumstances under which the courts should make new law. Above all, however, the case has one simple significance: 'It will', in the words of Jonathan Hirst QC, Chairman of the Bar Council, 'mean that a claimant who can prove loss, as the result of an advocate's negligence, will no longer be prevented from making a claim. We cannot really say that is wrong' (*Bar News*, August 2000, p. 3).

Notes

The case of *Moy v Pettmann Smith (a firm)* (2005) gives some comfort to advocates regarding advice provided to clients at the door of the court; that is, when, at the last moment before a case begins, an offer to settle the case is made by the other side and a lawyer has to advise his or her client under some pressure of time whether to accept it. The House of Lords decided that advice given by lawyers in such circumstances does not have to be absolutely perfect in order to be avoid being safe from an action for negligence by a dissatisfied client.

QUESTION 37

Evaluate the role of the expert witness in the English legal system.

How to Read this Question

The process word here is 'evaluate'. You should not simply describe the role of the expert witness but weigh up its value, using multiple points of view. In doing so, you should rely on evidence.

How to Answer this Question

Various approaches could be used in answer to this question. Provided that a structured response is given, and that it provides what the question asks for, it will be satisfactory. The answer here has been structured as follows:

- ❖ Explain the historical setting of expert witnesses.
- ❖ Identify the potential danger of unreliable expert evidence.
- ❖ The challenges posed in the field of costs: *Webster & Ors v Ridgeway Foundation School* (2010).
- ❖ The recommendations of the Jackson Review.
- ❖ The challenges of esoteric information and theories.
- ❖ The **Law Commission paper (2009)**.
- ❖ Conclusion – the inherent difficulties of partisan evidence.

Up for Debate

In the recent Supreme Court case of *Jones v Kaney* [2011] UKSC 13; [2011] 2 WLR 823, the immunity of the expert witness was removed (in line with the earlier removal of advocates' immunity, discussed above). The court was divided on this point. Do you think there is any justification for retaining expert witness immunity?

Answer Structure

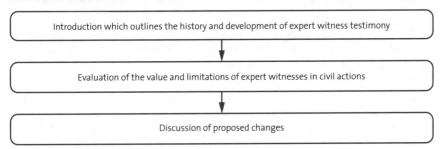

Introduction which outlines the history and development of expert witness testimony

Evaluation of the value and limitations of expert witnesses in civil actions

Discussion of proposed changes

ANSWER

Historically, witnesses in court cases were called to give evidence as they had personal knowledge of the particular facts of the case before the court. In the nineteenth century, the courts established the role of experts who were called to assist the court about recondite matters that the court would not be expected to know about or understand. Where experts appeared as witnesses about scientific or artistic matters, as opposed to lawyers reading parts from books, the quality of their testimony could be tested through cross-questioning. The role of the expert witness, though, has not developed in an entirely unproblematic way.

In 2007, Gene Morrison, a conman from Hyde, in Cheshire, was convicted of 22 crimes, including deception offences and perjury, after having posed in court for years as a forensic psychologist. He had used the title 'Dr' but when asked by police from which university he gained that qualification, he replied (on film) 'I have forgotten that.' Worryingly, he was able to have given testimony in over 700 cases without being exposed by lawyers or judges as a fake.

Many legal disputes need the evidence of experts. Expert opinion is much more than what an American judge once condemned as 'only an ordinary guess in evening clothes'. Every week thousands of specialists like consultant doctors, accountants, authorities on art, and shipping experts deliver testimony. Such expertise makes the discovery of truth much easier. But it does present occasional problems.[16]

An incompetent expert can cause more misery than a psychotic gang member. When justice is miscarried because someone has given sham evidence from the witness box, the repercussions can be catastrophic: people get imprisoned, companies collapse and children can be taken from parents.

The relatively unregulated nature of expert evidence also presents problems in the field of costs. In *Webster & Ors v Ridgeway Foundation School* (2010)[17] a minor celebrity headmistress claimed £200,000 for appearing as an expert witness for a school being sued by a pupil left brain damaged in a hammer attack by classmates. Marie Stubbs charged the enormous fee for writing a 30-page report assessing the school's health and safety policies and for a three-day court appearance. Ms Stubbs and another expert were criticised by the judge, who said, 'I was not greatly assisted by either witness …. It is not the role of the witness simply to become an extra advocate for the party which calls him or her'.

In his *Review of Civil Litigation Costs* (December 2009) Lord Justice Jackson asks for improved control of costs and the use of experts (**Part 6, section 38**). He notes (p. 43) that experts' reports can generate 'excessive costs'.

---

16 This paragraph provides a helpful link between the value of expert witnesses and the possible problems associated with their use.

17 The use of examples such as this can make explanation easier, demonstrates knowledge and adds additional weight to arguments.

An abiding challenge in the field of expert evidence is that a judge or a jury has to evaluate intricate testimony to do with science, technology or finance, and to conclude which side of a case is supported by stronger evidence. Sometimes a trial does not get as much expertise as is later seen to be helpful. In February 2007, in a retrial, Ian and Angela Gay were acquitted of having killed the three-year-old Christian Blewitt, by poisoning him with salt. In this second trial, a new medical expert witness presented an alternative theory about Christian's fatally high sodium level. He showed how the boy's blood–salt concentration could have been attributable to osmoreceptor dysfunction – a medical condition that results in the body not being able properly to regulate its sodium levels.

In civil cases, one problem has sometimes been a profusion of specialist testimony, leaving the court, as one judge said adapting a line of Milton, 'dark with excessive brightness'. To avoid a trial becoming overborne by an abundance of obscure expertise, a court now has the power under the **Civil Procedure Rules**[18] to direct that evidence is given by a single expert to serve 'both sides' of the case. **Rule 35.7(3)** states that where the parties cannot agree who should be the expert, the court may select the expert from a list provided by the parties, or chosen in another manner 'as the court may direct'.

Another point about expert evidence is that those giving it have a duty to justice above their duty to the person paying for their services. In criminal cases, expert witnesses have an obligation to assist the court, and they must remain objective and express only genuinely held opinions which are not biased in favour of either party.

Experts should ensure that developments in scientific thinking and techniques are not kept from the court, even where they remain at the stage of a mere hypothesis. This duty is facilitated by the **Criminal Procedure Rules** which enable opposing experts to consult together before the trial and, if possible, to settle their points of agreement or disagreement with a summary of their reasons.

Similarly, in civil trials, experts must be more than hired proponents of their side's case. The Practice Direction on **Civil Procedure Rule 35** states that 'it is the duty of an expert to help the court' and that this duty 'is paramount and overrides any obligation to the person from whom the expert has received instructions or by whom he is paid'. The rules are strict and demand that an expert should provide objective, unbiased opinion, and should not assume 'the role of an advocate'.

In its paper *The Admissibility of Expert Evidence in Criminal Proceedings in England and Wales, Consultation Paper No 190* (2009), the Law Commission expresses concern that defendants are at risk of being wrongly convicted on the evidence of 'charlatan' and 'biased' expert witnesses. A series of notorious cases in which convictions have been overturned after concerns over 'flawed' expert evidence 'represent the tip of the iceberg'.

....

18 Reference to the **CPR**, both Civil and Criminal (below), demonstrates knowledge of the changes introduced in regard to the use of expert witnesses.

The Commission recommends that magistrates and judges act as gatekeepers and screen expert witnesses by applying a list of criteria, to be encapsulated in a new statutory test, before they can give evidence in court. The purpose of the test would be to ensure that juries are not exposed to unreliable experts.

A major danger to be averted is the problem of the partisan expert witness; the person hired to put a particular slant on the evidence as opposed to giving entirely profes- sional neutral testimony. That sort of witness has been highlighted by Lord Justice Leveson, who has referred (*The Times*, 17 November 2009) to an orthopaedic surgeon who was known by the initials NWA – 'never work again' (because that was the evid- ence he always gave about the impact of an injury on a litigant) – and his frequent opponent in cases, another surgeon known by the initials BTW – 'back to work', because his expert evidence was always that the injured party was well enough to return to work. It is clear that, in general, more systematic caution is required in relation to the value of expert evidence.

Common Pitfalls

❖ The word 'forensic' means related to a court, though it is often wrongly used as if it has something to do with science. Forensic science is science related to court cases. It is a common pitfall to restrict discussion in questions such as this to expert evidence related only to science.

❖ The way that costs issues affect justice, i.e. the question of whether it is necessary to pay for a range of potentially very expensive experts in each case, is an important issue and is commonly omitted in poor answers.

Aim Higher

Highly creditable answers will introduce some good case illustrations that exemplify the relevant theoretical points, for example, *Webster & Ors v Ridgeway Foundation School* (2010), and will display a sound knowledge of recent reform proposals such as *The Admissibility of Expert Evidence in Criminal Proceedings in England and Wales, Consultation Paper No 190* (2009).

QUESTION 38

What was the Legal Services Act 2007 designed to achieve, and how successful has it been?

How to Read this Question

This is a question which seeks knowledge and understanding of how a piece of legislation in 2007 sought to change the delivery and regulation of legal services with a view to making improvements for both citizens and lawyers. The question therefore requires an understanding of business models, organisational ideas and the way that the rules affect consumers and professionals. In asking how successful the law has been, the question seeks an evaluative mode from candidates on the material that they have used in the first part of their answer.

How to Answer this Question

Note that this is a question in two parts. Sometimes questions like this are divided into (a) and (b) but sometimes, as here, there is just a simple division with no numbers or letters. Where that happens it is safe to assume that unless there are specific maximum marks allocated for each part of the question, then the different parts have equal marks awardable for answers to them. You should make it very clear in an answer where the second part of it begins.

Answer Structure

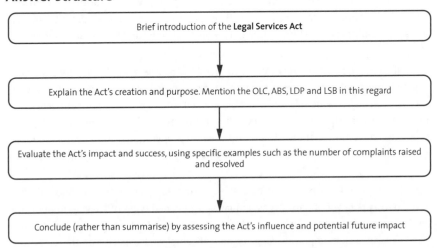

It is possible to answer this question by going through each major item of the Act's purposes, explaining each one, and then evaluating it before moving on to the next item. This, though, moving from expository mode to evaluative mode, can be an unnecessary challenge in the examination. It is usually better, as below, to go through each of the necessary exposition stages in one series of paragraphs before moving to be evaluative across all of the relevant territory. It is very important, as ever, for the introduction to be succinct in a question such as this, and for the conclusion to do something other than summarise what has been already stated.

ANSWER

The **Legal Services Act 2007** heralded major changes in the law. The changes prescribed were an attempt at comprehensive reform of the way legal services are delivered and regulated.

In 2003, Sir David Clementi was appointed by the Government to conduct an independent review of the regulation of legal services. He found that many areas were in need of restructuring and development, and agreed with the Government's earlier conclusion that the existing regulatory framework was 'inflexible, outdated and over-complex'. Sir David highlighted concerns about the complaints handling systems, and the restrictive nature of business structures. The Act in 2007 was designed thereafter to rectify the faults identified in the *Clementi Report*.

The Act created a single and fully independent Office for Legal Complaints (OLC) to remove complaints handling from the legal professions and restore consumer confidence in the legal profession. This established a new ombudsman scheme as a single point of entry for all consumer legal complaints. The Office commenced work in 2010. The Legal Ombudsman provides a free complaints resolution service to members of the public, very small businesses, charities and trusts. The Legal Ombudsman can deal with complaints about the following types of lawyers (and generally those working for them): barristers, law costs draftsmen, legal executives, licensed conveyancers, notaries, patent attorneys, probate practitioners, registered European lawyers, solicitors and trademark attorneys.

Alternative Business Structures (ABSs), to enable consumers to obtain services from a single business entity that brings together lawyers and non-lawyers, were introduced by the Act to meet, in Clementi's terms, a 'market need' and to increase competitiveness and improve services. These structures permit substantial non-lawyer ownership, together with external commercial investment. ABSs became operational from 2011 and Premier Property Lawyer, the conveyancing arm of myhomemove, was the first to register as such.

Legal Disciplinary Practices (LDPs) have been permitted since 2009, and allow firms to have up to 25 per cent of partners as non-lawyers or varied types of lawyers. In April 2010, the Bar announced that barristers could: become managers of LDPs; work in partnerships; work in both a self-employed capacity and an employed capacity at the same time (although not in the same case); hold shares in LDPs; share premises and office facilities with others; investigate and collect evidence and witness statements; attend police stations; and conduct correspondence.

A new Legal Services Board (LSB) was established under the Act to act as a single, independent and publicly accountable regulator with the power to enforce high standards in the legal sector. It replaced a variety of regulators with overlapping powers. The LSB's supervision extends to anyone providing legal services, including claims handlers, notaries, licensed conveyancers, patent and trademark attorneys and will writers. The chair of the Board is a layperson.

Under the Act, the LSB has a duty to promote the various regulatory objectives such as: protecting and promoting public interest; supporting the constitutional principles of the rule of law; improving access to justice; protecting and promoting the interests of consumers; promoting competition in the provision of services; encouraging an independent, strong, diverse and effective legal profession; and increasing public understanding of the citizen's legal rights and duties.

Turning now to evaluate the success of the Act in achieving its aims, it can be seen that the resultant changes have been mixed.

In 2013, the Office for Legal Complaints reported that, since its 2010 inception, it had had 185,000 contacts with complainants and had resolved 16,500 cases. In 2012–13 the Ombudsman resolved a total of 7,630 cases. While the number of people contacting the OLC is in decline, from 76,000 in 2011–12 to 71,000 in 2012–13, the resolution rate is still not high.

This enablement of non-law firms to own legal practices, commonly called 'Tesco Law' by the media, began in 2011 under regulations permitted by the 2007 Act. The Co-operative Society became one of the first organisations to obtain a licence and become an ABS. Irwin Mitchell, a large legal practice, and Quindell, a stock exchange Alternative Investment Market (AIM) listed company, acquired ABS licences. The Solicitors Regulation Authority (SRA) has issued over 250 ABS licences to date, including many substantial ones such as Slater and Gordon, the Australian quoted law firm, acquired the legal practice of Russell Jones & Walker in April 2012. They have since acquired four more law firms.

Whether the new business structures will proliferate is difficult to predict. Professor Stephen Mayson of the Legal Services Policy Institute of the University of Law noted in 2013 that in 2011 about 40 licences were issued, and progress seemed slow. The licences seem now to be being granted at the rate of about 100 a year, which, while not many compared with the 10,726 practising solicitor firms in England and Wales, is a fairly quick growth for a new business model. In 2014, the SRA significantly cut its backlog of ABS licensing applications from 142 in January 2013 to 52 in April 2014. The average age of work-in-progress ABS applications is now three months, with 10 per cent between six and nine months old, and none older than nine months.

A survey of barristers published by the Bar Standards Board in 2014, *Barristers' Working Lives*, showed that nearly one in five criminal and family barristers are considering joining ABSs with non-lawyer owners, while four out of ten of all barristers plan to apply, or are thinking of applying, for authorisation to conduct litigation. The survey revealed that many barristers are struggling to cope with the impact of legal aid cuts in publicly funded work, and that the earnings of two-thirds of self-employed criminal barristers had fallen in recent years.

Slater and Gordon specialise as an insurance complainant practice and, compared with the top English law firms, are very small. Their turnover for the 2013 accounting year was Aus$297.6m (£178.2m) and profit Aus$41.9m (£25.1m), according to their published accounts. The Slater and Gordon business model may well be appropriate for similar practices in the UK, but it is probably less likely to be adopted by the large City corporate law practices.

A new franchise – QualitySolicitors – was formed in 2008 to enable law small or medium-size firms to become members of a federated national organisation to compete with large firms that had adopted the ABS model. Their objective was to have 1,000 member law firms across the country in every high street by 2014, but the number by 2014 was, in fact, under 300. In 2014, QualitySolicitors announced an expansion drive after a multimillion-pound financial injection from its private-equity owner, Palamon Capital Partners. A two-year association with the national stationery and book retailer, WH Smith, to place QS staff in branches had not eventuated into a working model by June 2014.

In conclusion, it is difficult to make a case that the **Legal Services Act 2007** has resulted in substantial and unalloyed advantage to citizens, clients and lawyers. There is no evidence that the regulation of lawyers is demonstrably better than it was under the old regime. The new rules on business structures are beginning to cause both legal and non-legal professions and individual firms to consider how to compete in the context of the changes that have been taking place since October 2011. Although the Act has had a few years to impact on the world of legal services, change in a system that evolved over many centuries can often take longer to become manifest.

Common Pitfalls

A common pitfall in answer to a question such as this is for the candidate to be significantly unequal in his or her writing on the two different parts of the question. The two parts of a candidate's answer, dealing with explaining the Act's purposes and then evaluating the Act, do not need to be exactly the same but they should be of comparable length and detail. If the examiner was only going to award a maximum of 40 per cent for this question's expositional part, and up to 60 per cent for the evaluation, then that would be made clear on the printed exam paper.

Aim Higher

Excellent answers will exhibit knowledge and understanding of the topic's finer detail. For example, the Law Society did not ignore the ABS threat to its members and, in 2008, it commissioned a report by Lord Hunt, which was published in 2009 and titled 'The Hunt Review of the Regulation of Legal Services'. In his report (p. 102) Lord Hunt, in considering how ABSs might work and be regulated, asked: 'How will the inevitable conflict between economic benefits and ethical concerns be resolved?' An example of this conflict might arise where a firm decided to settle a major piece of litigation, believing that it was in the best interest of the client to do so. The practice's shareholders might suffer a consequential loss of potential profit. Under company law the shareholder may be able to sue the directors for making such a decision. The Australian firm Slater and Gordon, the first legal practice in the Western world to be listed on a stock market, worked with its regulator to solve that conundrum. Its constitution states that 'where an inconsistency or conflict arises between the duties of the company, the company's duty to the court will prevail over all duties'. This position has yet to be fully tested in Britain.

QUESTION 39

What reasons prompted the major reform of the family justice system in 2014, and what challenges will the system face in the future?

How to Read this Question

This is a question which seeks knowledge and understanding of the reasons why parts of the legal system have changed and how the changes aim to meet a particular objective, or set of objectives, concerning legal or social policy. A well-prepared candidate will have very good information on the background to the major reforms to the family court and civil process system, what changes were made to improve things, and a good current legal awareness of what sort of problems are yet to be dealt with by the new system.

How to Answer this Question

Note that this is a question in two parts. Sometimes questions like this are divided into (a) and (b) but sometimes, as here, there is just a simple division with no numbers or letters. Where that happens it is safe to assume that unless there are specific maximum marks allocated for each part of the question, then the different parts have equal marks awardable for answers to them. You should make it very clear in an answer where the second part of it begins.

Answer Structure

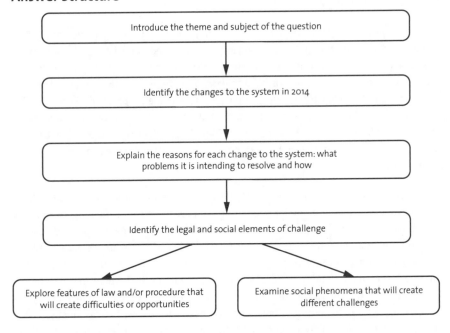

```
        ┌─────────────────────────────────────────────┐
        │  Introduce the theme and subject of the question  │
        └─────────────────────────────────────────────┘
                            │
                            ▼
        ┌─────────────────────────────────────────────┐
        │      Identify the changes to the system in 2014     │
        └─────────────────────────────────────────────┘
                            │
                            ▼
        ┌─────────────────────────────────────────────┐
        │  Explain the reasons for each change to the system: what  │
        │       problems it is intending to resolve and how       │
        └─────────────────────────────────────────────┘
                            │
                            ▼
        ┌─────────────────────────────────────────────┐
        │   Identify the legal and social elements of challenge    │
        └─────────────────────────────────────────────┘
                    ╱                       ╲
                   ▼                         ▼
  ┌──────────────────────────────┐  ┌──────────────────────────────┐
  │ Explore features of law and/or procedure that │  │ Examine social phenomena that will create │
  │  will create difficulties or opportunities    │  │         different challenges         │
  └──────────────────────────────┘  └──────────────────────────────┘
```

Introduce the general theme with information about the work of the family justice system, then move on to identify several parts of the system that have changed in 2014 and, with each one, the reason why the new system was introduced. In answering the second part of the question you should be able to identify both legal and social elements of challenge – in other words, some elements of family law or procedure that will create challenges and some elements of social phenomena like the scale of cases which will also cause different challenges.

ANSWER

About 270,000 new family cases arise each year dealing with issues such as local authority intervention, divorce, domestic violence and adoption.

In 2011 the independent Family Justice Review made many recommendations for reforming the family justice system. These were aimed at cutting delay and improving the way the system functions as a whole.

Following these recommendations, a single Family Court was created on 22 April 2014. On the same day, most of the family justice provisions in the **Children and Families Act 2014 (CFA 2014)** also came into force. The court replaces an old three-tier court system in family cases which produced an unnecessary complexity of process.

Since the middle of the twentieth century, the range of family law issues had widened considerably and the jurisdiction to deal with the various issues was spread across different types of court within the English legal system. Under the new system, a single Family Court is the venue for almost all family cases.

The new court was established by the **Crime and Courts Act 2013**, and the **Family Procedure (Amendment No. 3) Rules 2013/3204**. It streamlines jurisdiction as there is no longer a separate family jurisdiction in the magistrates' courts and county courts. This means citizens and lawyers do not need to work out whether to make an application to the county court or magistrates' court; applications are made simply to the Family Court – a national court which now sits in the same buildings as the county and magistrates' courts where family cases used to be heard. The Principal Registry of the Family Division still exists as a division of the High Court in the Royal Courts of Justice dealing with major cases and appeals.

At the centre of the new system of family justice are certain principles. These include, first, making it a requirement for separating couples to attend a meeting to find out about mediation before they are allowed to take disputes over finances or child custody to court (unless exemptions apply – such as in cases of domestic violence). Second, sending a clear signal to separated parents that courts will take account of the principle that both should continue to be involved in their children's lives where that is safe and consistent with the child's welfare. Third, ensuring expert evidence in family proceedings concerning children is permitted only when necessary to resolve the case justly, taking account of factors including the impact on the welfare of the child. Historically, the delay in cases where a local council applied to take a child into care if it thought the child was at risk was very lengthy – over a year in some cases. So, under a fourth new principle, there is a 26-week deadline for care and supervision proceedings.

The requirement for divorcing couples to attend a mediation information and assessment meeting (MIAM) is now embodied in legislation (**CFA 2014, s10**) as it was thought that the need to maximise the opportunities to get fully consensual agreements was desirable.

Although civil partnerships were previously permitted for same-sex couples under the **Civil Partnership Act 2004**, same-sex couples were still separated from different-sex couples who alone could marry. The **Marriage (Same Sex Couples) Act 2013** came into force 13 March 2014 and was designed to allow all couples to marry and be accorded an equal legal status.

Concerning the second part of the question, what challenges will arise in future, there are several important themes that confront those using the family justice system.

One challenge is developing a legal process suitable for the scale and diversity of separating couples. There are now about 60,000 marriages ending each year. Research by the Marriage Foundation has shown, however, that of five million *unmarried* couples in Britain, some 61,700 couples will split in a year, so the number is almost the same as for married couples, while unmarried couples are only one in five of the total.

There are legal rights for unmarried couples but these are different from those of married couples, and so the legal system operates for each type according to different precepts. Sir James Munby has said reform is 'desperately needed', though governments have so far failed to act. Part of the reform will necessitate an answer as to whether unmarried couples should have equal rights with married ones, and whether they should be together for a set time before any new rights are established.

A second challenge arises from the huge rise in people acting without lawyers in the absence of legal aid – the consequences of how this forces judges to change their court approach is yet to be addressed. Family judges have predicted a move to a more inquisitorial approach, with judges taking a more active role. He has insisted that he is not advocating a European Continental inquisitorial system, but courts must grapple with the fact that now litigants had not chosen, as occasionally they did in better economic times, to dispense with lawyers; today most unrepresented litigants were reluctantly unrepresented and this has an effect on how they handle their own case. Sir James says that this is already happening: judges are more interventionist and no longer sit 'sphinx-like' above the battle saying nothing until they pronounced judgment. He says that 'In the modern world, that simply will not work. It will not produce justice; it will just produce injustice.'

A third challenge for the future is to ease the unnecessary workload of the Family Court and the emotional aggravation entailed in adversarial divorce. One key change promotive of this aim would be for divorce to become a purely administrative process – divorce 'over the counter' – where couples consent and where there are no children. It is arguably unnecessary for judges to be involved. An additional and related type of reform would be the removal of 'fault' from divorce and the disconnection of divorce procedure from the procedure related to disputes over children and money. If couples were no longer required to show 'unreasonable behaviour', with a district judge going through what Sir James Munby has described as 'the ritual of considering anaemic allegations … and whether they do or do not amount to unreasonable behaviour', the process would be cleaner, less emotionally harmful to the parties and more expeditious.

Whether, and if so, the extent to which, these challenges are met will hinge as much on governmental attitudes as opinion within the legal profession and judiciary.

Common Pitfalls

A common pitfall in answer to a question like this is falling into the temptation to be over-recitative of changes without being properly explanatory about why those changes were introduced and how the changes sought to overcome the previous difficulties.

Aim Higher

Excellent answers will include wider contextual features of the family justice system. For example, an enhanced transparency is also a feature of the new system. In January 2014, Lord Justice Munby published *Practice Guidance: Transparency in the Family Courts: Publication of Judgments* on publication of judgments for judges in the Family Courts. The aim of the Guidance, which came into effect in February 2014, is to improve public understanding of the court process and confidence in the court system. The Guidance will have the effect of increasing the number of judgments available for publication.

7

Judges and Juries

JUDGES

Judges obviously occupy a central role in the legal system with regard to both civil and criminal law and, for that reason, questions about the judiciary are found in most examination papers on English legal system courses. There are, across all the ranks, 3,800 judges in England and Wales, and 30,000 magistrates. It is frequently claimed that judges represent the views of a highly limited section of society, being mainly white, middle-aged men. The point to consider, however, is whether this social placement has a deleterious effect on the decisions that the judges make. If judges are simply the mouthpieces of the law and their decisions represent no more than the automatic outcome of a strictly logical process of reasoning, then the actual social situation and background of the judge is immaterial, for the decisions are contained in the law itself. If, on the other hand, legal reasoning is not as prescriptive as outsiders generally consider it to be and judges actually have a substantial measure of discretion in the way in which they reach their decisions, then the social placement of the judiciary does become a matter to be critically analysed with regard to the decisions that they reach. Law becomes not the expression of some imminent authority, but the expression of individual and, perhaps more importantly, group prejudice.

For the above reasons, it is important to avoid reliance on superficial and anecdotal assertions as to the lack of awareness of judges, in favour of a reasoned and well-supported critique of the nature of legal reasoning, before attention is focused on the social background of the judiciary. The answers offered in this chapter locate weaknesses in the process of legal reasoning as of central importance and, indeed, as prior to any critical understanding of how judges operate.

JURIES

The role of the jury in the English legal system is the subject of contentious debate. You should be familiar with recent research on this theme and some particular questions which have been addressed by researchers: for instance, how often do juries return 'perverse' verdicts, and are such practices desirable? Are juries capable of properly following the details of complex trials? Be careful to observe how much the question you are answering requires a factual account or explanation of procedure, as opposed to evaluative, argumentative material. In any event, you will need a good knowledge of the legal and historical aspects of the jury in order to be able to rehearse the controversial parts of this topic.

In 2010, a major empirical study found that juries virtually always acted in a fair way. The research, conducted by Professor Cheryl Thomas at University College London, *Are Juries Fair?*, is the most in-depth study into the issue ever undertaken in the UK (available at: www.justice.gov.uk/publications/are-juries-fair.htm).

One contemporary issue of particular importance relates to the use information technology, by jurors researching cases on the internet and by members of the general public commentating on cases while trials are be conducted.

The **Criminal Justice Act 2003** contained provisions allowing for trials in cases of serious crime to take place without juries. The provision was to act as a safeguard against 'jury nobbling' – where jurors are intimidated or bribed into voting for an acquittal. Non-jury trials had been used in Northern Ireland in the 1970s during a period of civil strife when there were fears of jury nobbling, but outside of that situation cases of serious crime had been tried by juries for over four centuries. The power provided for in the **2003 Act** was not used until February 2010.

In the juryless trial, the judge acts as both judge and jury: he resolves matters of law and has to do 'mental gymnastics' (*The Times*, 1 April 2010), as one barrister put it, if he excludes evidence as inadmissible – trying to put it out of his mind and to pretend that he has never seen it. In a jury trial, the jury is sent out by the judge when there are technical legal arguments about controversial evidence and does not hear any evidence that has been excluded or even know that it has been excluded. After less than three months (about half the time a jury trial for such a complex case would have lasted) the defendants were found guilty by the single judge and given a range of sentences from life imprisonment to 15 years.

Checklist

You should be familiar with:

- the way in which judges are appointed and the role of the Lord Chancellor in their appointment;
- how judges can avoid the strict operation of precedent and their powers in relation to the interpretation of statutes;
- the difference between individual and corporate prejudice;
- the social background of the judiciary;
- possible ways of diminishing perceptions of judicial bias;
- the historical justification for trial by jury;
- the rules concerning eligibility (including disqualification and excusal);
- the powers of the prosecution and defence to alter the composition of the jury;
- the practice of jury vetting and issues of selection procedure and impartiality;
- the arguments for and against retaining the jury for criminal trials.

QUESTION 40

Evaluate the procedure for appointing members of the Supreme Court under the **Constitutional Reform Act 2005**.

How to Read this Question

This question is straightforward in that it requires an explanation of the specific procedure for appointing judges to the Supreme Court. The only tricky part of the question is the requirement for evaluation.

How to Answer this Question

This question requires candidates to evaluate the provisions in the **Constitutional Reform Act (CRA) 2005** in relation to the appointment of judges to the Supreme Court. It consequently requires candidates to explain the procedure for appointing its members. However, it should be noted that the key requirement in the question is 'evaluation'. It is not therefore simply a matter of describing the appointments procedure; some assessment of how it might function is also required, which in turn necessitates some critique of the previous system that the current procedure replaced.

A possible structure for dealing with the issues might be as follows:

- ❖ set out what were the perceived problems in the previous appointments procedure;
- ❖ detail the appointments procedure of the new system, focusing in particular upon the role of the Lord Chancellor;
- ❖ offer some evaluation, even if limited, of the new system.

Answer Structure

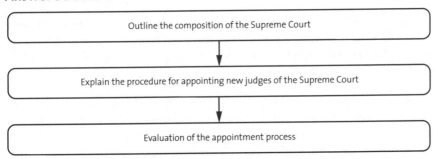

Outline the composition of the Supreme Court

Explain the procedure for appointing new judges of the Supreme Court

Evaluation of the appointment process

ANSWER

Section 23 of the **CRA 2005** established the Supreme Court of the United Kingdom, and set out its composition[1] as being made up of 12 judges, appointed by the Queen. One of the judges is President and one Deputy President of the court. **Sub-section 23(6)** provided

---

1   This demonstrates that the need to provide some description of the composition of the new court prior to attempting to evaluate the procedure for appointing new members has been recognised.

that the judges of the Supreme Court, apart from the President of the Supreme Court and the Deputy President of the Supreme Court, will be called 'Justices of the Supreme Court'.

Section 24 provided for the first judges of the Supreme Court to be the Lords of Appeal in Ordinary holding office at the date of commencement, i.e. the members of the former House of Lords. Thus was continuity maintained, as the members of what was the House of Lords became the first justices of the new Supreme Court when the Supreme Court opened for business in the newly refurbished Middlesex Guildhall building on 1 October 2009.

In the past, criticism has been made of the way in which judges were appointed to the House of Lords, and indeed at any level in the judicial hierarchy. It was suggested that the appointments were, to say the least, lacking in transparency and subject to the control of the judiciary and the senior members of the legal profession. As a consequence of the secret nature of the 'soundings' that were taken on candidates and their perceived right of veto, it was sometimes suggested that the senior judiciary constituted a self-selecting oligarchy. In response to such criticism, the Supreme Court has its own independent appointments system.

Appointment of Judges to the Supreme Court

As regards future appointments to the Supreme Court, **s 25** sets out two possible routes to qualification. These are:[2]

(1) having held high judicial office for at least two years;
(2) having been a qualifying practitioner for at least 15 years.

Although appointment to office is by the Crown, **ss 26, 27, 28, 29, 30** and **31** and **Sched 8 CRA 2005** set out the procedure for appointing a member of the Supreme Court.

The Lord Chancellor must convene an ad hoc selection commission if there is, or is likely to be, a vacancy. Subsequently, the Lord Chancellor will notify the Prime Minister of the identity of the person selected by that commission, and under **s 26(4)**, the Prime Minister *must* recommend the appointment of that person to the Queen.

Schedule 8 contains the rules governing the composition and operation of the selection commission, which will consist of the President of the Supreme Court, who will chair the commission, the Deputy President of the Supreme Court and one member from each of the territorial judicial appointment commissions (see below), one of whom must be a person who is not legally qualified. The next most senior ordinary judge in the Supreme Court will take the unfilled position on the selection commission if either the President or Deputy President is unable to sit.

Section 27 sets out the process which must be followed in the selection of a justice of the Supreme Court. The commission decides the particular selection process to be applied,

....

2   As the question demands evaluation of the procedure for appointing judges, it is important to describe the procedure before attempting any evaluation.

the criteria or competences against which candidates will be assessed, but in any event the requirement is that any selection must be made solely on merit. However, **sub-s 27(8)** does require that the commission must take into account the need for the Court to have among its judges generally at least two Scottish judges and usually one from Northern Ireland. The Lord Chancellor, as provided for by **sub-s 27(9)**, may issue non-binding guidance to the commission about the vacancy that has arisen, for example on the jurisdictional requirements of the Court, to which the commission must have regard.

Under **sub-ss 27(2)** and **(3)** the commission is required to consult:

- ❖ senior judges who are neither on the commission nor willing to be considered for selection;
- ❖ the Lord Chancellor;
- ❖ the First Minister in Scotland;
- ❖ the Assembly First Secretary in Wales;
- ❖ the Secretary of State for Northern Ireland.

Sub-section 28(1) provides that after a selection has been made the commission must submit a report nominating one candidate to the Lord Chancellor, who then must also consult the senior judges (or other judges) who were consulted by the commission, the First Minister in Scotland, the Assembly First Secretary in Wales and the Secretary of State for Northern Ireland.

Section 29 sets out the Lord Chancellor's options after he has received a name from the commission and carried out the further consultation under s 28.

The procedure may be divided into three possible stages:

Stage 1: where a person has been selected and recommended by the appointments commission. At this stage the Lord Chancellor may:

- ❖ accept the nomination and notify the Prime Minister;
- ❖ reject the selection;
- ❖ require the commission to reconsider its selection.

Stage 2: where a person has been selected following a rejection or reconsideration at stage 1. In this event the Lord Chancellor can:

- ❖ accept the nomination and notify the Prime Minister;
- ❖ reject the selection but only if it was made following a reconsideration at stage 1;
- ❖ require the commission to reconsider the selection but only if it was made following a rejection at stage 1.

Stage 3: where a person has been selected following a rejection or reconsideration at stage 2. At this point, the Lord Chancellor *must* accept the nomination unless he prefers to accept a candidate who had previously been reconsidered but not subsequently recommended for a second time.

In effect this means that the Lord Chancellor's options are as follows. He can:

❖ accept the recommendation of the commission;
❖ ask the commission to reconsider; or
❖ reject the recommendation.

Where the Lord Chancellor requires the commission to *reconsider* its original selection, the commission can still put forward the same name with additional justifications for its selection. In such circumstance the Lord Chancellor will either accept the recommendation or reject it. Alternatively the commission can recommend another candidate, whom the Lord Chancellor can accept, reject or require reconsideration of.

However, if the Lord Chancellor *rejects* the original name provided by the selection commission, it must submit an alternative candidate giving reasons for their choice. At this point the Lord Chancellor can either:

❖ accept the second candidate; or
❖ ask the selection commission to reconsider.

On reconsideration the commission can either resubmit the second candidate or propose an alternative candidate. At this point the Lord Chancellor must make a choice. He can either accept the alternative candidate or he can then choose the reconsidered candidate.

Under **sub-s 30(1)**, the Lord Chancellor's right of rejection is only exercisable where in his opinion the person selected is not suitable for the office concerned. The right to require reconsideration is exercisable under three conditions:

❖ where he feels there is not enough evidence that the person is suitable for office;
❖ where he feels there is not enough evidence that person is the best candidate on merit; or
❖ where there is not enough evidence that the judges of the Court will between them have enough knowledge of, and experience in, the laws of each part of the United Kingdom, following the new appointment.

Should the Lord Chancellor exercise either of these options he must provide the commission with his reasons in writing (s 30(3)).

While it can be seen that the appointment commission for the Supreme Court will be specifically convened for its purpose, all other judicial appointments will be made under the auspices of a new independent judicial appointments commission, which it is hoped will remove the criticisms levelled at the previous appointments process, that it too lacked openness. In conclusion, while the proposed system of appointment certainly appears more open than the system that preceded it, how it operates in practice remains to be seen.[3]

....

3   Clear evidence of evaluation of the new procedure.

Common Pitfalls

❖ It should be noted that the former Law Lords have moved premises and become Justices of the Supreme Court. The House of Lords, as a chamber of Parliament, still exists, but it no longer houses the highest court in the English legal system.

❖ It should be remembered that there is a particular ad hoc process for appointment to the Supreme Court.

Aim Higher

❖ Look to locate the emergence of the Supreme Court in the context of the doctrine of the separation of powers.

❖ Be prepared to explain the structure/membership of the Supreme Court.

❖ Be able to explain the distinct process of appointment to the Supreme Court in some detail.

QUESTION 41

Why does the social composition of the judiciary matter?

How to Read this Question

This question is short but involves a consideration of apparently non-legal information. It is the type of question that asks candidates to consider whether the particular class/race/gender background of the judges leads to a bias in their decisions. It has assumed a contemporary importance given the continued increase in judicial review and the incorporation of the **European Convention on Human Rights (ECHR)** into UK law, in the form of the **Human Rights Act (HRA) 1998**. This question still requires a reference to the late Professor Griffith's views in *The Politics of the Judiciary*, 5th edn, 1997.

How to Answer this Question

A good answer might take the following form:

❖ examine the actual constitution of the judiciary, referring to any available statistics;

❖ consider why the composition of the judiciary matters, paying particular regard to judicial review and the **HRA 1998**;

❖ refer to Professor Griffith's claim as to the biased nature of the judiciary;

❖ adduce an argument to the contrary;

❖ offer some proposals as to how the perceived problems might be remedied.

Answer Structure

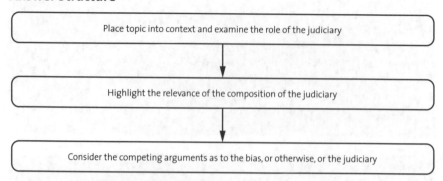

Place topic into context and examine the role of the judiciary

Highlight the relevance of the composition of the judiciary

Consider the competing arguments as to the bias, or otherwise, or the judiciary

ANSWER

Central to the general idea of the rule of law is the specific proposition that it involves the rule of *law*, rather than the rule of *people*. From this perspective, judges are seen as subservient to, and merely the instruments of, the law; and the outcome of the judicial process is understood as being determined through the straightforward application of legal rules, both statute and precedent, to particular factual situations. In applying those rules, the judge is expected to act in a completely impartial manner, without allowing his personal preferences to affect his decision in any way. A further assumption is that in reaching a decision, the judge is only concerned with matters of law and refuses to permit politics, economics or other non-legal matters to influence his decision. The law is assumed to be distinct from, and superior to, those non-legal issues and the assumption is that the judge operates, in the words of Professor JAG Griffith, as a 'political, economic and social eunuch'. In reality, however, judges have a large measure of discretion in determining which laws to apply, what those laws actually mean and how to apply them. Equally, judges are by necessity involved in political issues when they are called upon to provide judicial review of the actions of the state and its functionaries. Although some judges have denied the political nature of such decisions, others have actually welcomed and justified the growth in judicial review, on the grounds that it permits the judiciary to protect individuals from the abuse of the power by what they perceive as an over-mighty state and an otherwise uncontrolled executive. This overtly political role, which sets the courts up against the state, has been increased by the enactment of the **HRA 1998** which effectively places the courts in the position of acting as the protectors of individual rights from incursions by the state. Although the Act expressly declines to challenge the supremacy of Parliament by denying the courts the power to strike down particular legislation as being unconstitutional, it does permit them to make declarations to the effect that such legislation is incompatible with the human rights protected under the Act. Such declarations, and there are bound to be some, if not many, will inevitably place the judiciary in a political, not to say confrontational, relationship with Parliament.[4]

---

4   Here the topic is put into context and the non-legal role of the judiciary is highlighted.

In the light of this potential creative power, it is essential to ensure that the judiciary satis-factorily represents society at large, in relation to which it has so much power, and to ensure further that it does not merely represent the views and attitudes of a self-perpetuating elite. This desideratum could be reformulated in the form of a stark question: Are judges biased, and do they use their judicial positions in such a way as to give expression to that bias?[5]

Bias can operate at two levels. The first is personal bias and occurs where individual judges permit their own prejudices to influence their understanding and implementation of the law. Such bias is a serious matter and reprehensible, but the very fact that it is indi-vidual makes it more open to control and, in the long run, less serious than the accusation of corporate bias that some observers, such as Professor Griffith, level against the judi-ciary. Corporate prejudice involves the assertion that the judiciary, as a body, do not decide certain types of cases in a fair and unbiased way; rather that as a consequence of their shared educational experience, shared training and practical experience at the Bar, along with shared social status, they have developed a common ideology comprising a homogeneous collection of values, attitudes and beliefs as to how the law should operate and be administered. The claim is that because, as individuals, they share the same preju-dices, this leads to the emergence of an in-built group prejudice which precludes the pos-sibility of some cases being decided in a neutral way.

The essence of Griffith's argument is that judges in the UK are in the position of being required to make political choices in the many cases that come before them which require a determination of public interest. This situation will necessarily become more frequent as the judges are required, under the **HRA 1998**, to weigh individual rights against public interest. His further point is that in determining what constitutes the public interest, the judges give expression to their own values, which are in turn a product of their position in society as part of the Establishment, the group in society which is the location of estab-lished authority.

It is claimed that the most obvious examples of the judiciary's overzealous solicitude for the state's interests occur when those interests come into conflict with individual inter-ests or the right to public information. Griffith claims that in such cases, the courts will tend to give undue preference to the state and cites various examples, such as the unilat-eral withdrawal of rights of trade union representation at the GCHQ and the total ban on publication of extracts from the *Spycatcher* book being simply the most recent of a number of notorious cases demonstrating the courts' readiness to promote the interests of the state and the Government above those of the individual.

It is hardly surprising to find that Professor Griffith's attack on the judiciary has met with opposition.[6] One notable response (and presumed rebuttal) was provided by Lord Devlin

....

5   Examples are provided as a means of demonstrating the competing pressures which the judiciary may find itself under, highlighting the importance of the composition of the judiciary.

6   A balanced argument is provided by considering not only Prof Griffith's arguments but also those of Lord Devlin.

in a review article on Griffith's book, *The Politics of the Judiciary* (1978) 41 MLR 51. Lord Devlin pointed out that in most cases, and on most issues, there tended to be plurality rather than unanimity of opinion and decision among judges. He also explained any apparent Conservative bias on the part of judges as a product of age rather than class and that in any case, even if the judiciary were biased, its bias was well known and allowances could be made for it. It has to be stated that Lord Devlin's response is extremely complacent and, in the light of the alleged terrorist cases mentioned previously, worryingly so.

It is apparent that senior judges are still being appointed from the same limited social and educational elite[7] as they always have been and that this gives rise to the accusation, if not necessarily the reality, that the decisions made by this elite merely represent the interest of a limited and privileged segment of society, rather than society as a whole. It is arguable that even if the accusations of those commentators such as Professor Griffith are inaccurate, it remains appropriate and, indeed, essential that in order to remove even the possibility of those accusations, the present structure of the judiciary be examined and altered. It is to be hoped that the establishment of the Judicial Appointments Commission, with its control over the appointment of judiciary, will open up the whole process to much welcome scrutiny in the future. There is one further point that has to be considered in relation to Griffith's attack on the judiciary, and that is the fact that, with the advent of the **Human Rights Act 1998** and the New Labour Government of 1997, many on the political left appear to see the judges as the stalwart defenders of human rights in the face of an onslaught by the authoritarian state. This is particularly the case in relation to anti-terrorist legislation, which many see as draconian in its operation and effects.

QUESTION 42

Critically examine the law governing the circumstances in which judges should excuse themselves from presiding in a case because of a possible partiality.

How to Read this Question

This question involves a consideration of the circumstances under which judges should decline to sit in a particular case, i.e. when judges should recuse themselves. It is one of the rules of natural justice that a person should not be the judge in an action in which they have a personal interest, and the Latin expression of this rule, *nemo judex in causa sua*, goes back a long way.

How to Answer this Question

This question involves a consideration of the circumstances under which judges should decline to sit in a particular case. It is one of the rules of natural justice that a person should not be the judge in an action in which they have a personal interest, and the Latin expression of this rule, *nemo judex in causa sua*, goes back a long way. Answers should be able to provide an explanation of the historical context in which the question is set, but

---

7   The long-standing argument of the judiciary being from a very narrow class is discussed and the importance of not limiting selection to an elite section of society is highlighted.

the question really demands an examination of the contemporary situation, starting with the various actions relating to the application to extradite the former Chilean dictator Augusto Pinochet and going on to consider the *Locabail* (2000) action. A good answer might adopt the following structure:

❖ an explanation of the *nemo judex* rule citing cases that show how it has been applied in the past;

❖ an explanation of how the law understands bias as it affects the judiciary considering *R v Gough* (1993);

❖ a fairly detailed explanation of the facts and law in the *Pinochet* case (1999);

❖ a consideration of the post-*Pinochet* applications and the Court of Appeal's ruling in the *Locabail* case.

Answer Structure

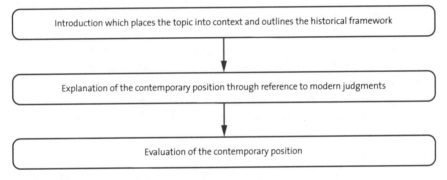

Introduction which places the topic into context and outlines the historical framework

Explanation of the contemporary position through reference to modern judgments

Evaluation of the contemporary position

ANSWER

The English legal system has a rule that no one may be a judge in their own cause, that is, they cannot judge a case in which they have an interest. This is sometimes known by the phrase *nemo judex in causa sua*. Thus, a judge who is a shareholder in a company appearing before him as a litigant must decline to hear the case (i.e. recuse themselves): *Dimes v Grand Junction Canal* (1852). Even if a judge is unaffected by his interest in coming to a decision, it would still be wrong to preside in such a case because it might look as if the judge was improperly swayed. Thus, in the famous *dictum* of Lord Hewart, it is of fundamental importance that 'Justice must not only be done but should manifestly and undoubtedly be seen to be done' (*R v Sussex JJ ex p McCarthy* (1924), at p. 259).[8]

This rule was given another dimension in *Re Pinochet Ugarte*.[9] General Pinochet, a former ruler of Chile, was in England on a visit when he was arrested for crimes of torture and mass killing allegedly orchestrated by him in Chile during the 1970s. His extradition had been requested by Spain. The legal question for the English courts was whether General Pinochet enjoyed a diplomatic immunity.

---

8 The introduction places the topic into context by illustrating the traditional approach of the courts.
9 Discussion of this case places the topic into a contemporary context.

His case was eventually rejected by the House of Lords (by a 3:2 majority) in November 1998. Pinochet's lawyers then alleged that the Lords' decision was invalid as one of the majority Law Lords, Lord Hoffmann, could not be seen to be impartial, because he had a connection with the organisation Amnesty International, which had been granted leave to intervene in the proceedings and had made representations to the Lords through counsel. Lord Hoffmann, at this time, was an unpaid director of the Amnesty International Charitable Trust. Amnesty International was in favour of General Pinochet being brought to trial. In January 1999, on an appeal brought by Pinochet, another panel of Law Lords set aside the decision of the earlier hearing on the basis that no one should be a judge in his own cause.

Whereas previously, only pecuniary or proprietary interests had led to automatic disqualification, the House of Lords held that if the absolute impartiality of the judiciary was to be maintained, there had to be a rule which automatically disqualified a judge who was involved, whether personally or as a director of a company, in promoting the same causes in the same organisation as was a party to the suit.

Following a number of other cases in which lawyers sought to challenge a judgment on the grounds that, through a social interest or remote financial connection, the judge was potentially biased, the Court of Appeal gave authoritative guidance on this area in *Locabail (UK) Ltd v Bayfield Properties Ltd and Another* (2000). In respect of five decisions in which the judge's impartiality was questioned, the Court of Appeal ruled on general principles as follows:

(a)   a judge who allowed his judicial decision to be influenced by partiality or prejudice deprived a litigant of the right to a fair trial by an impartial tribunal, and violated a most fundamental principle on which the administration of justice rested;

(b)   the most effective protection of his right was, in practice, afforded by disqualification and setting aside a decision where real danger of bias was established;

(c)   every such case depended on its particular facts, real doubt being resolved in favour of disqualification. It would, however, be as wrong for a judge to accede to a tenuous objection as it would be for him to ignore one of substance;

(d)   in determination of their rights and liabilities, civil or criminal, everyone was entitled to a fair hearing by an impartial tribunal.

The Court of Appeal ruled that there was one situation where, on proof of the requisite facts, the existence of bias was effectively presumed and, in such cases, it gave rise to automatic disqualification, namely, where the judge was shown to have an interest in the outcome of the case which he was to decide or had decided: see *Dimes v Proprietors of the Grand Junction Canal* (1852), *R v Rand* (1866) and *R v Camborne Justices ex p Pearce* (1955).

In *R v Gough* (1993) the House of Lords had stated that the relevant test for recusal was whether there was, in relation to any given judge, a 'real danger' or possibility of bias.[10] When applying the real danger test, it would often be appropriate to inquire whether the

---

10 This case is important as it sets out the circumstances in which a judge is required to excuse him/herself.

judge knew of the matter relied on as appearing to undermine his impartiality. If it were shown that he did not, the danger of its having influenced his judgment was eliminated and the appearance of possible bias dispelled. It was for the reviewing court, not the judge concerned, to assess the risk that some illegitimate extraneous consideration might have influenced his decision. However, in *Director General of Fair Trading v Proprietary Association of Great Britain (re Medicaments and Related Classes of Goods (No 2))* (2001) the Court of Appeal took the opportunity to refine the common law test as established in *R v Gough*. Previously, the court determining the issue had itself decided whether there had been a real danger of bias in the inferior tribunal. Subsequently, in line with the jurisprudence of the **ECtHR**, the test was to be whether a fair-minded observer would conclude that there was a real possibility of bias. In other words, the test moved from being a subjective test on the part of the court to an objective test from the perspective of the fair-minded observer. This approach was adopted by the House of Lords in *Lawal v Northern Spirit Ltd* (2003), stating that 'public perception of the possibility of unconscious bias is the key' for determining whether the judges should recuse themselves or not.

In *Locabail* the court expressed the view that it would be dangerous and futile to attempt to define or list factors which might, or might not, give rise to a real danger of bias, since everything would depend on the particular facts, could not conceive of circumstances in which an objection could be soundly based on the religion, ethnic or national origin, gender, age, class, means or sexual orientation of the judge. Nor, at any rate ordinarily, could an objection be soundly based on his social, educational, service or employment background or history, nor that of any member of his family; nor previous political associations, membership of social, sporting or charitable bodies; nor Masonic associations; nor previous judicial decisions; nor extra-curricular utterances, whether in textbooks, lectures, speeches, articles, interviews, reports, responses to consultation papers; nor previous receipt of instructions to act for or against any party, solicitor or advocate engaged in a case before him; nor membership of the same Inn, circuit, local Law Society or chambers.[11]

By contrast, a real danger of bias might well be thought to arise if there were personal friendship or animosity between the judge and any member of the public involved in the case; or if the judge were closely acquainted with any such member of the public, particularly if that individual's credibility could be significant in the decision of the case; or if in a case where the credibility of any individual were an issue to be decided by the judge, he had, in a previous case, rejected that person's evidence in such outspoken terms as to throw doubt on his ability to approach such a person's evidence with an open mind on any later occasion.

Common Pitfalls

Bias or apparent bias can occur through a political association in some contexts. It is a common pitfall among poor answers to omit from discussion cases such as *Re Pinochet Ugarte* (1999), which examine the political aspects of apparent bias.

....
11 The question clearly asks for critical evaluation, which is provided by such discussion.

Aim Higher

The Court of Appeal decision in *Locabail (UK) Ltd v Bayfield Properties Ltd and Another* (2000) added many dimensions of subtlety to the rules governing when a judge should recuse himself or herself from a case; an excellent answer will identify and explain these rules.

QUESTION 43

Critically examine the way juries are empanelled.

How to Read this Question

The key word in this question is 'critically'. Such wording does not invite the candidate to 'rubbish' the jury selection process; rather it requires them to engage in an impartial assessment of that process, focusing on both the merits and demerits of the system.

How to Answer this Question

This particular question asks for attention to be focused on the process of empanelling a jury, rather than the jury system generally, and seeks to elicit information about how the composition is determined and how it can be interfered with. The following procedure would address those issues:

- ❖ detail the process whereby a jury is actually selected, distinguishing between 'panels of jurors' and juries;
- ❖ consider how random this process is in practice;
- ❖ consider the need for racially mixed juries and whether randomness is always fair;
- ❖ consider rights of the defence and prosecution to challenge potential jurors;
- ❖ explain the process of jury vetting and consider its general legitimacy;
- ❖ offer a conclusion as to whether randomness is fundamentally necessary or, indeed, valuable per se.

Answer Structure

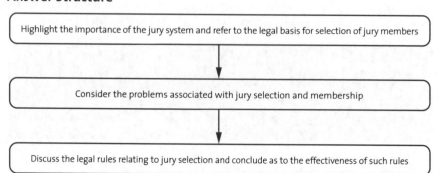

Highlight the importance of the jury system and refer to the legal basis for selection of jury members

Consider the problems associated with jury selection and membership

Discuss the legal rules relating to jury selection and conclude as to the effectiveness of such rules

ANSWER

The procedure for determining the actual composition of the jury to hear any particular case is as follows. An officer of the court summonses a randomly selected number of qualified individuals and, from that group, draws up panels of potential jurors for various cases. The actual jurors are then randomly selected, by means of a ballot in open court.

The **Juries Act 1974**, as amended by the **Criminal Justice Act 1988**, the **Criminal Justice and Public Order Act 1994** and the **Criminal Justice Act 2003**, sets out the law relating to juries.[12] It provides that any person between the ages of 18 and 70, who is on the electoral register and who has lived in the UK for at least five years, is qualified to serve as a juror. The dependency on electoral rolls to determine and locate jurors, however, raises a very real shortfall from the ideal assumptions made in relation to the jury system. The problem arises from the fact that electoral registers tend to be inaccurate. Generally, they have misreported the number of young people who are in an area, due to the fact that such people tend to have a greater degree of mobility than older people and, as a result, tend not to appear on the electoral roll of the place they currently live in. Electoral registers have also under-reported the true number of members of ethnic minorities, who have simply declined to notify the authorities of their existence.

Prior to the **Criminal Justice Act (CJA) 2003**, the general qualification for serving as a juror was subject to a number of exceptions.

For example, a number of people were deemed to be ineligible to serve on juries on the basis of their employment or vocation. Among this category were judges, justices of the peace, members of the legal profession, police and probation officers, and members of the clergy or religious orders. Those suffering from a mental disorder were also deemed to be ineligible. **Paragraph 2** of **Sched 33** to the CJA 2003 removed the first three groups of persons ineligible, the judiciary, others concerned with the administration of justice and the clergy, leaving only mentally disordered persons with that status.

In an endeavour to maintain the unquestioned probity of the jury system, certain categories of persons are disqualified from serving as jurors. Among these is anyone who has been sentenced to a term of imprisonment, or youth custody, of five years or more.

Certain people were excused as of right from serving as jurors on account of their jobs, age or religious views. Among these were members of the medical professions, Members of Parliament and members of the armed forces, together with anyone over 65 years of age. **Paragraph 3** of **Sched 33** to the CJA repeals s9(1) of the **Juries Act 1974** and consequently no one will in future be entitled to excusal as of right from jury service. However, it remains the case that a person may avoid jury service if they can show that there is a 'good reason' why their summons should be deferred or excused.

---

12 Demonstrates knowledge of the legal basis of the composition of juries and goes on to highlight important aspects of eligibility and selection.

The traditional procedure for determining the composition of the jury was improved by the introduction of a central summoning bureau, based at Blackfriars Crown Court Centre in London.[13] The new bureau uses a computer system to select jurors at random from the electoral registers and issues the summonses, as well as dealing with jurors' questions and requests. The aim of the new procedure is to ensure that all jurors are treated equally and fairly and that the rules are enforced consistently, especially in regard to requests to be excused from service.

Under s12(6) of the **Juries Act 1974**, both prosecution and defence have a right to challenge the array, where the summoning officer has acted improperly in bringing the whole panel together. Such challenges are rare, although an unsuccessful action was raised in the *Danvers case* (1982).

As regards individuals, the defence until fairly recently had the right to issue peremptory challenges, that is, challenges without reason, to potential jury members, up to a maximum of three. In spite of arguments for its retention on a civil liberties basis, the right was abolished in the **Criminal Justice Act 1988**. The defence, however, still has the power to challenge any number of potential jurors for cause, that is, with reason; however, following the attempt of the defence to exclude numerous classes of people from the jury in the *Angry Brigade* trial in 1972, the Lord Chief Justice issued a Practice Direction in which it was laid down that potential jurors were not to be excluded on account of race, religion, politics or occupation.

In *Danvers*, the defence had sought to challenge the array on the basis that a black defendant could not have complete confidence in the impartiality of an all-white jury. The question of the racial mix of a jury has exercised the courts on a number of occasions. In *Ford* (1989), the trial judge's refusal to accept the defendant's application for a racially mixed jury was supported by the Court of Appeal, on the grounds that 'fairness is achieved by the principle of random selection', as regards the make-up of a jury, and that to insist on a racially balanced jury would be contrary to that principle and would be to imply that particular jurors were incapable of impartiality.

Of perhaps even more concern than challenges by the defence is the extent to which the prosecution can challenge potential jurors for, in addition to the right to challenge for cause, the prosecution also has the option of excluding particular individuals simply by asking them to 'stand by' until a jury has been empanelled. The manifest unreasonableness of this procedure, in view of the limited power of the defence, led to the Attorney-General issuing a *Practice Note* ([1988] 3 All ER 1086) to the effect that the Crown should only exercise its power to stand down potential jurors in the following two circumstances:

(a) to prevent the empanelment of a 'manifestly unsuitable' juror;
(b) where the Attorney-General has approved the vetting of the potential jury members, and that process has revealed that a particular juror might be a security risk, and the Attorney-General has approved the use of the 'stand by' procedure.

....

13 Demonstrates up-to-date knowledge.

This latter point leads, naturally, to another contentious subject, that of jury 'vetting', the process in which the Crown checks the background of potential jurors. The practice of vetting potential jurors developed after *Angry Brigade* (1972), but did not become public until the **Official Secrets Act** case, known as the *ABC Trial*, in 1978. Subsequently, the Attorney-General published the guidelines for vetting panels. The most recent guidelines were published in 1988 and, interestingly, they support the general propositions that jury members should normally be selected randomly from the panel and should be disqualified only on the grounds set out in the **Juries Act 1974**. The guidelines do, however, make reference to exceptional cases of public importance where potential jury members might properly be vetted. Such cases are broadly identified as those involving national security, where part of the evidence may be heard *in camera*, and terrorist cases.

In conclusion, therefore, it can be seen that juries are by and large random, subject to some particular and important shortcomings. However, as has been suggested above, randomness is not necessarily a virtue in itself, especially if it leads to ethnically unrepresentative juries.

QUESTION 44

Assess the impact of the **Criminal Justice Act (CJA) 2003** on who can be required to attend for jury service.

How to Read this Question

This question is not difficult in itself, but if you have not prepared for it, there is simply no way in which you can answer it: there is no way a candidate could bluff their way through the detail required in the question. Examiners set these closed questions as ways of requiring candidates to cover a whole syllabus and effectively punishing those candidates who have indulged in the very risky game of 'question spotting'. Many examples of 'nice' open questions have been provided in this text, but it has to be remembered that most exams will contain questions such as this. The advice is, if you don't know the material required, don't attempt the question. Move on to something you do know more about.

How to Answer this Question

This question requires respondents to consider the changes in requirements for jury service introduced by the **CJA 2003**, but that in turn requires a consideration of the very important case of *R v Abdroikov* (2005), in which the House of Lords used its powers under the **Human Rights Act (HRA) 1998** to effectively overturn the expressly stated will of Parliament. A possible structure for answering the question would be as follows:

- ❖ an introduction explaining the previous system and its inherent shortcomings;
- ❖ a detailed account of the provisions introduced by the **CJA 2003**;
- ❖ in relation to eligibility, reference *must* be made to *R v Abdroikov* (2005);
- ❖ the best answers will make some comment on the use of the courts' powers under the **HRA 1988** to avoid express statutory provisions.

Answer Structure

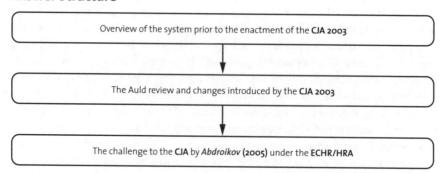

Overview of the system prior to the enactment of the **CJA 2003**

The Auld review and changes introduced by the **CJA 2003**

The challenge to the **CJA** by *Abdroikov* **(2005)** under the **ECHR/HRA**

ANSWER

Prior to the **CJA 2003**, the general qualification for serving as a juror was subject to a number of exceptions and as a result it had been suggested that jury service almost amounted to a self-selecting system, under which those who did not wish to serve were under no real compulsion to do so, just as long as they could provide a reason for not serving. Following the recommendations of the Auld review of the criminal justice system in 2001, the Government enacted the **CJA 2003** with the declared intention of not only increasing the numbers of people who would in future be required to serve as jurors, but also limiting the available excuses for not serving. However, as will be seen below, these intentions have been effectively undermined by the judges of the House of Lords.[14]

Ineligibility

A variety of people were deemed to be ineligible to serve on juries on the basis of their employment or vocation. Among this category were: judges, Justices of the Peace, members of the legal profession, police and probation officers and members of the clergy or religious orders. Those suffering from a mental disorder were also deemed to be ineligible. **Paragraph 2** of **Sched 33** to the **CJA 2003** removed the first three groups of ineligible persons, the judiciary, others concerned with the administration of justice, and the clergy, leaving only mentally disordered persons with that status.

The above reform came into effect in April 2005. However, the eligibility provisions of the **CJA 2003** were challenged, as being contrary to **Art 6** of the **European Convention on Human Rights**, in *R v (1) Abdroikov (2) Green (3) Williamson* (2005),[15] three otherwise unrelated cases. Each of the appellants appealed against their convictions on the grounds that the jury in their respective trials had contained members who were employed in the criminal justice system. The juries in the trials of the first and second appellants had contained serving police officers. The jury in the trial of the third appellant had contained a person employed as a prosecuting solicitor by the Crown Prosecution Service (CPS). Their proposal was that, as prior to the **CJA 2003** there would have

....

14 Highlights the pre-**CJA** system and the background to its introduction.
15 Consideration of the challenge to the changes introduced by the **CJA** made under the **ECHR/HRA**.

been no doubt that the presence of such people on juries would have been unlawful, so their presence in the current cases ran contrary to the need for trials to be free from even the taint of apparent bias.

The Court of Appeal rejected such arguments as spurious, holding that the expectations placed on ordinary citizens in relation to jury service had to be extended to members of the criminal justice system. However, by a majority of three to two the House of Lords held that the appeals of Green and Williamson should succeed, but that Abdroikov's appeal must fail. Lords Rodger and Carswell, in the minority, held that all appeals should fail. In reaching its decision the majority looked at the reports of previous committees which had been tasked with examining the operation of juries. Thus they referred to the findings of the 1965 committee chaired by Lord Morris of Borth-y-Gest which recommended that the police and those professionally concerned in the administration of the law should continue to be ineligible. Then in 2001, Auld LJ reviewed the issue and recommended that everyone should be eligible for jury service save for the mentally ill. He recognised that the risk of bias could not be totally eradicated and envisaged that any question about the risk of bias on the part of any juror could be resolved by the trial judge on the facts of the case. His recommendation was given effect by the **CJA 2003 s 321**. However, as the House of Lords made clear, Auld LJ's expectation that each doubtful case would be resolved by the trial judge could not be met if neither the judge nor counsel knew that the juror was a police officer or CPS solicitor. The House of Lords recognised that there were situations where police officers and CPS solicitors would meet the tests of impartiality; however, that did not mean they would always do so or do so automatically.

Disqualification

In an endeavour to maintain the unquestioned probity of the jury system, certain categories of persons are disqualified from serving as jurors. Among these are anyone who has been sentenced to a term of imprisonment, or youth custody, of five years or more. In addition, anyone who, in the past ten years, has served a sentence, or has had a suspended sentence imposed on them, or has had a community punishment order made against them, is also disqualified. The **CJA 2003** makes a number of amendments to reflect recent and forthcoming developments in sentencing legislation. Thus, juveniles sentenced under **s 91** of the **Powers of Criminal Courts (Sentencing) Act 2000** to detention for life, or for a term of five years or more, will be disqualified for life from jury service. People sentenced to imprisonment or detention for public protection, or to an extended sentence under **s 227** or **s 228** of the Act, are also to be disqualified for life from jury service. Anyone who has received a community order (as defined in **s 177** of the Act) will be disqualified from jury service for ten years. Those on bail in criminal proceedings are disqualified from serving as a juror in the Crown Court.

Excusal

Certain people were excused as of right from serving as jurors on account of their jobs, age or religious views. Among these were members of the medical professions, Members of Parliament and members of the armed forces, together with anyone over 65 years of age. **Paragraph 3 of Sched 33** to the **CJA 2003** repeals s 9(1) of the **Juries Act (JA) 1974** and consequently no one will in future be entitled to excusal as of right from jury service.

It has always been the case that if a person who has been summoned to do jury service could show that there was a 'good reason' why their summons should be deferred or excused, s 9 of the JA 1974 provided discretion to defer or excuse service. With the abolition of most of the categories of ineligibility and of the availability of excusal as of right, it is expected that there will be a corresponding increase in applications for excusal or deferral under s 9 being submitted to the Jury Central Summoning Bureau (see below).

Grounds for such excusal or deferral are supposed to be made only on the basis of good reason, but there is at least a measure of doubt as to the rigour with which such rules are applied.

A Practice Note issued in 1988 (now *Practice Direction (Criminal: Consolidated)* (2002), para 42) stated that applications for excusal should be treated sympathetically and listed the following as good grounds for excusal:

(a) personal involvement in the case;
(b) close connection with a party or a witness in the case;
(c) personal hardship;
(d) conscientious objection to jury service.

However, a new s 9AA, introduced by the CJA 2003, places a statutory duty on the Lord Chancellor, in whom current responsibility for jury summoning is vested, to publish and lay before Parliament guidelines relating to the exercise by the Jury Central Summoning Bureau of its functions in relation to discretionary deferral and excusal.

The aim of the guidelines should be to ensure that all jurors are treated equally and fairly and that the rules are enforced consistently, especially in regard to requests to be excused from service, and thus to reduce at least some of the potential difficulties mentioned above.

8 Alternative Dispute Resolution

INTRODUCTION

This part of the English legal system has undergone significant development in recent times. English Legal System courses tend to focus too much attention on the operation of the traditional court system. While the courts are of fundamental importance, one should not overlook the increasing importance of alternative methods of deciding disputes. It should never be forgotten that tribunals actually deal with more cases than the county courts and High Court combined. The use of specialist tribunals to decide problems has a long history in England, but it has to be realised that the huge growth in the number of tribunals is a product of the growth of the interventionist welfare state and represents, at one level, an attack on the traditional legal system. These alternative mechanisms may also be seen as highlighting the weaknesses in the adversarial court system, in that they emphasise conciliation over conflict and, to that extent at least, they may well represent an advance on the traditional system of dispute resolution. It should also be borne in mind, however, that such informal procedures themselves are not without weaknesses.

Litigation is an extremely costly procedure. This is so not just for the parties concerned in any action who have to pay the costs of their legal representatives, but also for the state which has to provide the legal framework within which the action is taken, that is, courts, judges and other staff. This has been a great impetus for potential litigants to resort to alternative dispute resolution (ADR) and, in particular, to mediation – the use of a neutral third party to assist the disputants to reach a compromise. Most civil cases are settled at the door of the court, but by the time they arrive there, most parties have spent much time and money. Mediation aims to encourage disputants to reach such an agreement earlier. One private mediation company, Mediation UK, already mediates in over 5,000 neighbour disputes a year.

Checklist

You should:

- have at least a minimal understanding of the social historical process that has seen the substantial development of tribunals;
- have particular knowledge of the operation of a substantial number of tribunals;
- be able to compare the advantages and disadvantages of alternative dispute resolutions, as against traditional court mechanisms;

- be able to distinguish and write about arbitration, mediation and conciliation;
- be prepared to answer a specific question relating to the **Arbitration Act 1996**;
- be prepared to answer a question on the county court small claims procedure (this may stand you in good stead for questions on court structure or civil procedure as well).

QUESTION 45

Explain the operation of tribunals as alternatives to the court system.

How to Read this Question

This is a straightforward question that really invites candidates to provide a standard answer, but it should always be remembered that questions can be much more demanding than this one. For example, although this particular question would benefit from mention of the **Tribunals, Courts and Enforcement Act (TCEA) 2007**, it could be answered adequately without it. Alternative questions might well focus on the Act, and in that case such general answers as this one would be worthless.

How to Answer this Question

This question invites a relatively straightforward comparison of tribunals and courts, but would benefit from some knowledge of the proposals to reform the operation of tribunals. The answer should include at least some of the following points:

- ❖ consideration of the usual advantages cited for tribunals – cheapness, speed and informality;
- ❖ consideration of the foregoing in the light of the disadvantages of the system;
- ❖ some note of the fact that the same areas can be cited as advantages and disadvantages, at one and the same time;
- ❖ comparison of the operation of tribunals with that of the courts;
- ❖ a brief consideration of the proposals contained in the **TCEA 2007** as far as they relate to tribunals.

Answer Structure

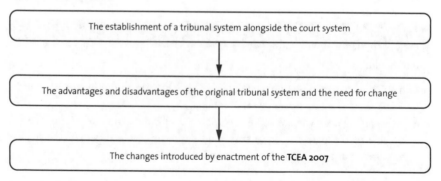

The establishment of a tribunal system alongside the court system

↓

The advantages and disadvantages of the original tribunal system and the need for change

↓

The changes introduced by enactment of the **TCEA 2007**

ANSWER

The reason generally put forward for the establishment and growth of tribunals in Britain since 1945 is the need to provide a specialist forum to deal with cases involving conflicts between an increasingly interventionist welfare state, its functionaries and the rights of private citizens.[1] It is arguable, however, that the large-scale development of this special area of dispute resolution marks a diminishment in the general rule of law, to the extent that it has led to a transfer of power from the ordinary courts. A number of advantages are usually cited in favour of the use of tribunals, rather than the ordinary court system. These advantages relate to the cost, speed, efficiency, privacy and the lack of formality involved in such proceedings. It is important, however, that these supposed advantages are not simply taken at face value for, although they do no doubt represent significant improvements over the operation of the ordinary court system, it is at least arguable that some of them are not necessarily as advantageous as they appear at first sight and that others represent potential (if not actual) weaknesses in the tribunal system.

The ordinary system of courts, with the important exception of the magistrates' courts, are staffed by people who have had a specifically legal education and training, as may be seen from the requirement for judges to be qualified legal practitioners of some standing. With regard to the tribunal system, however, this is not the case.

Tribunals are usually made up of three members, only one of whom, the chair, is expected to be legally qualified. The other two members require no specific legal qualification or expertise. The lack of legal training is not considered a drawback, given the technical administrative, as opposed to specifically legal, nature of the provisions they have to consider. Indeed, the fact of there being two lay representatives on tribunals provides them with one of their perceived advantages over courts, for, to the extent that the non-legal members may provide specialist knowledge, they enable the tribunal to base its decision on actual practice as opposed to abstract legal theory, and thus enable decisions to be taken on practical grounds rather than on the basis of mere legal formalism.

An example of this can be seen in respect of the tribunals responsible for deciding matters relating to employment under the **Employment Rights Act 1996**. In practice, such tribunals are normally made up of a legally qualified chairperson, a representative of employers and a representative of employees. As a consequence, the tribunal has access to the practical experience of the lay members, together with knowledge of the circumstances involved in any particular dispute from both sides of the employment relationship. Such practical experience and expertise provides a basis for the decisions of the tribunal and gives such decisions a degree of pragmatic legitimacy.

A lack of formalism is also evident in the general procedure of tribunals, with the intention of making them less intimidating than full-blown court cases. Informality is shown in the fact that the strict rules relating to evidence, pleading and procedure, which apply in courts, are not binding or applied in tribunal proceedings. An example of this relaxation of strict

....

1 Background to the establishment of a tribunal system.

court procedure is evident in the fact that tribunals are not bound by the strict rules of precedent. Of equal importance is the perhaps conflicting, if not contradictory, need for consistency of treatment, which is one of the major justifications of the system of precedent.

When these matters relating to the lack of formality are linked with the fact that tribunal proceedings tend not to be accusatorial, they generally lead to the conclusion that complainants do not need to be represented by a lawyer in order to present their grievance. They may represent themselves or be represented by a more knowledgeable associate, such as a trade union representative or a friend.

The fact that complainants do not have to rely on legal representation, in turn, makes the tribunal procedure less expensive than using the traditional court system, and this reduction in expense is further enhanced by the additional facts that there are no court fees involved in relation to tribunal proceedings and that costs are not normally awarded against a party who loses the case.

A further perceived advantage of the tribunal system is the speed of its operation, together with the certainty that a dispute will be heard on a specific date.

The final advantage usually cited is the fact that proceedings can be taken before a tribunal without necessarily triggering the publicity that might follow from a court case.

All of these factors, making the use of the tribunal system less intimidating as well as much less expensive than using the normal court system, serve to encourage individuals to pursue their grievances in circumstances where they might not be willing to take action in the courts and, thus, they can be seen as serving the praiseworthy function of increasing access to the law and legal remedies.

In August 2001, Sir Andrew Leggatt published his review of the tribunal system and after commenting on the lack of coherence in the system, his most important recommendations were as follows:[2]

❖ to make the 70 separate tribunals into one Tribunals System;
❖ to ensure that the tribunals operate independently of their sponsoring departments by having them administered by one Tribunals Service;
❖ to improve the training of chairpersons and members in the interpersonal skills peculiarly required by tribunals;
❖ to clarify the appeals procedure;
❖ to consider the effectiveness of lay members. It was felt that there is no justification for any members to sit, whether expert or lay, unless they have a particular function to fulfil, as they do in Employment Tribunals.

Subsequently, in March 2003, the Lord Chancellor's Office announced the Government's intention to follow Sir Andrew Leggatt's recommendations and to institute a

2　Proposals for change to the tribunal system, Tribunals for Users: One System, One Service, August 2001.

new unified Tribunals Service. The new organisation formally came into being in April 2005 and was launched operationally in April 2006 and was followed by new legislation in the following year.

The Tribunals, Courts and Enforcement Act (TCEA) 2007

In pursuance of the Leggatt review, the stated intention of this Act (**TCEA 2007**) was the creation of a new, simplified, statutory framework for tribunals, which was to be achieved not just by the bringing together of existing tribunal jurisdictions but by the provision of a new structure of jurisdiction and new appeal rights.

Unified structure

The Act provides for the establishment of a new unified structure to subsume all tribunals, except for the Employment and Asylum and Immigration tribunals which will remain independent. This unification is to be achieved through the creation of two new tribunals, the First-tier Tribunal and the Upper Tribunal and in pursuit of that end the Act gives the Lord Chancellor power to transfer the jurisdiction of existing tribunals to the two new tribunals. Chambers at the first-tier level will hear cases initially and the role of the upper chambers will be mainly, but not exclusively, to hear appeals from the first tier.

Appeals

The Act specifically recognises and attempts to deal with the previous unclear and unsatisfactory routes of appeal in relation to tribunals' decisions. Under its provisions, in most cases, a decision of the First-tier Tribunal may be appealed to the Upper Tribunal and a decision of the Upper Tribunal may be appealed to a court. However, it also provides that any such appeal must relate to a point of law and may only be exercised with permission from the tribunal being appealed from or the tribunal or court being appealed to.

Common Pitfalls

❖ This question requires some attention to be focused on the **TCEA 2007**.
❖ This topic is currently in flux and students should be aware of any future changes.

Aim Higher

Marks will be available for a consideration of the implementation of the **TCEA 2007**.

QUESTION 46

Explain the operation of the ombudsman system.

How to Read this Question

This is another straightforward question that invites candidates to provide a standard answer covering the topic in question.

How to Answer this Question

The Parliamentary Commissioner for Administration (hereon the Commissioner) is better known as the ombudsman, whose function under the **Parliamentary Commissioner Act (PCA) 1967** is to investigate complaints relating to maladministration. The Commissioner deals with problems in relation to central government and the health service, but other ombudsmen have been appointed under the **Local Government Act (LGA) 1974** to oversee the administration of local government in England and Wales. In dealing with this question, the following points should be addressed:

❖ a brief history of the concept of ombudsmen;
❖ the statutory basis of the Commissioner's powers;
❖ the meaning of maladministration;
❖ the filter role of MPs;
❖ the powers of the Commissioner;
❖ criticisms/limitations of the system;
❖ the spread of the system to other areas;
❖ case studies should be provided to support analysis.

Answer Structure

```
┌─────────────────────────────────────────────────────────────────────┐
│     Introduction to the ombudsman system, in particular origins and history     │
└─────────────────────────────────────────────────────────────────────┘
                                    │
                                    ▼
┌─────────────────────────────────────────────────────────────────────┐
│      Consideration of modern-day ombudsfolk, their role, processes and powers      │
└─────────────────────────────────────────────────────────────────────┘
```

ANSWER

The concept of the ombudsman is Scandinavian in origin and the function of the office holder is to investigate complaints of maladministration: that is, situations where the performance of a Government department has fallen below acceptable standards of administration.

The ombudsman procedure is not just an alternative to the court and tribunal system; it is based upon a distinctly different approach to dealing with disputes. Indeed, the **PCA 1967**, which established the position of the first ombudsman, provides that complainants with rights to pursue their complaints in either of those arenas will not be able to make use of the ombudsman procedure.

The first ombudsman, appointed in 1967, operated – and the present Commissioner, Julie Mellor, still operates –under the title of the Parliamentary Commissioner for Administration and was empowered to consider central government processes only. Since that date, under the **LGA 1974** a number of other ombudsmen have been appointed to oversee the administration of local government in England and Wales.[3] Scotland and Northern Ireland have their own local government ombudsmen fulfilling the same task.

Although maladministration is not defined in the **PCA 1967**, it has been taken to refer to an error in the way a decision was reached, rather than an error in the actual decision itself. Indeed, s12(3) of the **PCA 1967** expressly precludes the Commissioner from questioning the merits of particular decisions taken without maladministration. Maladministration, therefore, can be seen to refer to a procedure used to reach a result, rather than the result itself. In an illuminating and much-quoted speech introducing the **1967 Act**, Richard Crossman, the then leader of the House of Commons, gave an indicative, if non-definitive, list of what might be included within the term maladministration, and included within it: bias, neglect, inattention, delay, incompetence, ineptitude, perversity, turpitude and arbitrariness.

Members of the public do not have the right to complain directly to the Commissioner, but must channel any such complaint through an MP. Complainants do not have to provide precise details of any maladministration; they simply have to indicate difficulties they have experienced as a result of dealing with an agency of central government. It is the function of the Commissioner to discover whether the problem arose as a result of maladministration. There is a 12-month time limit for raising complaints, but the Commissioner has discretion to ignore this.

The powers of the Commissioner to investigate complaints are similar to those of a High Court judge: to require the attendance of witnesses and the production of documents; wilful obstruction of the investigation is treated as contempt of court. On conclusion of an investigation, the Commissioner submits reports to the MP who raised the complaint and to the principal of the Government office which was subject to the investigation. The Commissioner has no enforcement powers, but, if his recommendations are ignored and existing practices involving maladministration are not altered, he may submit a further report to both Houses of Parliament, in order to highlight the continued bad practice. The assumption is that on the submission of such a report, MPs will exert pressure on the appropriate minister of state to ensure that any necessary changes in procedure are made. Annual reports are laid before Parliament and a Parliamentary Select Committee exists to oversee the operation of the Commissioner.

Two reports from the Commissioner are worthy of particular consideration.[4] The first one, issued in February 1995, related to the effect of the delays in determining the route for the Channel Tunnel rail link. As a consequence of the four-year delay on the part of the Department of Transport in deciding on a route, the owners of properties along the various possible routes found the value of their properties blighted and the properties themselves even unsaleable. The situation was not finalised until the Department announced its final selection in 1994. According to the Commissioner:

....

3   This discussion clearly indicates knowledge of the expansion of the use of ombudsmen.
4   The value of reference to real-life examples of the work of ombudsmen should not be underestimated.

The effect of the Department of Transport's policy was to put the project in limbo, keeping it alive when it could not be funded.

As a consequence, he held that the Department:

had a responsibility to consider the position of such persons suffering exceptional or extreme hardship and to provide redress where appropriate.

The unusual thing about this case, however, was the reaction of the Department of Transport, which rejected the findings of the Commissioner and refused to provide any compensation. It was this refusal which led the Commissioner to issue his special report, consequent upon a situation where an 'injustice has been found which has not or will not be remedied'. Even then, the Department of Transport did not give way, until pressured to do so by the Parliamentary Select Committee on the Parliamentary Commissioner for Administration. Eventually, payments of £5,000 were made to those owners whose houses had suffered from property blight.

The second report, entitled *Equitable Life: A Decade of Regulatory Failure*, came out in July 2008 and set out ten specific findings of maladministration: one against the former Department of Trade and Industry, four against the Government Actuary's Department and five against the Financial Services Authority, in relation to their regulation of Equitable Life Assurance Society, whose financial mismanagement had led to the loss of pensions for a substantial number of people. On the basis of those findings the Ombudsman recommended, first, that the public bodies concerned should apologise for their failures. More importantly, however, her second recommendation was that the Government should fund a compensation scheme, with the aim of putting those who had suffered in the position they would have been in had they not invested in Equitable Life policies. Effectively this would have meant paying compensation to remedy any financial losses, which would not have been suffered had those people invested elsewhere than with Equitable.

Eventually in October 2010 it was announced that payments would be made, but would be limited to a total of £1.5 billion.

In offering an evaluation of the ombudsman procedure, it may be claimed that, all in all, the system appears to work fairly well within its restricted sphere of operation, but there are major areas where it could be improved. The more important criticisms levelled at the Parliamentary Commissioner for Administration relate to:

(a) the retention of MPs as filters for complaints. It is generally accepted that there is no need for such a filter mechanism;

(b) the restrictive nature of the definition of maladministration. It is possible to argue that any procedure that leads to an unreasonable decision must involve an element of maladministration and that, therefore, the definition as currently stated is not overly restrictive. However, even if such reverse reasoning is valid, it would still be preferable for the definition of the scope of the Commissioner's investigations to be clearly stated and be stated in wider terms than at present;

(c)   the lack of publicity given to complaints. If more people were aware of the procedure and what it could achieve, then more people would make use of it, leading to an overall improvement in the administration of governmental policies;

(d)   the reactive role of the ombudsmen. This criticism refers to the fact that the ombudsmen are dependent upon receiving complaints before they can initiate investigations. It is suggested that a more proactive role, under which the ombudsmen would be empowered to initiate investigation on their own authority, would lead to an improvement in general administration, as well as an increase in the effectiveness of the activity of the ombudsmen.

Common Pitfalls

The Parliamentary Commissioner should be the focus of any answer and should not be confused with other 'ombudsmen' if they are considered.

Aim Higher

Case studies will support analysis and the more up-to-date the case the better. The *Equitable Life* case will get good marks.

QUESTION 47

'For most people most of the time, litigation in the civil courts, and often in tribunals too, should be the method of dispute resolution of last resort.'

▶ Consider what alternatives to the court system are available and why they should be used.

How to Answer this Question

This question is more general than the previous ones, but it still requires a consideration of arbitration as well as mediation and conciliation. Detail is necessarily less, but the question still requires a substantial understanding of the processes. The following structure might prove satisfactory:

❖   consider the operation of arbitration as compared to the ordinary courts (refer specifically to the **Arbitration Act 1996**);

❖   consider the distinction between mediation and conciliation, as well as detailing how and when they are likely to be used;

❖   consider especially how the courts will use costs awards to ensure that the Alternative Dispute Resolution (ADR) is used;

❖   conclude by placing these various ADR mechanisms within the framework of the general legal system.

Answer Structure

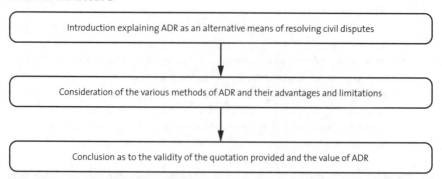

Introduction explaining ADR as an alternative means of resolving civil disputes

Consideration of the various methods of ADR and their advantages and limitations

Conclusion as to the validity of the quotation provided and the value of ADR

ANSWER

As the question suggests there are a number of valuable alternatives to using the courts. These Alternative Dispute Resolution mechanisms have many features that make them preferable to the ordinary court system in many areas. For one thing they tend to be much less formal and less stressful that the court system. However, perhaps their main advantages are that they are less antagonistic than the ordinary legal system, being designed to achieve agreement between the parties involved and they are, by and large, much cheaper than the courts.

Arbitration

The first and oldest of these alternative procedures is arbitration. Arbitration is the procedure whereby parties in dispute refer the issue under contention to a third party for resolution, rather than institute legal proceedings in the courts. This practice is well established in commerce and industry;[5] its legal effectiveness has long been recognised by the court. In contemporary business usage, it is a matter of common practice for commercial contracts to contain express clauses referring any future disputes to arbitration.

Commercial arbitration proceedings are now governed by the **Arbitration Act 1996**. This Act significantly alters the relationship between the parties, the arbitrator and the courts. Whereas, previously, the courts ultimately dominated the procedure, now their role has been reduced to providing safeguards against improper actions on the part of the arbitrator, and the determination of points of law. So, now the parties to any dispute are at liberty to provide their procedures for resolving it.

Mediation

Mediation and conciliation are the most informal of all ADR procedures. Mediation is the process where a third party acts as the conduit through which two disputing parties communicate and negotiate in an attempt to reach a common resolution of a problem. Mediation has an important part to play in family matters, where it is felt that the adversarial

---

5   This emphasises that arbitration is most used by commerce rather than individual litigants.

approach of the traditional legal system has tended to emphasise, if not increase, existing differences of view between individuals and has not been conducive to amicable settlements.[6] Thus, in divorce cases, mediation has traditionally been used to enable the parties themselves to work out an agreed settlement, rather than having one imposed on them from outside by the courts. It is important to realise that there are potential problems with mediation. The assumption that the parties freely negotiate the terms of their final agreement in a less than hostile manner may be deeply flawed, to the extent that it assumes equality of bargaining power and knowledge between the parties to the negotiation. Mediation may well ease pain, but, unless the mediation procedure is carefully and critically monitored, it may gloss over and perpetuate a previously exploitative relationship, allowing the more powerful participant to manipulate and dominate the more vulnerable, and force an inequitable agreement. Establishing entitlements on the basis of clear legal advice may be preferable to apparently negotiating those entitlements away in the non-confrontational, therapeutic atmosphere of mediation.

Conciliation

Conciliation takes mediation a step further and gives the mediator the power to suggest grounds for compromise and the possible basis for a conclusive agreement. Both mediation and conciliation have been available in relation to industrial disputes, under the auspices of the Government-funded Advisory Conciliation and Arbitration Service (ACAS)[7] and have an important part to play in family matters. The essential weakness in these two procedures, however, lies in the fact that although they may lead to the resolution of a dispute, they do not necessarily achieve that end. Where they operate successfully, they are excellent methods of dealing with problems, as essentially the parties to the dispute determine their own solutions and, therefore, feel commitment to the outcome. The problem is that they have no binding power and do not always lead to an outcome.

The foregoing has considered a variety of alternative mechanisms for dealing with legal problems which have been developed in response to particular shortcomings in the ordinary court system and, perhaps, they point to a fundamental need to reform the operation of those law courts and to regularise the whole provision of dispute resolution devices under the law.

As part of the civil justice reforms, the general requirement placed on courts to actively manage cases includes 'encouraging the parties to use an alternative dispute resolution procedure if the Court considers that to be appropriate and facilitating the use of such procedure'. **Rule 26.4** of the **Civil Procedure Rules (CPR) 1998**[8] enables judges, either on their own account or at the agreement of both parties, to stop court proceedings where they consider the dispute to be better suited to solution by some alternative procedure,

....

6   An important point which highlights the failings of the court system in maintaining a positive relationship between disputing parties.

7   Helpful use of an example, demonstrating knowledge and providing clarity of explanation.

8   Demonstrates knowledge and understanding of the means through which the state promotes and supports **ADR**.

such as arbitration or mediation. **CPR 44.3(2)** provides that 'if the court decides to make an order about costs (a) the general rule is that the unsuccessful party will be ordered to pay the costs of the successful party; but (b) the court may make a different order'. **CPR 44.3(4)** provides that 'in deciding what order (if any) to make about costs, the court must have regard to all the circumstances, including (a) the conduct of the parties'. **Rule 44.3(5)** provides that the conduct of the parties includes '(a) conduct before, as well as during, the proceedings and in particular the extent to which the parties followed any relevant pre-action protocol'. If, subsequently, a court is of the opinion that an action it has been required to decide could have been settled more effectively through ADR, then under **r 44.5** of the **CPR**, it may penalise the party who insisted on the court hearing by awarding them reduced or no costs should they win the case.

The potential consequences of not abiding by a recommendation to use ADR may be seen in *Dunnett v Railtrack plc* (2002).[9] When Dunnett won a right to appeal against a previous court decision, the court granting the appeal recommended that the dispute should be put to arbitration. Railtrack, however, refused Dunnett's offer of arbitration and insisted on the dispute going back to a full court hearing. In the subsequent hearing in the Court of Appeal, Railtrack proved successful. The Court of Appeal, however, held that if a party rejected ADR out of hand when it had been suggested by the court, they would suffer the consequences when costs came to be decided. In the instant case, Railtrack had refused to even contemplate ADR at a stage prior to the costs of the appeal beginning to flow.

It is possible to refuse to engage in mediation without subsequently suffering in the awards of costs. The test, however, is an objective rather than a subjective one, and a difficult one to sustain, as was shown in *Hurst v Leeming* (2002).

In *Halsey v Milton Keynes General NHS Trust* (2004), the Court of Appeal emphasised that the criterion was the reasonableness of the belief.

Common Pitfalls

Avoid the temptation either to ignore arbitration or, alternatively, just to focus on that aspect of ADR.

Aim Higher

Higher marks may be gained by reference to any contemporary reports on mediation which tend to appear regularly. Also reference to how the courts use cost awards to ensure people do use ADR will be advantageous.

---

9   Reference to this decided case provides powerful evidence of the value of **ADR**.

Index